The Travel Agent

Second Edition

Michael Bottomley Renshaw

Business Education Publishers Limited

1997

© MICHAEL BOTTOMLEY RENSHAW

ISBN 0 901888 00 2

First published in 1992
Second Edition 1997

Cover design by Mark Lucas

Published in Great Britain by
Business Education Publishers Limited,
Leighton House,
10 Grange Crescent,
Stockton Road,
Sunderland,
SR2 7BN

Telephone 0191 567 4963
Fax 0191 514 3277

Printed in Great Britain by Athenaeum Press Limited

Foreword

by Norman Richardson
Hon MA(Dunelm) Hon MBA Hon CGIA CBIM FTS FinstTT D MCIM
Chairman of the ABTA National Training Board

The last forty years have experienced tremendous growth in all sectors of Travel and Tourism, already seen as the largest Industry and Employer of our World - a view well underpinned in a recent report by the prestigious WTTC, a global coalition drawn from all the segments making up this vast Industry - in which wealth creation is identified to the unbelievable gross output of trillions of US dollars and involving 130 million employees in all the sectors.

Not least in the developments over the years has been the emergence of Retail Travel as a dynamic and flourishing element of our U.K. economy - employing tens of thousands of people with a turnover of billions of pounds. This sector of the industry has developed from relatively humble beginnings to a point where there are now Travel Agency outlets on every High Street in the country. This expansion and evolution has reflected that of Travel and Tourism as a whole for it has been the ever-increasing desire of the general public to see all the continents of our world which has fuelled this remarkable expansion of sales outlets.

As more and more people are able to enjoy world-wide holiday and travel opportunities the industry servicing them must have staff at all levels who are trained and qualified.

Here the role of ABTA (the Association of British Travel Agents) has been far-seeing - not only as a U.K. Trade Association for Travel and Tour Operating Principals and Agents but in encouraging, for over four decades, a disciplined and structured approach to training and educational opportunities for members at all levels.

Through this encouragement there are now courses and programmes in Travel and Tourism Training and Education in Colleges of Further Education, Polytechnics and Universities throughout the country and it is now well accepted that the ABTA National Training Board is one of the most significant of any Trade Association world-wide.

However the retail sector itself is diverse and complex and it is vital that those who work in it understand how the Travel and Tourism industry operates as a whole and the part travel agents play.

This book meets an important need in bringing together in an interesting and detailed way much important material, providing a comprehensive and understandable view of the role of the Travel Agent.

Michael Bottomley Renshaw - the author - has for many years - indeed over some three decades - made an important contribution to the development of Training and Education in Travel and Tourism. He was instrumental in establishing the first courses in Retail Travel Agency Training in the early 1970s and as Director of Studies for Travel

Management in New College Durham has helped to develop the whole structure of BTEC courses in this discipline area. He has been an important contributor to the success of the U.K.'s first undergraduate degree programme in Travel and Tourism Management developed and operated jointly by New College Durham and Newcastle Polytechnic in association with the ABTA National Training Board.

Through his teaching, course leadership and academic study of Travel and Tourism and now with the publication of this book he has helped, and will continue to help, many hundreds of young people to discover successful careers in the great industry of Travel and Tourism.

In this book, Michael has drawn, not just on his own many years as a practitioner and teacher in Travel and Tourism, but on the experience and understanding of numerous Senior Executives and Managers in the industry.

With their help Michael has produced a book which will, I am sure, come to be required reading for all those involved or interested in the way in which the Travel and Tourism industry operates.

Norman Richardson

May 1992

Forward to the Second Edition

by Malcolm Hewitt,
President and Group Managing Director,
A. T. Mays Ltd.

The global march of the travel and tourism continues apace, as the business segments itself firmly as the world's largest industry.

This book, the Travel Agent, by distinguished author Michael Renshaw, is probably the most definitive guide to the sometimes complex, exciting and challenging business of retail travel.

The pace the industry moves at is rubber stamped by the fact that this book requires up-dating only five years since its last publication.

A. T. Mays too has changed dramatically in the last five years. We have signed a strategic alliance with Inspirations, linked with independent consortiums, ARTAC WorldChoice to form the largest travel agency network in the UK and Ireland and opened a shop in Moscow, Russia. Our next move is a change of corporate name and identity.

As the industry moves towards the next millennium, it is becoming increasingly necessary for students of travel to be well informed about the retail business. The major issues of the day are covered in this excellent book, such as vertical integration, product distribution, retail theory and practice, regulation and new technology.

As a strong supporter of travel education in the UK, A. T. Mays is delighted to endorse the extensively up-dated 2nd edition of the Travel Agent, the most valuable source of reference on the retail business for travel students from foundation level to degree.

I would take this opportunity to wish readers of this book every success in their careers in the retail travel business.

It is fitting to finish this foreword with a thank you to Michael Renshaw. By the time many of you read this, Michael will have retired from his full-time academic teaching position at New College Durham. He has helped launch careers in travel for thousands of students, and no doubt he will continue to do the same in his part-time teaching and training role.

Malcolm Hewitt

June 1997

Preface

For many years students studying travel and tourism have had to rely on only a few standard text books. These books, whilst fulfilling an essential need, have been very general in content, often attempting to cover every aspect of tourism. For the study of individual industry sectors, such as retail travel, detailed information has been very difficult to come by. This book attempts to solve this problem by concentrating on travel agencies, a sector which, for many students, provides the first career destination.

It is intended that the book should evolve as a story of the travel agent from its early beginnings to its present day role. Initially the focus is one of 'setting the scene' by placing the agent in an industrial context within the marketing chain of distribution, then comparing the roles of the players within the chain. The book analyses the various types of agent, each with its own specific market to cover and, by breaking down the travel market into its component parts, gives the reader some idea of the dimensions and value of the business available, major product areas and agency shares.

To understand the role and function of the travel agent it is necessary to appreciate the development that has taken place since the end of the Second World War and to appreciate how closely it is linked to advances in transport and accommodation services.

The book then considers the distribution system that now exists and the options that suppliers have in getting their products to the consumer. The suppliers of the travel product, known in the trade as the 'Principals' of the travel agent, can exercise choice in the way their products are distributed to the consumer. What are the factors that influence that choice and what advantages and disadvantages derive from each channel available to them? Opinion from the major suppliers of travel agents was sought on major areas for concern and the possible future role agents may play.

If the agent is to be classed as a member of the distribution system readers must understand what distribution is and the channels through which products reach the consumer. In this part of the book we look at distribution and channel theory within marketing and relate that theory to every day practices in the travel agency business.

The next chapter examines the travel agency industry, outlining its present structure, problems and issues. In particular, we consider the greater emphasis given to marketing by travel agents in the last decade. New innovations such as preferred operator selection, the holiday credit card clubs and phonecentres have come about partly because of the growth of the sector both in size and power and as a result of increasing competition.

Technology now plays a major role in the travel and tourism business. The suppliers, especially the airlines, have pioneered technological advances in reservation systems and automatic ticketing machines. U.K. travel agents have been the largest users of British Telecom's Prestel Viewdata service and while many still see new technology as both complex and confusing, it is essential that agents install such systems if they are to meet the challenge of the future. The spectre of 'home buying' and sales through independent computer machines located at non-travel points are said to be a most serious potential threat to the future existence of agents, but is this really so?

Before entering education I was employed for some eleven years in the industry within the travel agency sector. Since entering lecturing, travel agency operation has been a key element of my teaching and for students, agencies often provide their first employment destination. It would be difficult to guide, advise and promote the sector to young people if I had serious misgivings about its role, value and future. The writing of this book therefore gave a valuable opportunity to find some answers to these questions.

Michael B. Renshaw
Durham
May, 1992

Preface to the Second Edition

When I wrote this first edition, only some six years ago, ABTA was still operating its "closed shop" rules of entry, Airtours was just beginning to show its teeth, Pickfords and Hogg Robinson travel shops lined the High Street, excavation had just started on the Channel Tunnel and the Internet sounded like science fiction. How times change and how quickly. The travel business in breathtaking, stand still for a while, stop reading travel trade press and you can be hopelessly behind. That is why it was essential to up-date this book so soon to enable travel students and employees and those interested in the industry to keep apace.

The basic structure of the book remains the same but the text, including every statistic, table and figure, has been up-dated. Over the past five years the inexorable expansion of the major multiple travel agents has continued with the number of regional multiples and small independent agents declining. Forced to compete with heavy discounting some have given up the fight or banded together within consortia and franchise groupings. The Monopolies and Mergers Commission, at the request of independent grouping and consumer organisations continue to investigate vertical integration fearing that the consumer is being unfairly enticed into buying a product or purchasing insurance that may not be in their interests. It will probably be by 1998 before they report.

New technology appears in virtually every travel press publication, threats to unnerve the most optimistic travel consultant predict the fall of the agent due to home shopping for leisure travel and direct sales for corporate customers. Yet the most research shows that in general the public and business travellers still want to speak to a person rather than a faceless computer screen. It can take ages to "serf the Internet" looking for the appropriate information and in many cases leads up a "blind alley". So for the time being the prospects are still good for the travel agent provided they move ahead and adopt the new technology to promote and sell their own services. In this way they get the best of both worlds and long term survival is more sure.

Michael B. Renshaw
Durham
June 1997

Acknowledgements

This book evolved from the work done to complete a Master of Philosophy Degree under the supervision of the University of Surrey. In the initial stages of this work the ideas and support of Victor Middleton, now visiting Professor at Oxford Polytechnic and, nearer home, Norman Richardson, Chairman of the ABTA National Training Board, were invaluable in providing the focus of study. When Victor left the University I was grateful to be placed in the professional and expert hands of Professor Steve Wanhill, a leading authority on tourism matters both in the U.K. and abroad. His advice and guidance have been much appreciated. To all those in the travel industry who gave up their valuable time to speak to me in person on the issues raised in the work I give my grateful thanks. Their openness and frank opinions have provided a unique insight into the workings and business relationships within the industry, thus providing me with the opportunity to produce something new. In addition the historical information search would have been impossible without access to the archives of the *Travel Trade Gazette* to whom I am indebted. I would also like to thank Frances Brown who edited the manuscript, Paul Callaghan as general series editor, Gerard Callaghan who produced the graphics and Caroline White and Moira Page who helped to produce this book. Finally my thanks go to the Principal and Governors of New College Durham and to Durham County Council for granting me a full year's secondment for research and the support in time and money to complete the project.

Michael B. Renshaw,
Durham, May, 1992.

Acknowledgements to the Second Edition

The production of this second edition has been helped by many people. I would particularly like to thank Malcolm Hewitt, President and Group Managing Director of A. T. Mays Ltd. for his foreword and the many industry professionals who have provided me with help, advice and insight. My thanks also go to those involved at Business Education Publishers for their work in producing the book and in particular to Moira Page and Gerard Callaghan for their editorial work, Mark Lucas for the cover design and Paul Callaghan as general series editor.

Michael B. Renshaw,
Durham, June, 1997.

The Author

Michael Bottomley Renshaw was, until his recent early retirement, Director of Studies of the Division of Travel, Tourism and Leisure at New College Durham. He was a Fellow of the Institute of Travel and Tourism and a Founder Member of the Tourism Society. After moving into education from Thomas Cook he was involved in the launch of the first ever ABTA recognised Joint Diploma in Travel and Tourism. This became the "blueprint" for all Further Education travel courses across the UK. Since then, over a twenty five year period, courses have expanded from Youth Training through to degree level. He has been responsible for starting off the careers of thousands of travel students and has created valuable links between education and the travel industry through work placements and employment.

Industry Acknowledgements

I am indebted to the following industry representatives without whose generous help this work would not have been possible.

Adkin C,	Director Travel Management, Thomas Cook
Arscott D, R.,	Executive Secretary, Pacific Asia Travel Association, United Kingdom Chapter
Aspinall J,	U.K. Sales Manager, Hertz Car Hire (1989)
Brett P,	Chairman and Chief Executive, Thomson Travel
Bruce-Mitford M,	Chairman, Association of Independent Tour Operators (1989)
Boyle J,	Chairman, Falcon Holidays (1989)
Cambata R, S.,	Greaves Travel Ltd
Chandler H,	Travel Club of Upminster (1989)
Chapman D,	National Travel Trade Manager, British Rail
Coles A,	Product Marketing Manager, Hertz Car Hire (1989)
Curtis-Brignell D,	Director of Marketing and Sales, Best Western Hotels
Cust N,	Sales & Marketing Director, Superbreak
Daykin R,	Sales Manager, Warner Holidays Ltd. (1989)
Dooley R,	Managing Director, Travel Bazaar (1989)
Ellett S,	Scheduled Services Manager, Dan Air, (1989)
East M,	Managing Director, Eastcastle Management Consultants
Farrell A,E.,	U.K. Passenger Sales and Marketing Manager, North Sea Ferries
Gurrusa C,	Head of Leisure, British Airways.
Harmi Travel,	Wolverhampton
Heape R,	Director Products and Marketing, British Airways Holidays
Horsman A,	Marketing Manager, Saga Holidays Ltd. (1989)
Jenkins N, J.,	Director, Unijet Travel
Jones D, A.,	Head of Air Fare Services, Hogg Robinson
King J,	Managing Director, Wallace Arnold

Mayhew L,	Head of Distribution, British Airways (1989)
McDermott C,	General Sales Manager, P&O Cruises
McNally R,	Managing Director, Exchange Travel (1989)
Moffat J,	Managing Director, A.T.Mays
Moss P,	Sales Administration Manager, Pan Am (1989)
Playford A,	Marketing Manager, Trusthouse Forte (1989)
Price S,	Managing Director, Rainbow Holidays
Pyle H,	Operations Director, Marketing, Mount Charlotte Thistle Hotels
Ramsdale S,C., Ms,	Retail Sales Manager, Newcastle Chronicle
Richardson N,	Chairman, ABTA National Training Board
Sawbridge P,	Managing Director, Smiths Shearings (1989)
Short D, R.,	Managing Director Retail Division, Page & Moy
Smith J,	President, ABTA (1989)
St. Clair K,	Managing Director, Sol Holidays (1989)
Swinglehurst E,	Historian
Turton G,	Sales Manager, National Express (1989)
Upton R,	Managing Director, Neilson Travel (1989)
Walsh D,	NAITA, Briggs & Hill
Welsh K,	Sales & Marketing Director, Pickfords Travel
Woodcraft A,	Marketing Manager, Tjaereborg

Industry Acknowledgements to the Second Edition

I am indebted to the following industry representatives without whose generous help this second edition would not have been possible.

Ashbridge K,	UK Regional Marketing Manager, Sabre Europe.
Atkins J,	Sales Director, Rainbow Holidays
Bennett K,	Director of Marketing & PR., National Express

Brett P,   Chairman and Chief Executive, Thomson Travel

Coulson B.I.C.,   General Manager, Passenger Shipping Association

Farrell A.E.,   Passenger Manager UK, P & O North Sea Ferries

Flynn R,   Head of Distribution British Airways

Heape R,   Director, British Airways Holidays

Herbert P.R.,   Managing Director, Siesta/Travel Europe

Hewitt M,   President and Group Managing Director, A.T. Mays

Low B,   Editor, Business Travel World

McLean A,   Undergraduate, Civil Aviation Authority

Meli S,   Marketing Communications Co-ordinator, Worldspan

Nardi R,   Solicitor, Association of British Travel Agents

Short D.R.,   Director, Page & Moy

Stott D,   Account Manager, Thomas Cook Direct

Watkinson C,   Head of Personnel, Association of British Travel Agents

Abbreviations

ABC   Advance Booking Charter

ABT   Automatic Ticket and Boarding Pass

ABTA   Association of British Travel Agents

AITO   Association of Independent Tour Operators

ANTOR   Association of National Tourist Office Representatives

ARTAC   Alliance of Retail Travel Agents Consortia

ATOC   Association of Train Operating Companies

ATOL   Air Travel Organisers Licence

ATRF   Air Travel Reserve Fund

BEA   British European Airways

BOAC   British Overseas Airways Corporation

BTA   British Tourist Authority

CAA	Civil Aviation Authority
CAB	Civil Aeronautics Board
CRS	Computer Reservation System
CTAC	Creative Travel Agents Conference
EDI	Electronic Data Interchange
EFTPOS	Electronic Funds Transfer at Point of Sale
ET	Electronic Ticketing
GBTA	Guild of Business Agents
GDS	Global Distribution System
GNER	Great North Eastern Railway
HMSO	Her Majesty's Stationery Office
IATA	International Air Transport Association
ILG	International Leisure Group
IT	Inclusive Tour
ITA	Institute of Travel Agents
ITPS	Interactive Transaction Processing Systems
ITT	Institute of Travel and Tourism
ITX	Inclusive Tour Fares
MMC	Monopolies and Mergers Commission
NAITA	National Association of Independent Travel Agents
OPEC	Organisation of Petroleum Exporting Countries
PC	Personal computer
PNR	Passenger Name Record
PSA	Passenger Shipping Association
RPM	Retail Price Maintenance
STP	Satellite Ticket Printer
TOSG	Tour Operators Study Group
TTG	Travel Trade Gazette
TTI	Travel Technology Initiative
VDU	Visual Display Unit
VFR	Visiting Friends and Relatives

Table of Contents

Chapter 1   The Travel Agent

The Travel Distribution Framework 1
Principals in the Travel and Tourism Industry 2
   Principals as Manufacturers or Suppliers of a Service 2
The Principals' Means of Selling their Product 3
   Direct Sell 3
   Indirect Selling Through an Agent 3
   Sale to Tour Operators for Inclusion as Part of a Package . . 4
Tour Operators 4
   Vertical Integration by Tour Operators 6
   Travel Agents 6
   The Position of the Travel Agent in Law 7
   Agency Agreements 8
   Forms of Direct and Indirect Selling 8
   (a) Direct Selling 8
   Direct Response Marketing 8
   (b) Indirect Sell 9
   The 'Pull' Strategy 10
   The 'Push' Strategy 10
The Role and Function of Travel Agents 10
The General Public 10
   Personal Service 11
   Expert Advice 11
   Unbiased Advice on a wide Range of Products 12
   The Provision of Ancillary Services 13
   Convenience and Location 13
   Greater Choice of Products 14
The Principals/Suppliers 14
   A Major Channel of Distribution 14
   Savings in Time and Money 15
   An Important Marketing Point 15
The Business Community 16
   Personal Service 16
   Accuracy and Expertise 16
   Savings in Time and Money 17

Extended Credit Facilities 17
Types of Agency 18
  By Size of Organisation 18
  Multinationals 19
  National Multiples 19
  Regional Multiples or Miniples 19
  Independents 20
By Type of Business Conducted 20
  General/Leisure Agent 20
  Holiday Agents 22
  Business Agents 23
By Appointment 26
  ABTA Agent 26
  Non-ABTA Agents 26
  IATA Agents 27
  Non-IATA Agents 27
The Retail Travel Market 28
  Inclusive Tours 30
  Air 31
  Surface Transportation 31
Reasons for Development 33

Chapter 2   Travel Agency Development

Tourism and Change 35
  (i) Economic Trends 35
  (ii) Socio-economic Trends 38
  (iii) Demographic Trends 41
Transport Developments 43
  (i) Air Transport 43
  (ii) Shipping 46
  (iii) Road 48
  (iv) Rail 50
Tour Operators 51
  The 1950s - The Early Years 52
  The 1960s - The Market Expands 52
  The 1970s - The First Great Price Wars 54
  The 1980s - The Halcyon Days 55
  The 1990s - Retrenchment and Consolidation 57
  Direct Sell 59

Travel Agencies *61*
1950 to 1980 - The early years *61*
The March of the Multiples *64*
The Association of British Travel Agents (ABTA) *68*
The Early Development of ABTA *68*
Stabiliser *70*
Bonding *70*
Restrictive Practices *71*
EC Directive on Package Travel *73*

Chapter 3   *Travel Product Distribution*

Travel Industry Distribution Channels *75*
The Travel and Tourism Industry's Channels of Distribution *76*
1. Air travel *76*
Primary Distribution Channels *77*
Secondary Channels of Distribution *79*
2. Surface Transport Distribution *82*
3. Accommodation *92*
4. Inclusive Tours *96*
Aspects of Channel Economics *104*
The Costs Involved in Selling Travel and Tourism Products . . . *104*

Chapter 4   *The Importance of Distribution and Retailing to the Travel Agent*

Channels of Distribution in Travel and Tourism *109*
The Choice of Distribution Channel *110*
(a) Exposure to Target Markets *112*
(b) Performance Requirements *112*
(c) Influence *112*
(d) Flexibility *112*
(e) Supplier's Profit *113*
(f) Channel Needs *113*
Different Forms of Distribution *113*
(a) Channel Length and Width *113*
(a) Intensive Distribution *114*
(b) Selective Distribution *115*
(c) Exclusive Distribution *115*
Controlling the Channels of Distribution *115*
(a) Consensus Distribution *117*

(b) Vertically Integrated Distribution *117*

(c) Vertically Co-ordinated Distribution *117*

Travel Distribution as a System *118*

(a) The Respective Roles of Different Organisations
within the Distribution System *118*

(b) The Use of Power in the System *119*

(c) Co-operation and Competition *120*

Retailing Theory and Practice *121*

Aspects of Retailing Theory and Practice *121*

(a) Role and Function of Retailing *121*

(b) Institutional Change *122*

The Wheel of Retailing *123*

The Retail Life Cycle *123*

(c) Natural Selection *124*

The Retail Marketing Mix *125*

(a) Location and Opening Hours *126*

(b) Shop Design and Ambience *126*

(c) Merchandising *127*

(d) Pricing Policy *128*

(e) Personnel, Reservations and Payment Systems *128*

Aspects of Consumer Behaviour *129*

External Influences on the Buying Process *129*

(a) Social and Economic *129*

(b) Political *129*

(c) Motivations *130*

The Buying Process *131*

(a) Problem Recognition *132*

(b) Information Search *132*

(c) Evaluation of Alternatives *132*

(d) Purchase Decision *132*

(e) Post-purchase Behaviour *132*

Chapter 5   The Travel Agent

The Reasons for Change *135*

(a) Increase Market Share *136*

(b) Acquisition of Assets, Expertise and Goodwill *136*

(c) Economies of Scale *137*

(d) Brand Image *137*

(e) Geographical Spread *138*

The Effect of the 'March of the Multiples'
on the Industry as a Whole 138
  (a) The Structure of the Industry and the Relationship
    between Principals and Retailers 138
  (b) The Increasing Commoditisation of the Principals' Product . . 139
  (c) Parent Companies whose interests are Non-travel 139
  (d) The Squeezing out of the Independents 139
  (e) The Ability of the Multiples to Determine which Products
    are on offer to the General Public 140
The Effects of the 'March of the Multiples'
within the Agency Sector 140
  (a) Development of Corporate Image 141
  (b) Staff Development 141
  (c) Market Segmentation 142
  (d) Investment in New Technology 142
  (e) Product Discrimination 143
  (f) Customer Incentives 145
  (g) Own-label Products 148
  (h) Holiday Clubs 150
  (i) Direct Telesales 153
  Teletext 154
  Credit cards 154
  Advertising 154
  Third party promotions 154
Independent Agents 155
  (a) Excessive Competition 155
  (b) Reduced Market Share 156
  (c) Pressure on Profits 157
  (d) Formation of Consortia 157
  (e) Franchise Schemes 159
Business Relationships 161
  Agency Appointment Policy 161
  Commission/Overrides/Incentives 163
  Agency Support Services 165

Chapter 6   Technology and Change

New Technology and its Impact on Retail Travel 169
The Use of Technology by Suppliers and Agents 170
The Development of Computer Reservations Systems (CRS) . . . 171
  CRS Laser-disc/CD ROM Technology 174

Top four CRS Suppliers 1997 . . . . *175*

(i) Amadeus *175*

(ii) Galileo *176*

(iii) Sabre *176*

(iv) Worldspan *177*

Development of Viewdata *178*

(i) ATT&T Istel *181*

(ii) Imminus Fastrak *181*

(iii) Prestel *181*

Co-operation *182*

Competition Between CRS and Viewdata - Future Developments . . *182*

Payment Systems *183*

Competition Policy *184*

(i) Airline CRS Bias *184*

The Impact of New Technology on the Relationship
Between the Travel Agent and Customer *186*

The Travel Customer's Use of Technology *187*

Electronic Point of Sale and Self Ticketing *187*

Touch-Screen Kiosk *189*

Travel Shopping at Home *190*

Payment System between Customers and Agents *192*

Payment Systems between Customers and Suppliers *192*

Appendices   *193*

Bibliography   *217*

Index   *223*

List of Figures

Figure 1   Distribution channels - a comparison   2

Figure 2   Vertical integration within the Travel Industry chain of distribution, 1997   5

Figure 3   Airtours Plc   58

Figure 4   Travel agency takeovers/mergers in the 1980s   64

Figure 5   Basic channels of distribution in travel   75

Figure 6   Airline distribution channels - scheduled - business/leisure   77

Figure 7   Airline distribution channels - Charter/Leisure   82

Figure 8   Alternative channels for accommodation providers   93

Figure 9   Distribution channels for U.K. tour operators   97

Figure 10   Tour operators' conventional selling process   103

Figure 11   Tour operators' direct selling process   104

Figure 12   Distribution strategies as part of an overall marketing plan   108

Figure 13   Distribution channel types   114

Figure 14   Vertically integrated distribution in travel   117

Figure 15   The retail marketing mix for travel agencies   125

Figure 16   Kotler's 'five stage model' of the buying process   131

Figure 17   The travel buying process   133

Figure 18   An early Computer Reservations System (CRS)   171

Figure 19   A Global Distribution System (GDS)   173

Figure 20   An early example of the Viewdata system   178

Figure 21   The Viewdata 'Hard-Wiring' system   180

Appendices

Appendix A   ABTA Travel Agents Code of Condcut *193*

Appendix B   Job description for a travel sales consultant *202*

Appendix C   U.K. residents currency allowances, 1945-79 .   .   .   . *204*

Appendix D   U.K. residents population figures 1985-95 .   .   .   . *205*

Appendix E   Socio-economic groups *206*

Appendix F   ABTA membership growth *207*

Appendix G   ABTA Council structure *208*

Appendix H   Middleton's 'tourism channel' chart *209*

Appendix I   Examples of agency discount offers *210*

Appendix J   Example of a Holiday Club promotion leaflet *211*

Appendix K   Capabilities of a modern CRS *213*

Appendix L   How does Electronic Ticketing work *216*

Chapter 1

The Travel Agent

Travel agencies are today as well known as any other retailer in the high street such as chemists, clothes shops, electrical stores, banks and building societies. Not only in this country, but throughout the world, they provide the link between the providers of travel services, such as the airlines, shipping companies and tour operators and the potential customer. Yet this was not always the case. Prior to the 1950s travel agents were rare, used only by those in higher income brackets and hardly ever by the average person in the street. In the mid 1990s however there are just under 7,000 travel agencies in the United Kingdom. Many, such as Thomas Cook and Lunn Poly, are household names and advertise their services widely on television and in the media.

But what are travel agents, what do they do and where do they fit in the travel and tourism business? In this chapter we will attempt to answer these and other questions and we will begin by placing travel agents into context within the travel and tourism industry.

The Travel Distribution Framework

All industries which produce goods and services need a way of ensuring that their products reach their customers. In marketing terms this is known as 'the distribution framework' or 'the channel of distribution'. We shall discuss this aspect of travel retailing in some detail in Chapter 4. To begin, however, to help us understand the place of travel agents within the distribution framework it is useful to compare the travel industry with other similar industries involved in the supply of goods and services. Figure 1 shows a simplistic and uncomplicated comparison of the travel industry with other industries. As you can see there are a variety of routes, or 'channels', down which the product can pass on its way from the producer to the consumer. Some of these channels are described as 'direct channels' where producers sell their products directly to the customer. An example of this in the travel industry is when a passenger buys an airline ticket directly from an airline at the airport or buys a rail ticket at a station. Other means of distribution are termed 'indirect channels'. Here one or more 'intermediaries' are involved, for instance in travel when a passenger buys plane or rail tickets through a travel agency.

Figure l. Distribution channels - a comparison

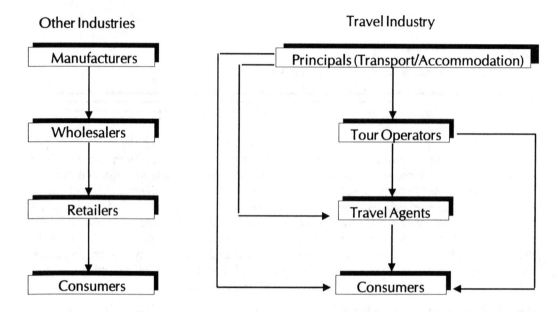

Although at first glance it may appear that the organisations in the travel industry chain of distribution fit neatly into these industrial categories there are in fact some essential differences in the way in which these companies conduct their businesses. As you will see as you learn more about each of these different businesses we need to be careful when we refer to organisations in the travel chain as manufacturers, wholesalers or retailers. We shall begin by examining the nature of the following types of organisation:

- Principals
- Tour Operators
- Travel Agents

Principals in the Travel and Tourism Industry

Principals as Manufacturers or Suppliers of a Service

At the head of the travel and tourism distribution chain are the organisations which provide the basic travel product or as we sometimes describe it, the 'core' product. In the travel and tourism industry such suppliers are called 'principals'. They provide such products as transport, accommodation and amenities. The word 'principal' in this context means first in rank or importance and without whose basic products there would be no further organisations down the chain of distribution. These organisations are therefore 'principals' to the tour operators and travel agents.

Travel and tourism principals are, however, unlike manufacturers in other industries. For in this industry the principal's product is somewhat different. For example, a customer cannot taste an airline seat or hotel bed before purchasing it or take it away and return it after use if it is unsatisfactory. From an operational view point the product is immediately perishable, gone forever once the date of travel is past. It is therefore our interpretation of what the product is that the principals are supplying, which decides whether or not we can describe principals as manufacturers.

As the principals do not build the aircraft or the hotels themselves they are not manufacturers in that sense, yet they do have a product to sell. Their product is a service and so an alternative to labelling travel principals as manufacturers would be to refer to them simply as 'suppliers of a service'. When a passenger steps onto a car ferry the product is the ship itself, its standards of passenger comfort, meals, cabins and amenities and, just like car manufacturers, ferry operators market a product to others below them in the chain of distribution.

The Principals' Means of Selling their Product

Travel and Tourism Principals can distribute their products in a number of ways. These are:

- Direct sell

- Indirect selling through an agent

- Sale to tour operators for inclusion as part of a package

Direct Sell

This involves the Principal in selling the product directly to the consumer. For example airlines sell seats through airline offices, the train operating companies sell tickets at railway stations, coach companies sell seats at bus stations and hotels sell overnight accommodation at the reception desk. In this way they are acting as retailers in their own right. Unlike many other industries such as the motor trade, there is no need to go through a network of dealers and retail outlets.

Indirect Selling Through an Agent

A second important channel of distribution for travel and tourism principals is through a travel agent. In this case the travel agent earns a commission on each sale. An important factor which you need to recognise, however, is that customers often do not realise that the principals bear the cost of the commission. You would pay no more for your holiday or your railway ticket if you had purchased it directly from the principal rather than through the travel agent. It is the tour operator or the railway company and not the customer that pays the commission to the travel agent. You should note however that some suppliers will take any commission charges they are likely to bear into account when fixing the price of their product.

Sale to Tour Operators for Inclusion as Part of a Package

The third important channel of distribution is where principals sell their products to tour operators who in turn combine them with other elements to produce an inclusive package. So for instance, Thomson Holidays buy aircraft seats from a charter airline and hotel beds from an hotelier and put them together with transfers from the airport to resort to produce an inclusive package holiday.

You should note that several principals also act as tour operators in their own right and create their own packages. For example, British Airways operate British Airways Holidays, some cruise and ferry operators have their own inclusive deal brochures and hotel chains often offer inclusive short breaks holidays.

Tour Operators

In 1987 an Inland Revenue publication on Travel Agents stated that :

> *"...tour operators can be described as assemblers of bought-in parts who produce the holiday package that the travel agent retails. They plan, organise, finance and sell the complete holiday package, which includes transport, accommodation and food."*
>
> *(Business Economic Notes, BEN 1, 1987)*

This definition is not strictly correct as tour operators can always sell directly to the customer and so miss out the travel agent completely. Depending, however, on how we interpret the word 'product', we could say that tour operators are in effect creating an entirely new product and as such we could legitimately class them as manufacturers or suppliers. In fact referring back to our chain of distribution we can see that tour operators act as one of the travel agent's principals.

In the U.S.A. tour operators are often called 'wholesalers' and a tour operator has been referred to as:

> *"A business entity that consolidates the services of airlines or other transportation carriers and ground service suppliers into a tour that is sold through a sales channel to the public."*
>
> *(Tour Wholesaler Industry Study, Touche Ross & Co, 1976)*

To refer to them as 'wholesalers' is somewhat ambiguous, however, as the dictionary defines wholesaling as *"the selling of articles in large quantities to be retailed by others"*.

Conventional wholesalers buy the product in very large quantities from manufacturers and 'break bulk' when they sell smaller amounts to retailers. An example of this would be 'cash and carry' wholesalers. Retailers purchase the product in smaller, yet still substantial amounts and pay the wholesaler up front. The retailer bears the risk of holding stock which may or may not be sold. Usually if it is not sold it is the retailer who carriers the cost because the stock cannot be returned to the wholesaler.

In tour operation this process is different. The tour operator sells on single units, an individual inclusive package, either directly or through the travel agent but only when the consumer chooses to buy. Looked on in this way tour operators could be seen as retailers, in the sense that they sell individual units to individual members of the public. They do not bulk sell to anybody, unless to a group and it is they, the tour operators, who take the risk.

If the tour operator decides to sell through a travel agent then the operator pays commission to the agent and builds this extra cost into the selling price. If the package is sold directly to the customer, when for instance the customer telephones the operator's reservations centre directly, there is usually no reduction in price and thus no saving to the consumer. In this way the agent's position is protected. Some operators, however, purposely cut out the agent and pass on the commission saving directly to the consumer. Examples of these 'direct-sell' operators include Portland Holidays (part of the Thomson Travel Group) and Eclipse (part of First Choice Holidays). Here the tour operators act as true retailers in that they are buying in stock, taking a risk, marking up the price and then selling on to the customer.

Figure 2. Examples of vertical integration within the travel industry chain of distribution (1997)

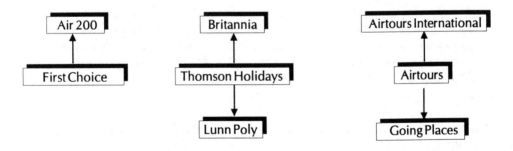

Vertical Integration by Tour Operators

Several tour operators have expanded their operations both up and down the chain of distribution, see Figure 2. This is known as 'vertical integration'. They have either bought an existing airline or developed one of their own, thus giving themselves a position at the top of the chain of distribution. One major tour operator, Thomson Holidays, has both an airline, Britannia, and a travel agency chain, Lunn Poly. Likewise Airtours owns the airline, Airtours International and Going Places, its travel agency chain.

Travel Agents

At the bottom of the distribution chain, dealing directly with the consumer, is the travel agent, often referred to as the 'retail travel agent' (Burkart & Medlik, 1981). There are, however, many aspects of the travel agent's business that differ from conventional high street retailing. Here are some examples:

- Unlike their high street neighbours travel agents carry no stock and therefore bear limited financial risk.

- Travel agents never actually purchase the product but simply act on behalf of consumers. The process involves no financial purchase and no mark-up before sale and usually there is no charge to the customer for using the travel agent's services.

- Agents receive commission on sales and are therefore more akin to insurance brokers or estate agents. Therefore if we use the title 'retail travel agency' we are technically incorrect.

In 1990 the Association of British Travel Agents (ABTA) attempted a definition of the role of the travel agent. It describes the travel agent as:

> *"...supplying prospective travellers with details of travel and related services (available through them from principals from whom they can secure documentation and tickets or issue these on their behalf) and, when requested, provide advice about the suitability of services available in relation to individual requirements."*

> *(ABTA, 1990).*

Note that no mention is made of the word 'retailer' and later in 1990, ABTA dropped the idea of defining travel agents, stating *"there is no legal definition necessary"*.

The dictionary defines 'retailing' as *"the sale of goods in small quantities"* so the problem here is that the travel agent sells a service rather than goods and until travel agents buy stock from principals, by for example taking sizeable proportions of tour operators' programmes of holidays, and are financially accountable for selling them, they should not be called retailers. Compare the way in which a travel agent works with the way a typical clothes shop operates. The clothes shop proprietor goes out to the manufacturers or wholesalers and makes a judgement on what he or she thinks will sell and at what price the product can be sold for. The proprietor then buys the goods, calculates a suitable mark-up and sells them to the public. Travel agents do not do this and, by not having to hold stock, they have less incentive to push products, they do not have goods which are already paid for sitting in the stockroom waiting to be sold.

Many people involved in the travel industry take a slightly different view and accept that the travel agent is a retailer. They argue that the travel agency has so many similarities with its high street neighbours that the term 'retailer' is justifiable. They suggest that the following similarities exist:

- they share the same prime sites;

- they have goods on display, although in the case of the travel agent these are intangible and in the form of brochures;

- they advertise products;

- they offer customer incentives e.g. cash discounts and low deposits;

- they employ sales staff;

- they go to a great deal of effort, especially in the larger travel agency chains, to be retail orientated and employ Sales and Marketing Directors often brought in from outside retailers or manufacturers;

- they have buyers who, like high street chain stores, negotiate deals with suppliers.

Supporters of the term 'retail travel agent' argue that these similarities are much more important than the concept and theory of retailing.

The Position of the Travel Agent in Law

In this section we shall consider the position of the travel agent in law as this will help you understand more clearly the travel agent's role. In law the primary duty of agents is to their principals (Corke, 1987), but agents also owe a duty of professional competence to their clients. In the travel business, as in any commercial situation, the contract of sale for a product is between the parties who are joined together by it, so for example, the sale of a seat on a scheduled flight involves a contract between the airline and the customer. If difficulties arise from the terms of the contract, then these need to be resolved between the airline and the client as the agent is not technically a party to the agreement. We shall see, however, that the agent may have a responsibity to ensure as far as possible that any dispute between a principal and a client is resolved satisfactorily and such responsibilities may be included in the agency agreement.

Agency Agreements

Agents are required to adhere to the terms of their agreements with their principals. These may be contained in a contract creating the agency, or arise from established custom and trade practice such as the ABTA Codes of Conduct. An example of the travel agent's duties can be seen within the ABTA Codes (see Appendix A) Code 1.12 Disputes (iii) states that "travel agents shall make every reasonable effort to deal with complaints of a minor and general character with a view to avoiding recourse to principals. When complaints are of such a nature that reference to the principal is necessary a travel agent shall use his best endeavours acting as an intermediary to bring about a satisfactory conclusion" To some extent in such circumstances the agent is faced with a conflict of interests. To whom the agent is answerable? If the principal appointed the agent then the customer may find that the agent's interests are biased towards that principal.

Forms of Direct and Indirect Selling

As we noted earlier travel industry suppliers have two basic alternatives by which they can distribute their products to their consumers:

(a)   direct selling; or

(b)   indirect selling using intermediaries.

(a) Direct Selling

We have already seen that 'direct sell' involves suppliers getting their products to their customers without the use of retailers as intermediaries. Examples of this method of selling in other industries include the sale of C.D.s and cassettes by mail order using direct television advertising or factory shops selling clothing or furniture directly to the general public. Apart from the advertising, the customer response and the sale there is no attempt on the part of the supplier to build up any two-way communication or an on-going relationship with the customer.

Middleton (1988) states that:

> "...direct selling is any form of selling to the general public that involves direct communication between producers and customers such as direct mail and telephone sales".

Direct Response Marketing

There is another form of direct selling, however, that does attempt to establish a relationship between supplier and customer and this is termed 'direct response marketing'. Here the supplier first attempts to make contact with prospective customers through a variety of advertising methods. Once customers have made a first purchase the supplier's aim is to keep them and to establish a rapport which will eventually result in the establishment of customers' brand loyalty to the supplier's product and so will generate repeat business for the supplier. As Middleton states:

> *"it is two-way communication linking producers and their targeted individual customers in continuing contact."*

This method of selling is used by tour operators such as Saga Holidays, Portland and Eclipse. Having established contact with a potential customer, these operators will feed the customer's details into a sophisticated computer database that will enable the operators to seek repeat business by targeting mail-shots of offers and brochures to customers.

Deutsch and Shepard (1988) describe it as:

> *"...a marketing strategy based on the premise that by gathering, maintaining and analysing detailed information about customers or prospects, marketeers can identify key market segments within their house files and/or prospect segments within outside rented lists and modify their marketing strategies accordingly".*

As we noted above, one of the companies most successful in this field is Saga Holidays of Folkestone and we shall examine this type of marketing in more detail in Chapter 3.

(b) Indirect Sell

Indirect selling simply means that before the product or service reaches the customer it passes through some intermediary such as the travel agent. Examples from other industries include a car manufacturer selling-on to car distributors and garages, or food manufacturers supplying wholesale warehouses who in turn sell-on to shops and finally to the customer.

In the U.K. most foreign package holidays are sold by this indirect method whereby customers use travel agents who deal with tour operators on their behalf. The travel agent effectively brings the customer and the supplier together so that a sale can take place. Sometimes intermediaries such as travel agents are referred to as 'middlemen', because they occupy a position in the distribution channel between the supplier and the final buyer.

Tour operators can adopt different strategies to market their products through travel agents. Two examples are:

- the 'pull' strategy
- the 'push' strategy

The 'Pull' Strategy

Here tour operators use direct mail techniques to reach the customer but instead of selling the product directly themselves they still use the retailer as their distribution outlet. This is known in marketing jargon as the 'pull' strategy as the supplier, for example a tour operator, promotes the product aggressively to the consumer, then directs the potential purchaser to the travel agent. In effect the operator is 'pulling' the customer to the agent.

The 'Push' Strategy

An alternative marketing approach is known as the 'push' strategy. Here tour operators promote their products aggressively to agents who in turn promote the products to the customer. In this instance it could be said that the operator is 'pushing' the agent to the customer.

The Role and Function of Travel Agents

In the previous section we have tried to define a travel agent, now we are going to consider the role and functions that a travel agent carries out. The basic role and function of a travel agent has been described as providing:

> *"... a convenient location where potential travellers may first obtain all the information necessary to make buying decisions and then conclude the purchase."*

> *(Foster, 1985)*

We shall begin by identifying some groups who benefit from the existence of travel agencies. These include:

- the general public
- the principals/suppliers
- the business community

The General Public

Over recent years a number of developments seemed to suggest that the travel agent's days were numbered. These included:

- advances in new technology which allow people to book holidays from the comfort of their own home;
- computerised booking machines which are appearing increasingly in airports, hotels and elsewhere;

- the development of the direct sell tour operator attempting to 'cut-out the middleman'.

Despite these factors most travel agents are still thriving and are still able to offer customers a number of important reasons for using them rather than buying direct. These include:

- Personal Service

- Expert Advice

- Unbiased Advice on a Wide Range of Products

- The Provision of Ancillary Services

- Convenience and Location

- Greater Choice of Products

Personal Service

Recent research suggests that most people still prefer the personal service they receive from a travel agent when arranging their holidays and travel needs. In a survey by Mintel in 1989 respondents rated personal service as the major factor in making their choice of which method of booking to use. Travel agents are clearly in an extremely strong position to meet this need, especially when, for example, the customer wants face-to-face advice on a holiday destination or choice of operators. In contrast the direct sell operator, despite being able to offer a cheaper price, (though not always with agency discounting) is usually restricted to speaking to a potential customer on the end of a telephone or to advising through correspondence.

'Service' is therefore the agent's major incentive in attracting customers into the agency. For this reason and others the role of the agency's sales consultants is crucial. To help you understand the role of the travel sales consultant we provide a typical job description in Appendix B.

The agency's sales consultants must provide the very best in personal service or they risk losing out to the direct sell operator in the future. For members of the general public then, a major advantage of booking through a travel agent is the possibility of building up a friendly and loyal relationship with sales consultants, to whom they will turn to for all their travel needs and hopefully recommend to their friends and relatives.

Expert Advice

Although not specifically mentioned in the Mintel survey another prime reason why the public go to travel agencies is to seek the advice of an expert in travel. Such expertise should include an extensive knowledge not only of the travel products and fares which are available but also of world geography. A trained travel consultant will also have reservation and ticketing skills which will make it easier for clients to obtain the products they seek.

A significant problem for travel agents is that often, because of the relatively low salaries they offer, they cannot employ sales consultants with sufficient experience. The more competent travel consultants often move into management, into other sectors of the business which pay more, or leave the industry completely. Consequently travel agency sales consultants are predominantly young and inexperienced. It is therefore difficult for them to offer the high level of expertise that can often be developed only from personal experience of visits to foreign destinations. Travel agents therefore have had to place increased emphasis on intensive training courses such as the ABTA Youth Training scheme or have had to recruit employees who have qualified from an ABTA approved college. The expertise of such staff comes from knowing where to look, manuals, guides, reference books etc. and using sophisticated computer systems rather than from their own direct experience.

Direct sell tour operators have an advantage in this respect as they have in effect only one product to sell and so can ensure that their sales staff have visited as many of their destinations as possible in order to give first hand experience of the holidays they are trying to sell to customers by telephone.

Unbiased Advice on a wide Range of Products

Travel agents should be able to give the public unbiased advice on a wide range of products and so allow the customer to make a well informed choice. Unfortunately sales consultants do not always give such unbiased advice as they are subjected to a range of incentives from the principals to sell their particular brands. Such incentives may be the result of a commercial agreement struck between the agency and the supplier in which the agency receives a higher commission if more of a supplier's product is sold. (This is explained in more detail in Chapter 5.) This is more problematic when the travel agency is 'Vertically Integrated' with a supplier, that is to say for example, the tour operator owns the travel agent. Sales consultants themselves can also be on commission, either personally or collectively as an office. Different products carry varying levels of commission linked to special deals or as a reward for achieving specific monetary targets.

Even ignoring any incentive that may be being offered to the travel consultant the choice presented to the customer will also depend on the personal experiences of the sales consultant. This may be influenced by whether or not the individual consultant has travelled with a particular operator or has booked previous customers with that operator.

In addition an individual consultant's perception of a tour operator will inevitably be affected by the service he or she receives when making the booking. For example, a consultant may often base a judgement on whether the operator is 'good' or 'bad' on factors such as the efficiency of the operator's computer reservation system, the speed with which tickets and invoices are received, the likelihood of the operator levying surcharges or making changes to the holiday and how well the operator deals with any complaints. Travel product suppliers have therefore to ensure that they are providing the highest levels of service and efficiency to the agent if they are to rely on sales consultants in travel agencies presenting their products in a favourable light to would-be customers.

This ability of travel agents to offer advice on a wide range of products sharply contrasts with that of direct sell reservation consultants who can only talk about their own product and will not wish, or be able to comment on, the products of their competitors.

The Provision of Ancillary Services

The travel agent also offers a range of ancillary services including the provision of:

- information on passports, visas and health requirements;
- recommendations and advice on insurance;
- travellers cheques and foreign currency;
- local transportation to the departure point;
- overnight accommodation;
- car hire.

Indeed under the ABTA Codes of Conduct it is an agent's responsibility to ensure that all necessary supporting information is given to customers to enable them to meet all travel regulations imposed by the U.K. and foreign governments. (Code 1.9) Direct sell operators and transportation suppliers can do this but it adds to their communication charges and administration costs and consequently most would prefer customers to undertake these responsibilities themselves.

Convenience and Location

The general public benefits from the convenient locations of most travel agents. With just under 7,000 agency branches in the U.K. in 1997, spread throughout every city, town, suburban area and village, most people have an agent within easy reach. It is only convenient, however, from a locational point of view as direct sell tour operators can obviously be contacted directly from the customer's home and tickets and other documentation will be dispatched through the post. In fact it could be less convenient to travel to your nearest agency trying to find a parking space on a cold wet day, or having to take time off from work to fit in with the agency's opening hours, than it would be to telephone the tour operator directly. Most of the direct operators have telephone lines open outside normal working hours and at weekends.

Greater Choice of Products

Travel agents save the general public time and money as they are willing, at no extra charge, to contact as many suppliers as the customer wishes in order to secure a booking. Most agents contact operators using quick and efficient computerised reservations systems. Such communication systems have, of course, to be paid for from the income derived from commissions earned by the agent. In fact it was not uncommon in the past for agents to levy a service charge on customers wanting them to make enquiries with many operators, but increased competition has seen this practice eliminated.

If customers know exactly what they want then contacting a direct sell supplier could be quicker and cheaper. Often, however, the customer wants some choice and needs advice. This would cost the individual customer both time and money if he or she had to make a number of telephone calls to a variety of operators. The cost to the customer of communication with the operator is clearly one of the major problems facing direct sell suppliers and some have made substantial investments in providing systems that cause the minimum of inconvenience to potential customers.

The Principals/Suppliers

For suppliers such as tour operators, airlines and ferry companies travel agents provide a widespread network of product distribution points. Just imagine the problem the principals would have in trying to provide booking facilities for their services if no agencies existed. Their only alternative would be to operate their own sales outlets and, for many, this would be completely out of the question because of the high costs involved. So even if travel agencies disappeared there would still have to be some form of local distribution agent acting on the supplier's behalf. Therefore the travel agent provides the supplier with the following:

- A Major Channel of Distribution
- Savings in Time and Money
- An Important Marketing Point

A Major Channel of Distribution

For tour operators, distribution is perhaps the most crucial business problem they face because if the customer does not know about the product, or as they say in marketing terms, it has low 'product visibility', then the operators have little chance of selling anything. Their only alternative is to use the media and advertise directly in newspapers or on radio and television. Such methods can be expensive and are risky. Even when a potential customer is identified the operator has still to follow up with the types of direct response activities described earlier.

Savings in Time and Money

We have already seen that travel agents can save the general public time and money and they benefit the supplier in a similar way. The agent saves suppliers' time because suppliers do not need to have staff tied up discussing travel choice or ancillary services with the customer. All their administrative effort can be concentrated on product development, operations and sales support to agencies.

British Airways and the Railway Train Operating Companies devote massive amounts of time and money to enquiries and reservations. If additionally travel agents were not selling their products on their behalf they would probably have great difficulty in being able to cope with the extra volume of sales without a substantial increases in staffing.

Of course suppliers must also support the agencies and this in itself takes time but now that computerised reservations systems exist there is very little human contact between supplier and agent. Such systems do cost the supplier money but they would still have to invest in such systems even if they dealt only with direct customers.

Nevertheless suppliers do incur additional costs in dealing through agents and these include:

- the costs involved in employing representatives to visit agencies; although these are at present being cut back to make efficiency savings.

- additional costs in printing many more brochures to supply all the agencies;

- most importantly, the commission payable to the agencies.

An Important Marketing Point

For many suppliers, especially those who have publicity materials such as brochures, posters and timetables, the travel agency is a free marketing point where all the supplier's point of sale material will be on view to the public. Agents will usually allow suppliers to place displays in their shop window and arrange for the operators' sales representatives to meet the public for special sales promotion days. In addition suppliers who have entered into special 'preferred' deals with the agency will be allowed to hold staff training sessions. (This will be explained in more detail in Chapter 5.) Sales promotions including special destination evenings and shows are often held jointly by agents and suppliers with the cost of such activities usually shared between the two.

The Business Community

The need to export goods and services abroad is crucial to the U.K. economy and businesses must send their representatives to both domestic and international destinations to obtain orders for their goods. Such representatives need travel advice, reservations, tickets and ancillary services and many now turn to the travel agent to fulfil this need.

Business organisations benefit in a number of ways from using a travel agent including:

- Personal Service

- Accuracy and Expertise

- Savings in Time and Money

- Extended Credit Facilities

Personal Service

Although perhaps not as important to the business traveller as to the general public, personal service is still an important attractive factor in deciding to use a travel agent. Often business travel agents assign specialist sales consultants to a specific business account in the hope that a rapport will be built between the two organisations. Sometimes this element of personal service extends to placing the sales consultant within the premises of the client organisation. For example Carlson Wagonlit Travel, one of the world's largest business travel agents have an office within Shell U.K. in London and American Express have an 'Implant' within ICI on Teeside. Of course a business organisation can, and many often do, obtain travel requirements, such as airline tickets or car hire, directly from the supplier but as this is usually done by telephone the 'personal' aspect of the transaction is sometimes lost.

Accuracy and Expertise

Perhaps the most demanding responsibility placed on the agent by business travellers is the need for accuracy and expertise and it can be of great benefit to the client organisation when it is supplied to the highest standards. The advantage to a client of using an agent, however, is clearly lost if the agent's sales consultant knows less than the travel suppliers or, even worse, less even than the business travellers themselves. There is just no margin of error in terms of accuracy as mistakes may cost the client organisation much time and money. It is extremely important therefore that the agent is able to offer such accuracy and expertise to the client, for without it the customer may just as well book directly.

Savings in Time and Money

If business travel agents did not exist then companies would have to deal directly with suppliers. This would cost them a great deal in time and money. For example, contacting airlines, hotels or car hire firms, in some cases not just domestic but worldwide, and arranging for ticket and voucher issue and payment are all expensive and time consuming and can all be done by the agent on the client's behalf.

Some business organisations employ their own travel managers whose job it is to deal directly with suppliers rather than to go through an agent. However, in recent years, as business travel agents have invested in the latest travel technology the role of the travel manager has been undermined: the only way a travel manager could compete with a travel agent in terms of speed and efficiency is if the firm itself invested in the same technology. To date most firms have found this to be an uneconomic proposition.

Extended Credit Facilities

Another benefit to business clients is that the business travel agent will usually offer extended credit as an incentive to gain and hold the client's business. Offering credit to a customer is of course an established business practice and such deals with travel agents are no exception. Usually a new business account must pay on invoice, but once the client is established with the agent, credit would be extended to seven days, a month or even longer. In the case of a very large business account the travel agent may have to offer this monthly facility from the outset in order to secure the account. This arrangement, whilst a benefit to clients, places a drain on agents' financial resources as they may not get equally favourable terms from their suppliers. Agents must be careful therefore that clients do pay within the agreed credit period or the agent will in effect be subsidising the client's account. Unfortunately some agents find that placing too much pressure on a client for payment may result in the loss of the account.

The **Economic Benefits to Society**

Before leaving this section it is worth pointing out that society as a whole benefits from the existence of travel agents even though we all do not use them. As organisations occupying high street locations they have to pay local rent, rates and taxes. They are also major employers with just under 7,000 agency units each employing on average five people. Such substantial commercial activity benefits the local, regional and national economy.

Table 1. Top leisure travel agents - by type and size, April 1997

Multinational	Branches	Parent Company
Thomas Cook	Worldwide	Westdeutsche Landesbank
American Express	Worldwide	American Express

National Multiples		
Lunn Poly	799	Thomson
Going Places	710	Airtours
A. T. Mays	390	Carlson
Thomas Cook	385	Westdeutsche Landesbank
Travelcare	240	CWS Travel Group

Regional Multiples		Region
Bath Travel	56	Southern England
United Norwest	55	North West England
Bakers Dolphin	51	South West England
Woodcock Travel	39	Yorkshire and N. Mids
Althams	28	North West England
Callers Pegasus	24	North East England

Source: Company

Types of Agency

We make many references in this book to the different types of travel agency that exist in the U.K. It is therefore important, in this first chapter, that you understand the characteristics of the various types of agency. We will attempt to do this by dividing the agency sector as follows:

- by size of organisation;

- by type of business conducted;

- by appointment.

By Size of Organisation

To the uninitiated the industry is now clearly split between a number of very large organisations known as 'multiple' travel agents and numerous small companies referred to as 'independents'.

Multiples can be further sub-divided into three categories, Multinational, National Multiples and Regional Multiples and these are shown in the Table 1.

Multinationals

Multinational agents are distinguished by the fact that their travel offices can be found worldwide. Thomas Cook for example is represented in most European countries, North America, the Middle East, the Indian sub-continent, the Far East, South Africa and Australasia. American Express is the U.S.A's equivalent to Thomas Cook and is part of a large banking and financial institution. Both these organisations are worldwide house-hold names and can provide 'on the spot' services for their customers which cannot be matched by other non-multinational agencies. In 1989 A.T. Mays, considered a national multiple, was taken over by the Carlson Travel Network of the U.S.A. Mays therefore became part of the Carlson global network of agencies and in effect part of a multinational, although the Mays name is not to be found over agency shops in other countries.

National Multiples

The 'National Multiple' category refers to those agencies which have offices spread across the length and breadth of the U.K. Many are household names like Going Places, Lunn Poly and A. T. Mays. They can be found in most high streets in the country next to other nationally known retailers which, although giving them a high profile, also means that they face higher rents. Their business comes from shoppers visiting city and town centres so their catchment area is difficult to define. In recent years a number of these multiples, especially Lunn Poly, have spread their offices into suburban areas to compete with local, well established, independent agents. Whilst most of the Multiples deal with the Leisure/Holiday market some deal exclusively with business travellers, leading companies include American Express, Carlson Wagonlit and Hogg Robinson. More will be said about these later in this chapter. Often owned by large parent companies, the Leisure Multiples dominate the market both in terms of branch offices and in volume of sales. For example, by the late 1980s the top five national multiples accounted for approximately 22% of the number of travel agency offices and 45% of sales. By 1995 this had grown to 35% of offices and a massive 65% of sales. Their expansion has become known as the 'March of the Multiples' and it is discussed it in some detail in Chapter 2.

Regional Multiples or Miniples

There is a distinct group of companies which have multiple offices but which are concentrated in one region of the country. They are referred to as 'Regional Multiples' or 'Miniples'. They often enjoy a high profile with local communities, business and media in their region.

Many have grown from a one-shop family business and have spread out across the locality to a natural boundary, for example a county line.

Like national multiples they occupy high cost, prime high street sites as well as having a presence in suburban areas. Some offer a business travel service but generally they tend to concentrate on the leisure market. With their strong local identity these organisations can be very successful when measured against national multiples but they are also vulnerable to takeover or merger.

Independents

The final category are the 'Independents'. Often they are a single shop agency, (although those with up to say six shops are also classed as independents), usually run by a sole proprietor or partners who are local and perhaps well-known in the area. In some cases the proprietors have left multiples to set up their own businesses. Alternatively the owners may be well-established local business people looking for a diversification of their commercial interests. Unlike the national and regional multiples, who usually occupy prime high street sites in city and town locations, independents are most likely to be found in city and town secondary streets and in suburbs and villages where overheads are not so high. Their business is often built up over a period of years, usually through recommendations from family, friends and previously satisfied customers. They are very susceptible to changes in the market and are vulnerable to takeover and merger from both regional and national multiples.

By Type of Business Conducted

We can categorise agents by the type of business they conduct and divide them into the following types:

- General/Leisure Agents
- Holiday Agents
- Business Agents

General/Leisure Agent

This category of agent will attempt to deal with all types of travel product from inclusive tours to rail and coach tickets. It will have acquired all the necessary licences and appointments to trade. One such licence is from IATA (International Air Transport Association) and it allows the agency to sell international airline tickets. This licence is quite difficult to obtain as IATA imposes strict rules on the number of qualified staff the agency must employ and also with regard to payment and security. A general agent should be able to find the answer to any customer problem or request. For example, the agent should be able to book a short coach journey from London to Birmingham, a rail ticket from Sydney to Adelaide, a theatre seat in London or car hire in Delhi. The majority of multiple agents fall into this category as do a number of well established independents.

Until the mid-1980s most of the large multiple travel agencies in the U.K. could be referred to as 'general agents' as they were fully licensed and sold the majority of products available. Being a general agent provides a number of advantages:

- One of the major advantages of this type of agent is its ability to meet all customer needs. This can greatly enhance the agency's public image. On many occasions a casual enquiry or low revenue purchase can lead at a later date to a much more profitable transaction.

- In providing this 'all-travel' service, sales staff need to be more knowledgeable and qualified and this can often help to create an atmosphere of 'professionalism'.

- This type of travel agency is frequently more highly regarded within the travel trade itself, giving it more influence and power in its relationships with its principals. This power and influence can help in negotiating better deals on commissions and in other matters.

Unfortunately this type of agent faces a number of disadvantages including:

- The problem of handling low cost, low revenue products such as coach or rail travel. It would probably take less time to process a high cost inclusive tour to the Far East than it would to arrange a through rail booking to a European destination with all its attendant reservations.

- The situation can often arise where a customer wanting to buy a high value product is kept waiting whilst sales staff are engaged in a complex timetable reading exercise for coach or rail travel. A possible outcome is that the customer decides not to wait and the booking is lost, most probably to the travel agency that deals exclusively with inclusive tours - the holiday shop.

- Additionally most staff have to be 'Jack of all trades but masters of none' unable to specialise in specific products. This can leave gaps in their knowledge and expertise despite the agency spending more money on their salaries and training.

One criticism levelled at general agents, especially the large multiples, is the lack of personal service they provide. This may be the result of a lack of loyalty to the company from sales staff who see themselves as being just one of thousands of employees. Recently, however, much more emphasis has been placed on customer service skills by these agents to rid themselves of this claim.

In the mid 1980s, however, one company, Lunn Poly, broke the mould and decided to adopt the 'Holiday Shop' concept, which involved the company in concentrating on the selling of inclusive tours. The company even sold off its business travel units to the then Pickfords Travel. Other multiples have also become more selective about the products they are prepared to sell. They pose themselves the question, "is it worth the time and effort for our staff to be engaged in low revenue earning activities?"

Rather than using the term general agent, some companies have formed a 'leisure division' which distinguishes their activities from business travel. Most multiple travel offices are now referred to as 'leisure shops'.

Holiday Agents

Holiday agents specialise in the inclusive tour market as their principal source of business and, to a large extent exclude other types of business.

Historically the typical holiday agent has been a very small independent agency operated by a sole proprietor or by partners. Often it was an extension of an existing business such as a newsagency or clothes shop. They are still very much in evidence today in the suburbs of cities and towns and in villages. Many have no ambition to expand into general agent activities and leave that sort of business to the multiples.

Many of these small independent travel agents remain holiday specialists because they would probably have great difficulty securing other licences such as those of IATA and Rail.

Agents which concentrate on inclusive tours enjoy some major benefits including:

- a high level of revenue per sale compared to that received from the sale of other travel products, and with limited markets and severe competition from multiples this concentration is essential for the survival of many of the small independents;

- the staff of the holiday agent are able to concentrate on selling one major product type, the inclusive package holiday. Consequently they will be less likely to be distracted by the need to know other products and their training can be geared so that the emphasis lies on tour operators, travel geography, resort information and customer care;

- inclusive tours have a relatively high commission earning potential and will often take only a few minutes of the sales consultant's time to sell, especially when the agent is able to use a computerised booking system;

- as the majority of holiday agents are small independents the proprietors are often local people who are well known to the local population. They will have many ex-school friends, families, relatives and will probably be members of the local Chamber of Commerce, Rotary or golf clubs. This gives them a unique advantage over their general agent rivals who, if they are a multiple, will often bring 'outsiders' in as Branch Managers;

- small independents frequently occupy secondary, off-high street sites and employ the minimum number of staff on salaries commonly lower than those on offer by the general agent. This keeps the holiday agent's overheads lower than those of its high street general agent competitors who invariably occupy prime sites.

There are, however, some drawbacks in being solely a holiday agent:

- the agency is unable to meet all requests from would-be customers. Frequently people will have to be told that they cannot be helped if they seek to book products other than inclusive package holidays and are then referred to general agents. This does little for the holiday agent's public image and unfortunately it may be the last time those particular customers are seen;

- a further problem for holiday agents is that travel industry principals do not always see them in quite the same way as general agents. Holiday agents, therefore, tend to have 'less muscle' in negotiating licensing or favourable commission deals;

- finally, as most small independent holiday shops are heavily dependent on the sale of inclusive package holidays they are more likely to suffer during a recession. In the recession of 1991 about nine travel agencies per week went out of business as they were unable to switch to other products for survival. Not only do economic forces hit the sale of package holidays particularly hard but political upheavals, such as the Gulf war, or natural disasters, such as flooding and earthquakes and man-made events such as the outbreak of diseases, can have a serious effect on bookings. There is little for the holiday agent to fall back on at such times and survival means living on reserves until these happenings pass by.

Business Agents

Some business agents are multiples in their own right whilst others are often part of a leisure multiple. There are also a number of very well established independents. Business travel is a highly competitive market which for new players is very difficult to break into.

Business agents derive their income from commercial clients and not the general public. Some of these clients are among the UK's largest organisations as can be seen in Table 2 and the value of business can run into millions of pounds. The business agent can therefore only secure these accounts by offering a highly specialised and expert service which will cover the full product range of a general agent.

Table 2. Top business travel agencies - by size in UK, January, 1997

Company	Offices	Implants	Major Accounts
American Express	53	129	British Aerospace British Council British Gas
Carlson/Wagonlit	54	62	Abbey National Boots IBM Shell UK
Hogg Robinson	33	120	BBC Esso BT

Source: Company/Business Travel World

In some cases, where the value of accounts is high, business agents will take office space within their clients' premises and install their own staff and computerised reservations equipment. This is termed an 'implant' operation.

Compared to leisure agents there are very few organisations which are purely business travel, however some are amongst the world's largest travel organisations such as American Express, Hogg Robinson and Carlson Wagonlit (see Table 2). The largest UK independent business travel agent is Portman Travel with 44 offices and implants followed by The Travel Company and Britannic Travel. Such agents have the advantage of being highly specialised with little or no diversification into other areas of business. Prime high street sites with extensive window display areas are of course not essential for business travel units and therefore business agents can normally be found occupying space in various types of general office accommodation.

The business agent has a number of benefits including:

- a steady flow of business throughout the year without the peaks and troughs experienced by leisure agents;

- additionally business travel is less susceptible to sudden changes in consumer demand. In times of recession, when the holiday market is depressed, many commercial clients have to increase their overseas travel to attempt to secure new contracts;

- as it is the employer who is paying for the travel and not the executives themselves, the type of product purchased can often be high cost, for example the 1997 cost of a single ticket on Concord from London to New York was £3,223 Most executive travel is by air and usually either in

first or club class (London to New York - First £2,492, Club £1,407)
They also often require high grade hotel accommodation and car hire all
of which generates high levels of commission for the business agent;

- by establishing a close relationship with individual commercial accounts
the business agent may also generate leisure travel business from the client company's staff and this is clearly a boon for those agents operating
in both markets.

- leading business agents are generally highly regarded within the travel industry and this helps to strengthen not only their image but also their
negotiating position when seeking to gain extra commission from principals.

There are, however, a number of major disadvantages facing agents who choose to operate
in this area and this keeps many travel agencies out of business travel and requires a
continual review of their operations by those who decide to become engaged in it. These
are as follows:

- it is an extremely competitive market with many of the major multiple
travel agents heavily involved. As mentioned previously Carlson Wagonlit, American Express and Hogg Robinson are the market leaders in
business travel. All of these organisations are trying to expand their business in a market which, when compared to leisure travel, has a relatively
low growth potential;

- because of the intense level of competition business agents have to provide costly extended credit and to substantially discount travel tickets.
Some commercial accounts demand an incentive payment based on the
amount of business they place with their business travel agent. This
makes life extremely hard for the agents who are in effect having to repay some of their hard earned commissions in order to keep the account;

- although overheads can be relatively low for their premises as business
agents do not require a high street site, other costs are high. For example
staff must be highly trained, well qualified and experienced as there is no
margin for error in business travel. Consequently salaries are higher;

- investment in expensive and sophisticated technology like the new global
computer reservations systems such as Galileo, Worldspan and Sabre are
essential if the business agent is to compete. The agent's services must be
promoted to the business community which means advertising, promotions for account staff and the employment of sales representatives. In
addition to these essentials the business agent may incur other costs in
providing services such as: free ticket delivery, special air fare advice,
24 hour service, free gifts, detailed itineraries, translation service, airport representation, V.I.P. handling, special business packages, incentive
schemes, corporate rates and reduced holiday rates.

The provision of all these services plus the need for personal and regular contact between the business agency's management and staff with their client accounts requires a major commitment by any agent thinking of entering this sector of the market.

By Appointment

There are two major appointments sought by travel agents in the U.K., the ABTA and IATA licences.

ABTA Agent

The vast majority of U.K. travel agents are members of ABTA. This means that the agent has applied for, and been accepted into the membership of the Association of British Travel Agents. Founded in 1950, ABTA is a voluntary association of travel agents and tour operators. (see Chapter 2) As it is usual for Tour Operators and other suppliers to request evidence of ABTA membership before they will enter into an agency agreement, this makes membership virtually an essential requirement. The agent must agree to abide by the Associations Articles of Association. One of the most important aspects of these articles is that it enforces a consumer protection scheme whereby all members must be insured against finanical failure. Other rules of ABTA membership include an assessment of the suitability of the owners of the agency, financial stability, employment of qualified staff and an acceptance of the ABTA Code of Conduct which has been produced in close co-operation with the Office of Fair Trading. (see Appendix A)

Non-ABTA Agents

Some agents either prefer the freedom to trade with whoever they choose or they have been rejected by ABTA. The non-ABTA agent does not have to conform to specified rules and regulations except those laid down by principals as part of an agency agreement. These agents may have difficulty in gaining agreements to sell foreign inclusive tours produced by ABTA operators because they are not members. Although the customers of non-ABTA agents will not enjoy ABTA's consumer protection schemes they will still be covered under the Civil Aviation Air Travel Organisers Licence (ATOL) if they take a package holiday by air. Other non-ABTA tour operators using surface travel are also required to take out customer protection schemes under the EC Package Travel Directive (see Chapter 2) The majority of non-ABTA agents will be non-licensed air ticket sales offices working for consolidators (which will be explained in Chapter 3) or ordinary retailers, who are often small shopkeepers selling mainly domestic products like Holiday Centres or coach tours for local bus operators.

IATA Agents

IATA agents have been accepted into the membership of the International Air Transport Association. The IATA agency investigation panel examines all agents applying for membership and will vet the agency's financial record and its financial standing, the qualifications and experience of its staff, the quality, security and accessibility of its premises and its ability to promote and sell international passenger air transportation. Once the agency has obtained the IATA licence it will be able to offer its customers the full services of world-wide air transportation. The majority of multiples and leading independents hold the IATA licence and it is essential for agents engaged in the business travel market. One of the benefits of holding this licence is that it can help to ensure an even flow of business throughout the year as international airline tickets tend to be less of a seasonal market than inclusive tour sales.

Table 3. Spending on tourism in Britain and abroad by U.K. residents 1985-1995

Year	In Britain £bn	Abroad £bn	Total £bn
1985	6.3	4.9	11.2
1988	7.9	8.2	16.1
1990	10.5	9.9	20.4
1993	12.4	13.0	25.4
1994	13.2	14.5	27.7
1995	12.8	15.7	28.5

Source: BTA/MQ6

Non-IATA Agents

The majority of small independent travel agents and a number of multiples specialising in the selling of inclusive package holidays do not hold the IATA licence. Although such agencies are unable to offer international scheduled airline travel they can deal with all domestic air services, Advance Booking Charters (ABCs), and 'seat-only' deals connected with the package tour market. Unfortunately, as they do not hold the IATA licence, they must redirect customers to other licensed agents when they are asked for international scheduled air tickets.

Table 4. Agency income from travel services, 1985-1994

Year	Total £bn
1985	4.5
1988	6.4
1993	6.2
1994	6.8

Source: Mintel/Keynote

The Retail Travel Market

In this section we will provide you with an approximate idea of the value of the U.K. travel market and the market share held by the major agents. We will begin by quantifying the total market value for both outbound and domestic tourism. These figures are available from the British Tourist Authority and the Office for National Statistics. Table 3 gives the figures from 1985-1995. These figures show that the travel market was worth approximately £28.5bn in 1995. From this figure we have excluded incoming tourism as this is a market in which the U.K. travel agents do not have a significant share.

One difficulty we face is being able accurately to quantify the share of this vast and growing market held by the major travel agents. There are three possible ways of doing this:

- by identifying the turnover figures for approx 7,000 U.K. agents;

- by using information from each supplier; or

- by using information supplied by major retail survey organisations such as Mintel and Keynote. For example Mintel believed that the total agency income derived from travel services in 1985 was around £4.5bn and that by 1994 Keynotes estimates were £6.8bn (Mintel, Keynote figures are shown in Table 4).

From these figures we estimate that the travel agency share of the total market, excluding incoming tourism, is about 24%. However, in making this estimate we must take account of two major considerations:

- tourism statistics as expressed in Table 3 include such items as shopping, entertainment and eating and drinking which are not within the travel agent's business income mix.

- a large proportion of expenditure on domestic tourism by the British holiday maker is spent directly with the supplier. For example, the vast amount of business generated by car travel to U.K. destinations or the purchase of transportation tickets directly from supplier locations at railway stations, coach stations and airports would not be passing through the travel agent's hands. This is illustrated by a BTA estimate that in 1986 only 6% of UK domestic tourists used a travel agency for their bookings compared to approximately 70% of those making overseas visits. Even by 1997 it was estimated that this figure had only increased to 8%.

Having now quantified the value of tourism products sold through a travel agent we can now go further and break it down by individual product type. We are helped in this by an agency remuneration survey carried out by ABTA in the early 1980s, the results of which produced an estimated share of each product as shown in Table 5. The figures have been updated to 1995 following a recent survey of leading travel agency multiples. These figures however do not include financial services such as the sale of travellers cheques and foreign currency now a significant earner for most large agencies.

Table 5. Leisure agency product breakdown, 1980-1995

Product	1980 %	1990 %	1995 %
Inclusive Tours	52.3	66.0	73.6
Air	33.0	20.0	14.0
Rail	2.7	2.0	1.5
Ferry	2.4	4.0	1.6
Insurance	0.8	2.2	5.6
Car Hire	0.3	0.2	0.6
Others (inclu cruise)	8.8	5.6	3.1
	100.0	100.0	100.0

Source: ABTA Remuneration Survey, 1983. Industry Sources, 1991, 1996

This survey reveals that inclusive tours have, throughout the 1980s and 1990s, been the most important source of travel agency income. Their reliance on package holiday sales makes travel agents extremely susceptible to changes in the market caused by unforeseen circumstances such as economic downturns, currency fluctuations or political instability in host destinations. One other notable feature is the increase in the revenue from sales of insurance which resulted from the introduction in the mid-eighties of incentives to agents to sell insurance. It is now common practice that in order to qualify for a cash discount the customer must take out the agency's insurance. As the agency gains a high commission level from the sale of insurance, often between 30 and 40% of the price of the insurance, this helps to offset the discount being given. This will be considered in more detail in Chapter 5.We now consider the factors which influence the travel agent's share of the market in the following sectors:

- inclusive tours,

- air,

- surface transport.

Inclusive Tours

Sales of inclusive tours through travel agents divide into the domestic market for U.K. residents and the outbound international market.

U.K. Domestic Market

It was estimated that in 1986 only 6% of the public used an agency to book their U.K. holiday. This percentage has increased slightly over the last decade as a result of attempts by ABTA, the U.K. Tourist Boards and domestic tour operators to stimulate interest in domestic holidays. As mentioned previously we now estimate that the share of domestic holidays being booked through agencies is still only 8%.

However, within certain U.K. domestic market segments and in particular in the short break inclusive tour market the position is quite the reverse. According to Rainbow Holidays the hotel-based short break market in 1989 accounted for approximately 4m people of whom 25% booked through an agent. By 1995/6 this had risen to 6.7m people of whom around 20% booked through an agent. About half of these customers booked an inclusive package from a specialist operator rather than from a hotel group and these specialist operators estimated that between 80% and 90% of business came from agency bookings!

Outbound International Market

By far the most important market for agents is the overseas inclusive tour market. Without this business most would not survive. It has been the bedrock of agency development since the first tour took place in the fifties. The value of overseas package holidays has been closely monitored over the years and we show it in Table 6. In 1980 for example, approximately 6.3 million inclusive tours were sold and of this figure some 80% were booked through travel agents generating revenue for the agents of just under £100m. By 1995 sales had risen to 15 million tours sold increasing revenue to an estimated 600m.

Table 6. Number of visits abroad by UK residents on inclusive tours 1970-1995

Year	Total (m)	Air (m)	Surface (m)	Market Value (£bn)
1970	2.7	2.1	0.5	n/a
1980	6.3	4.9	1.4	1.2
1985	8.5	6.4	2.1	1.9
1990	11.4	8.8	2.6	5.9
1993	13.6	10.6	3.0	6.9
1995	15.3	12.2	3.1	7.5

Source: MQ6/Mintel

Air

In 1988 the market for air travel to, from and within the U.K. was estimated at £5bn increasing to £8.4bn in 1993. Travel agents have played a major role in selling the air product. Around 75% of this figure relates to holiday travel and travel agents account for an estimated 90% of this type of booking. In fact around 80% of all air tickets purchased are bought through travel agents. This is shown in Table 7. British Airways estimate that approximately 72% of its worldwide business comes through travel agencies.

Table 7. Sources of all air ticket purchases, 1997

% of purchases

72	Travel Agents
16	Discount agents (consolidators etc), Tour Operators
12	Direct airline sales
100	

Source: British Airways

Surface Transportation

The markets for independent surface transportation including express coach, rail, sea and car hire are of significantly less importance to the agent.

Express coach

The express coach business is dominated by one supplier, National Express whose turnover in 1995 was approaching £160m. However we estimate that only about 35 to 40% of this business was generated through the high street travel agencies. This is due to the fact that it is regarded by some as low revenue, low priority especially in multiples where foreign inclusive package holiday customers are the prime target. However nearly half of all agencies hold a licence to sell National Express and are keenly supported by the smaller independent.

Rail

Although rail travel is a huge market, valued at around £24bn in 1995, it contributes only a small percentage of most agents' income. The exception are the specialised business travel units dealing solely with commercial accounts. To estimate agents income we must first remove the sales of season tickets, which agents cannot book, this reducing the potential to £17bn. The old British Rail Board estimated that agents were generating about 20% of ordinary ticket sales giving a value of around £340m. For certain types of rail ticket the agent's role is far more important, for example in the first class market they handle an estimated 40% of all passenger business.

Ferries

The value of the UK ferry market in 1996 was about £34m and P & O North Sea Ferries estimated that approximately 60% of all passengers travelling on their services out of Hull used a travel agent to book their ferry crossings. (This figure would have been lower for services using the Channel routes). It is easy, however, for passengers, especially in the off season, just to turn up at the ferry without a booking and be reasonably certain of getting aboard.

Cruising

The cruise market is a very lucrative source of commission earnings for agents. If we exclude line services such as the QE II from Southampton to New York and mini cruises by ferry operators, P & O estimated that in 1989 there was an annual market of approximately 125,000 passengers, this having more than doubled to some 429,201 passenger by 1996. The Passenger Ship Association (PSA) estimated the market value to be in the region of £511m of which P & O estimated 85% was generated through travel agents.

Car Hire

Britain's car hire market is estimated to be worth around £600m and is second only to Germany's within Europe. Much to the regret of leading car hire firms such as Hertz however, travel agents pick up only about 60% of the business.

Reasons for Development

In this final section of our introduction we will summarise a number of important external events and changes that have had a major influence on the industry's development since 1950. In the next chapter these points will be further developed.

Burkart and Medlik (1981) identified three major stimuli to the growth of tourism. These were:

- the wealth of the industrialised society;

- developments in transport;

- the organisation and servicing of travel.

Taken together these factors have been crucial to the dramatic growth of the travel agency sector since 1950. As ABTA reports, the sector has grown from 97 members when ABTA was formed in 1950 to a peak of 2,965 members with some 7,513 offices by the end of 1989. In the mid nineties it had slipped back to 2,430 members with 6,977 offices.

The Wealth of Industrialised Society

Since the end of the second world war the U.K. has enjoyed a period of relative growth and prosperity with only short periods of temporary recession. With this prosperity has come a significant increase in consumers' discretionary incomes. This has been particularly true of the working class who previously did not regard holidays and travel abroad as a part of day to day life.

Economic prosperity can be identified in many aspects of our lives. Improvements in education have seen better qualified young people able to seek higher paid jobs. They tend to have a keen interest in travelling abroad either to seek the sun or experience alternative cultures and history. Foreign holidays have become for many a way of life in the same way that the ownership of motor cars, washing machines and their own homes have become common place.

For those in higher income brackets the possibility of a second holiday, such as a winter sun break or domestic short break, has been added to the family holiday abroad each summer.

Developments in Transport

Linked to economic and social change have been developments in transport and the travel industry both of which will be discussed in greater depth in Chapter 2. Human ingenuity produced in the 1950s the first commercial jet aircraft offering speed and comfort undreamed of by the travelling public. By the 1970s the capacity of aircraft soared with the introduction of the Boeing 747 Jumbo jet carrying over 300 passengers. As a consequence the average cost per mile of air travel has actually reduced relative to the increase in the price of other products. Inclusive tour operators have emerged to take advantage of the availability of air travel and linked it to overseas hotel developments. On land the car has become the symbol of status and independence. In the U.K. private car ownership has risen from two million in 1950 to twenty million in 1994. Motorways have been built in an attempt to cope with this volume of cars and large technologically advanced jumbo ferries and hovercraft have been introduced to transport them to Europe. Elegant cruise ships have been built offering the highest standards of comfort, food and leisure facilities.

Road and rail organisations continue to compete for the surface traveller, each trying to improve on speed and performance by introducing new advanced equipment whilst maintaining a competitive price. The coach operators have taken advantage of motorway development by introducing high speed luxury vehicles offering reclining seats, enter-tainments, toilets and refreshment facilities. Rail travel on inter-city routes is by high speed trains such as the Inter-City 125 and on the East Coast the 225 Electric service. Rail coaches are more comfortable, quieter and trains include more modern catering facilities. The Channel Tunnel has brought the possibility of long distance through services to Europe including luxury travel to Brussels and Paris by the Eurostar service.

The Organisation and Servicing of Travel

To take advantage and to service all these developments organisations such as tour operators and travel agents have flourished. They have become an accepted part of the country's commercial life with many becoming household names and being controlled by multinational organisations. They have been helped by the media which has stimulated an interest in travel by producing weekly travel shows on television and radio, colour supplements in newspapers and magazines written by a new breed of travel writers. Travel agents have played an important role in this development, helping the emerging tour operators to distribute their new products and this brings us back to the focus of the book – has the travel agent lived up to the expectations of suppliers, is it providing the right level and type of service, has its role changed over the last forty years and can it survive in the future?

Chapter 2

Travel Agency Development

In this chapter we are concerned with the changes that have shaped the travel agency industry of today. We begin by looking at general economic and social trends which have shaped the market. Then we shall go on to consider the changes affecting transport and tour operation. Finally we will examine the developments which have influenced travel agents themselves.

Tourism and Change

(i) Economic Trends

The state of both the U.K.'s economy and those of potential tourist destinations can have a major effect on the level of tourism. This has been increasingly apparent over the last forty years. In the 1950s one of the major problems facing the U.K. was the need to redevelop the domestic economy following the devastation and financial ruin caused by the Second World War. The country was heavily in debt to the rest of the world and therefore needed to keep its currency under tight control to prevent an outflow of funds. Exchange controls were imposed which restricted the amount of currency people could take abroad and this clearly had the effect of dampening the demand for foreign travel from the U.K.

It was not until 1959 that these restrictions were eased and U.K. travellers were allowed a travel allowance of £250 per person. This was the amount that travellers were permitted to take out of the country and change into foreign currency. Until then the fluctuating travel allowance had been a barometer of Britain's economic solvency. It started at £100 immediately after the war and was even reduced to zero in 1947. It fluctuated wildly from £25 to £100 between 1948 and 1953. Later the so-called 'travel year' was abolished and travellers were allowed to retain unused foreign currency for future use.

A major shock came in 1966 when, with the economy worsening and the balance of payments deteriorating, the then Labour Government under the premiership of Harold Wilson imposed a £50 foreign travel allowance. This relatively meagre amount had to cover all costs paid to foreign suppliers and included such items as accommodation and coach transfers. For those travelling on inclusive tours it involved separating out the so-called 'foreign content' of the holiday. Tour operators were required to state the 'foreign content' in their brochures and when the holiday was booked this amount had to be deducted from the £50. The balance was then available to the tourist as spending money. Such restrictions seem almost incomprehensible in today's market. This restriction created immediate problems for those tour operators offering high cost accommodation. For example, if hotel accommodation abroad cost £40 this left travellers with only a £10 balance on their travel allowance plus a small amount of cash in sterling.

By law the travel agent who made the booking was required to enter the 'foreign content' in the customer's passport issuing a 'V form' which had to be attached to the booking file and could be checked by Bank of England inspectors. Tour operators responded by dropping all their up-market properties and substituted low cost, low grade accommodation. A further blow to the travel trade came in 1967 when the pound was devalued, pushing up the prices of foreign holidays. Fortunately this dampening of demand was followed almost immediately by the devaluation of the Spanish peseta, the currency of the major destination country, and this somewhat softened the effect of Britain's devaluation.

The late 1960s was one of the most difficult times for the travel trade. A major economic squeeze was combined with higher inflation which resulted in higher prices, fuel costs and excise duties. The severe problems facing the industry in the late 1980s and early 1990s are nothing new, as these economic troughs and peaks have bedevilled the industry throughout its post-war development. However, virtually all restrictions on currency movements were finally lifted by the Conservative Government in 1979 (see Appendix C).

The industry was also badly hit in 1973, when the members of the Organisation of Petroleum Exporting Countries, (OPEC), decided to raise the cost of oil by almost 100%. OPEC was the world's major supplier of oil and it acted as a price fixing cartel controlling both the price of oil and its level of supply. The Western industrialised nations, including the U.K., were once again thrown into recession. At the time it was predicted that over 500 travel agencies would go out of business as a result of the drop in consumers' disposable income and the rise in air fares caused by the increase in airline fuel costs. The inclusive tour market fell by 18% from 1973 to 1974. Capacity was severely cut back and operators were much more selective when considering which agencies to appoint as their distributors. By the late 1970s the U.K. had begun to recover and the holiday boom was on again. This boom, which lasted through the middle years of the 1980s, has been described by some as the industry's 'halcyon days'. It continued until 1988 when the government, alarmed by the consumer credit boom of 1986 and 1987 which had resulted in rising inflation, felt it necessary to impose a substantial increase in interest rates to curb excessive consumer demand. Once again the result was a squeeze on the holiday and travel business as people tried to economise on their discretionary spending.

The early nineties were difficult economic times for the travel business compounded by the Gulf War in 1991 during which period virtually all outbound tour business dried up. The UK's second largest tour operator, Intasun, failed causing a loss of consumer confidence in the holiday business. Due to economic measures taken by the Conservative

Government in the first half of the decade, including the reduction in bank base and mortgage rates, the economy started to show a slow revival and just before the General Election of 1997 was said to be the strongest in Europe. The currency, having lost ground over many years, was gaining strength in the first few months of 1997 prompting a return of the so-called 'feel good factor'.

Despite such fluctuations in the economic fortunes of the U.K., two factors in relation to holiday taking are clear. Long-term trends both in the numbers of holidays whether Inclusive Tours or Independently arranged have always been upwards and this is clearly illustrated in Table 8.

Table 8. Overseas holiday taking 1951-1995

Year	No (m)
1951	1.5
1961	4.0
1971	7.3
1981	13.3
1991	20.6
1995	28.1

Source: BTA

Finally, it must be remembered that currency exchange rates have a significant bearing on the attractiveness of foreign travel. Potential visitors will be deterred from visiting a country if the value of sterling is weak against the destination country's currency as this will make accommodation and local purchases expensive.

Of particular interest are the so-called 'sunshine currencies' – the peseta, lire and drachma. Although by March 1997 Sterling was strong against these currencies there have been highs and lows over the previous ten years as can be seen in Table 9. Spain, traditionally the most popular destination for British holidaymakers has had mixed fortunes, in the early nineties sterling was weak against the peseta making Spain increasingly less attractive as a cheap destination. This was also linked to other problems such as poor quality accommodation and unruly behaviour by British youths. However by 1995 sterling was recovering and together with the Spanish Government investing heavily in up-grading the resorts and increasing security, helped to restore the destination to its premier position.

Undoubtedly the success story in recent years has been Greece. Sterling has doubled in value against the drachma over the last decade making this destination very popular and good value for money. However, during 1995 and 1996 this position slowed down and at one point sterling was weakening against the Drachma illustrating the volatility of exchange rates. It must also be remembered that inflation in the host destination will offset savings gained on the currency exchange.

As aviation fuel is produced from oil and oil is traded in U.S. dollars on the World markets this makes its relationship with sterling important. When sterling weakens against the dollar as it did in 1993 the price of fuel can increase which then may be passed on to the holiday traveller. In addition it is crucial for the increasingly important American holiday market.

Table 9. Value of sterling against major holiday currencies 1987-97

Year	Peseta	Lira	Drachma	US Dollar
March 87	206.58	2094.75	215.68	1.61
March 90	176.60	2035.25	265.20	1.61
March 93	170.10	2302.25	322.70	1.43
March 95	203.10	2749.00	363.80	1.58
March 96	189.50	2387.00	367.50	1.52
March 97	231.80	2720.00	430.00	1.60

Source: Travel Trade Gazette

(ii) Socio-economic Trends

In 1956 James Maxwell, then General Manager of Thomas Cook, reported that a record number of people, some 1.4 million, had gone abroad in the previous year and yet this was to prove a mere fraction of the potential market. He estimated that at least ten million could afford to undertake foreign travel and that it was possible to achieve this figure in the space of ten years. In fact as we show in Table 10 this figure was not achieved until the mid 1970s. From then on however, the number of visits abroad by U.K. residents has climbed steadily to reach a staggering 41.9 million visits by the end of 1995 with spending estimated at some £15.7 billion pounds.

Table 10. Visits abroad by UK residents (all purposes)1956-1995

Year	Number of visits (m)	Expenditure (£m)
1956	1.4	-
1966	6.9	297
1976	11.6	1,068
1986	24.9	6,083
1990	31.2	9,916
1995	41.9	15,683

Source:BTA

During this period there has been a fundamental change in attitudes towards travel and holiday-taking. The fifties were seen as the decade when people really did get on the move. New developments were made in every area of transportation and accommodation and these were linked to an acceptance by governments of many countries of the importance of domestic and international tourism. The jet age arrived, opening up new routes for the emerging tour operators. Throughout the world more people from more countries visited each other using the ever increasing scheduled airline routes.

The complex mass of rules and regulations which had held back travel and tourism development was for the first time being addressed and reviewed by authorities in many countries bringing increased freedom to the new leisure travellers. Such changes included the relaxation of entry requirements, the lifting of visa restrictions and much freer import and export of currencies.

During the 1960s the traditional British seaside resorts, so long the backbone of U.K. tourism, began to 'wake up' to the growing continental challenge. They needed to bring themselves up-to-date to compete with European resorts which offered new luxury accommodation, modern leisure amenities and of course sunshine. It became more fashionable to take a foreign holiday, much to the distress of the U.K. tourism business.

The Director of the British Hotels and Restaurants Association said in June, 1960:

> "that much of the urge to holiday abroad comes from a strange snobbishness which arises from the fashionable hobby of keeping up with the Jones's. It is so much more impressive to be able to talk of the pension we found at some Mediterranean resort with an unpronounceable name, where sanita-

tion does not exist and where a visit to the chemist is almost a daily necessity than to admit to having had a grand holiday at a boarding house with good English food at one of our seaside resorts."

(TTG, 1960)

This new continental 'product', however, simply left the British hotelier unable to compete. New hotels and apartments, many with air conditioning, brand new swimming pools, evening entertainment and sightseeing excursions, all were combined with the experience of visiting a foreign country to sample the culture and meet the people.

At home the holidaymaker found domestic resorts offering pre-war accommodation often with the traditional 'British seaside landlady' with her outdated 'house rules'. The resorts themselves had poor leisure facilities which combined with the vagaries of British summer weather proved no contest for the Mediterranean resorts.

By 1973 the inclusive tour market represented over 65% of all consumer spending overseas. People were increasingly taking second and even third holidays in a year attracted by the low prices on offer for off season and short duration breaks.

The growth in overseas holiday taking was most pronounced among the 16 - 24 and 45 - 54 age groups. The emerging younger generation, born after the second world war, had a much greater desire to explore and visit other lands than their parents who had had to contend with wars, low pay, unemployment and the lack of cheap transport. More young people were better educated and their ability to earn higher incomes gave them not only the desire but the means to enjoy foreign holidays.

Tour operators emerged to meet their needs and an ever increasing number of groups travelled abroad. Of course, a minority caused some distress to fellow tourists and to local inhabitants through bad behaviour and it could be said that it was at this time that we began to see the emergence of the 'lager lout' generation.

For the 45 - 54 age group the increased demand for foreign holidays was the result of a higher standard of living and greater disposable incomes. Many families now had dual incomes with both husband and wife working. Their children had grown up and left the family home reducing their financial commitments. But most of all it was the growing availability of cheaper inclusive tours by comfortable and quick jet transport which stimulated demand from this group.

The eighties was said to be the decade when:

"the global village became a reality and the great British travelling public took its sunscreen and sandals to the four corners of the earth"

(Brookes, TTG, 1990)

Leading the way in the opening of new destinations was the United States of America with their holiday boom from the U.K. starting in the southern state of Florida. The creation of the new Walt Disney World near Orlando with nearby beaches in and around Miami began to tempt holiday makers away from the traditional resorts of the Mediterranean which were now suffering from the after effects of over twenty years of development. Spending twelve hours on an aircraft to reach your destination became more acceptable as holidaymakers wanted to try something new and exciting. A number of cruise companies offered special deals to attract customers to fly out to Miami and then to join a Caribbean cruise, turning it into the cruise capital of the world.

Other long haul destinations such as Australasia and Canada were also opened up as demand from the holiday traveller grew. But the big success story outside the U.S.A. was the Far East and in particular Thailand and Hong Kong. With their mixture of the exotic, cheap prices, good service and fine beaches both destinations proved to be extremely attractive to British holiday makers.

Virtually every holiday destination in the world started to appear amongst the hundreds of brochures now available and were featured in the ever increasing number of specialist holiday television programmes such as 'Wish you were Here' and 'The Holiday Programme'. This media coverage brought the exotic and long haul destination right into the living room of the would-be traveller. New, highly specialised tour operators grew up to meet this demand.

With growing sophistication the demands of holiday makers were changing and increasingly quality became an important issue. Many holiday makers were no longer prepared to be flown through the middle of the night to areas which in the high season resembled their own town centre on a Saturday night. Perhaps it was the seemingly continuous flow of tourists to the Mediterranean resorts which had made some tour operators, hoteliers and locals complacent. Whatever the reason, the public perceived a lowering of standards in the traditional Mediterranean resorts, all done, it was said, with the aim of keeping prices down. The U.K. tourism industry began to play on this perception saying that it was now time to abandon the Mediterranean package and return to the good old traditional British holiday. Trends were changing with activity and cultural holidays becoming more popular. The increasing wealth of certain sections of the population also led to a boom in time-share villas and apartments. For many holiday makers the package was out and the freedom to 'do your own thing' was in.

(iii) Demographic Trends

Another equally important factor which has played its part in moulding the market for travel and tourism over the last forty years has been Britain's changing demographic profile. Key Note analysts (1989) cite two specific events that have shaped population distribution during the period under review. First was the effect of the Second World War, which significantly reduced the birth-rate during the early and middle 1940s but which saw a baby boom in the late 1940s and 1950s. Second was the introduction of the birth control pill in the 1960s which, coupled with an increase in women working and a trend to postpone pregnancy until later in life, has had a significant effect on the birth-rate. Demographically this has meant that there is a heavy peaking of the population with a large population bulge among those born in post-war years who are now aged between forty and fifty. There is a corresponding reduction in population of those born in the early seventies, now aged between twenty and thirty (see Appendix D).

It is possible therefore to anticipate the changing volumes of potential purchasers in each age group and such market predictions can be further refined by cross referencing population changes to an analysis of income bands. The population is divided into 'socio-economic' groupings according to occupation and other factors (see Appendix E), and in recent years the BTA has analysed these groups in relation to their holiday taking. This is illustrated this in Table 11.

Table 11. Profile of British holiday takers, 1987-1995

Socio-econ Groups	% Of Adult Pop		% No Holiday		% UK Holiday		% Abroad Holiday	
Year	**87**	**95**	**87**	**95**	**87**	**95**	**87**	**95**
AB	17	17	9	8	21	21	33	28
C1	22	28	19	22	24	29	25	35
C2	29	22	29	22	30	24	26	19
DE	31	33	43	48	25	26	15	18

Source: BTA

The BTA's findings may not be what we expect. For example those in the top band, the AB group, had the highest proportion of overseas holidays in 1987 however, by 1993 they had been overtaken by those in the C1 category. It must be noted though that there was a shift of those people moving upwards from C2 to C1 category. This has been a significant trend over the last forty years where certain sections of society are upwardly mobile with children seeking to move into a higher socio-economic group than their parents. Such movements have continued to increase the market for those seeking to take overseas holidays. Overall the AB and C1 groups are the better educated, have better jobs, earn higher wages and thus have more disposable income to spend on holidays and travel.

Finally, it is worth noting that over the past twenty five years there has fluctuating trends in the number of working hours and an overall increase in holiday entitlement. For example, over the period from 1961 to 1987 the normal basic weekly hours worked by full-time manual employees fell from 42.8 to 38.9 hours, however, this increased again to 43 by 1994. Average annual holiday entitlement with pay for this group in 1961 was only two weeks but by the 1980s it had risen to three weeks and now it is estimated that over 90% of full-time manual employees are entitled to four weeks or more.

Transport Developments

(i) Air Transport

In the space of a little over a quarter of a century the airline industry has changed from being the preserve of a wealthy few, to being a common place form of transport for a large proportion of the population. Without doubt it was the introduction of the world's first commercial passenger jet, the Comet, in 1953 which completely transformed the business. It cut flying times dramatically and opened up a new era in civil aviation. Despite earlier technical difficulties it was to become the workhorse for the then British Overseas Airways Corporation (BOAC – which was later to become British Airways). Whilst modifications were being made to the Comet, BOAC introduced one of the most comfortable aircraft of all, the Britannia, affectionately known as the 'whispering giant'.

After the Second World War there was a surplus of ex-military propeller-driven aircraft and many were bought up by small independent airlines. These initially carried cargo but increasingly turned to passengers to expand their businesses. One such company, Airwork Ltd., in 1954 opened up a new network of air routes linking the South and East of England with the Continent using Viking and Dakota aircraft. This challenged the ferry operators on the cross channel routes. Aquila Airways gained approval to operate from Southampton to Genoa/Santa Margherita so opening up the Italian Riviera from only £19 single and £34 return. Silver City introduced a road, air and rail service to Paris and Brussels from £4.15s single with a journey time of 7hrs 40mins.

By the mid fifties attention had turned to the Atlantic and the possible introduction of the first jet flights. In 1939 a Clipper flying boat took twenty passengers from the U.S.A. to the U.K. in 4 days, yet by 1959 BOAC was flying from London to New York using Comets in 10hrs 30mins. Pan American quickly followed suit using the famous Boeing 707. This company promoted tourist fares, credit plans and low cost tickets aimed at families, and attempted to make it possible for the average American working man to take his family to Europe during a normal two week vacation. The jet airliner made it possible to fly routes never dreamed of before such as the first non-stop trans-polar air service operated by TWA flying from London to the west coast of America in eighteen hours. One problem for the newly emerging independent airlines in those early days was the dominance of the state operators on scheduled routes. This monopoly was not broken until 1960 when independents were given equal rights in applying for new services. Early operators included Cambrian, Jersey Airlines, Silver City and British United Airways, all now sadly part of history. In 1963 the monopoly on domestic routes was broken when British Eagle commenced operations from London to Glasgow and Belfast.

As more independent charter flights came on stream to take tourists to foreign destinations, the state carriers recognised their weakness in this sector of the market. In 1963 British European Airways (BEA) decided to sell the inclusive tours of some of the top U.K. operators using seats on its scheduled services. Tours were selected from a number of leading ABTA operators and sold under a newly formed Silver Wing Holiday brand. This marked a significant change in policy by BEA, then the state carrier, and BEA were later to merge with BOAC to form British Airways, who still continue to be involved in inclusive tours. The development of air charter services was of course closely linked to the emergence of the inclusive tour and until 1967 this was hampered by a licensing rule known as 'Provision One'. This stated that inclusive tours could not be sold below the normal scheduled return fare. The reasoning behind this provision was an attempt to protect the existing scheduled routes from charter competition, which if allowed to offer a cheaper deal, would undermine the profitability of the scheduled network. In that year, however, the authorities decided to allow certain operators to offer tours to the Continent and East Africa at below normal scheduled fares. This marked the beginning of the end for 'Provision One' and heralded a new era for independent charter operators.

In 1969 two very significant events took place with the maiden flights of two aircraft which were to change the face of passenger aviation. The first was the introduction of the now famous 'Jumbo' jet, the Boeing 747, capable of carrying over 300 passengers. This huge aircraft was capable of offering a variety of classes including its famous upper-deck, reached by a spiral staircase from below which could contain sleeperettes, bar, lounge or working area. This was followed by the supersonic 'Concorde', a joint Anglo-French development which involved a U.K. government investment of over £600m. Both aircraft stimulated great public interest and provided yet another spur to aviation development. Concorde did not actually carry passengers on scheduled services until 21st January 1976 when British Airways introduced the plane onto its London - Bahrain service. Later it was allowed into the U.S.A. through Washington D.C., but there was great resistance by the people of New York who complained about its high noise level. After months of protest the US authorities finally relented, allowing it to land at John F. Kennedy airport.

Until the 1970s price had always been an inhibiting factor in the attempt to encourage more people to fly. Prices on scheduled routes were often held at an artificially high level as a result of the virtual monopoly which scheduled carriers enjoyed. These carriers, and in particular the so-called 'national flag carriers' would meet within their own association, IATA, and fix fares which would then be recommended to their respective Governments. A challenge to this establishment came from Freddie Laker, an airline and tour operator, who wished to introduce a low cost, walk on, no frills 'Sky train' service from London to New York for only £75. It took him six years to get the necessary approval from the American and British authorities before he could introduce his service in September 1977 at the then remarkable fare of £59 one way, about a quarter of the normal rate. His services lasted until 1982 when his business collapsed – the result, he alleged, of unfair co-operative price cutting by his competitors. At the time of his collapse, Laker's fare was still only £109 single from London to New York, yet a year after he left the market his remaining competitors had taken it up to £257. Despite his unfortunate demise Laker brought to commercial aviation a process of fare reductions which has continued throughout the 1980s and 90s.

Group charters in which flights were sold without accommodation were permitted prior to 1973 provided that each passenger was a member of a genuine club or society. These were known as 'affinity' charters as each member was supposed to have an affinity with the other passengers. They were operated by many of the leading scheduled carriers but unfortunately the system was severely abused with fictitious groups being established or groups chartering flights where passengers were not genuine members or had substituted for members. This practice, particularly prevalent over the North Atlantic, allowed certain groups to enjoy cut price travel while the rest of the travelling public had to pay higher scheduled rates. The American Civil Aeronautics Board (CAB) intervened and caused a major row between the Governments whose airlines were involved. This dispute was finally settled in 1973 when the U.K.'s Civil Aviation Authority (CAA) introduced the Advanced Booking Charter (ABC), which did away with the need to belong to a club. Now all that was required for a cheap charter fare was that the traveller had to book in advance, make full payment with the booking and unable to claim a refund should he or she cancel before the flight. This move immediately strengthened the market and encouraged the development of tour operators who specialised in this sector, including Jetsave and Poundstretcher, the seat-only brand of British Airways.

When Laker folded in 1982 it seemed as if British Airways' domination of the U.K. end of the North Atlantic route was complete; however, fresh competition emerged through Richard Branson's Virgin Atlantic and Harry Goodman's charter carrier, Air Europe. Branson, the founder of Virgin records, tried not to fall into the same trap as Laker by taking on the scheduled giants and his policy has been one of 'small is beautiful'. Goodman, founder of the tour operating giant, Intasun, in contrast took up the Laker challenge and was aided by the U.K. Government's decision to allow traditional charter operators the right to apply for and operate scheduled routes. Throughout the 1980s Goodman built up Air Europe. The recession and the Gulf War, however, combined to undermine his operation. A severe downturn in business coupled with his failure to re-finance lead to the collapse of the airline in 1991.

Table 12. Air passengers travelling abroad by UK airlines, 1968-1995

Year	Scheduled (m)	Charter (m)
1968	7.1	2.7
1973	10.9	8.4
1978	13.9	7.7
1983	13.2	13.0
1988	20.2	21.2
1993	29.8	24.8
1995	34.9	20.4

Source: CAA

Thomson's Britannia Airways remains the major supplier of seats to the package tour holiday market. By the 1990s the difference between scheduled and charter operators with regard to type and age of aircraft had completely closed. No longer are the charter companies seen as offering an inferior product. Their aircraft are as modern, and in many cases, newer than those operated by scheduled carriers. Both the charter companies and the tour operators have come of age.

The airline business has shown sustained and remarkable growth over a twenty seven year period from 1968 to 1995 with international scheduled service passengers increasing by nearly 400% and non-scheduled services, which include inclusive tour charters, growing by over 600% and this is shown in Table 12.

(ii) Shipping

The primary changes in the shipping industry over the last forty years have been the gradual rundown of the ocean liner services as a result of the development of air transport and the emergence of a new and vibrant cruise and ferry sector. There are now virtually no ocean liner services out of the U.K., the exception being the QE II service from Southampton to New York in the summer season. In contrast multi-million pound cruise ships offer the highest standards of comfort and entertainment whilst car ferries have become almost mini-cruise ships in their own right.

In 1953, the minimum off season first class fare from Southampton to New York on Cunard's Queen Elizabeth was £130. Orient Line, at the time yet to merge with P & O, sailed up to six large liners every month from Southampton to Sydney from £76. At this time sea travel still far exceeded air transport in terms of the numbers of passenger carried. These were the halcyon days of the shipping operators with ports such as Southampton and Liverpool bristling with ships and activity. Daily boat trains departed from London terminals packed with passengers and luggage. Famous companies fought for business using prestige ships such as Cunard's *Queen Elizabeth* and *Queen Mary*, French Lines' *France*, and the United States Lines' *United States*. New York harbour was filled with ships from many nations and many operators such as Greek Line, Hamburg America, Matson, Holland America. Today the wharves are virtually empty and in fact it is very difficult for passengers who choose not fly to America to find an alternative by sea.

When, in 1959, the number of passengers travelling by sea to the United States dropped for the first time to below one million, shipping owners realised that they had a fight on their hands. Their response to the airlines offering high speed was to capitalise on the higher standards and quality that the cruise liners could offer and to combine this with lower fares. Shaw Saville announced a six million pound order for a new round-the-world liner. French Lines' 60,500 ton *France* was launched and the £10 million Union Castle flagship *Windsor Castle* started its regular service between the U.K. and South Africa. By the mid-sixties, however, services were starting to close. Cunard withdrew its two major vessels because of size and expense as by 1966 it was losing £7m a year on its transatlantic routes. In that year liner services dropped 10%, the lowest number of services since 1948, and operators once again sought to improve selling and marketing techniques in an attempt to survive. The final nail in the coffin of liner services was the oil price rise of 1973. Large ships were just not economic to operate. The *France* went out of service after only thirteen years. Passenger shipping out of Liverpool stopped altogether and Southampton traffic was reduced to a trickle. The airlines had won a decisive victory and a renaissance of liner services is highly unlikely.

Fortunately for the emerging travel agents however, exactly the opposite was happening in respect of cruise and ferry operations. Perhaps it was the influence of Max Wilson, a South African financier, which marked the turning point when he formed the Travel Savings Association (TSA) in 1964. The original concept was not welcomed by ABTA being a 'cruise now, pay later' scheme sold by door-to-door salesmen. Although the scheme did not last long it introduced many new sales ideas to cruising both from an operational and marketing point of view. For example, the undoubted success of the *Reina Del Mar* ship of Union Castle was largely the result of Max Wilson's influence. It was a relatively low cost, high quality, one class cruising ship which built up a very loyal following.

The pioneering of cruising with custom built ships from the new port of Miami was another major development. By 1978 it had grown from scratch to fourteen ships sailing regular cruises and carrying more than 500,000 passengers a year. Leading cruise operators now firmly focus on the lucrative American market and futuristic new ships have already been introduced with others in the planning stage. However in the mid nineties the UK has made a remarkable comeback and is now considered to be the second most important market for cruise operators with an estimated value of some £380 million. To emphasis the confidence in the UK market P&O took delivery of a new superliner, the Oriana in 1995. Even the major tour operators joined in with Airtours creating the Sun Cruises brand and buying two ships, Seawing and Carousel, at a cost of around £50 million.

Ferries

New technology and the advance of the motorcar have been the major stimuli for the rapid development of car ferry services. The design concept of the 'roll-on/roll-off' vessel revolutionised services creating higher capacities and allowing quicker turnaround times. As the popularity of motoring holidays grew, particularly to France and the near Continent, new companies and new routes emerged. Ports such as Dover and Harwich were expanded and rebuilt to provide better facilities including improved waiting areas, airport style check-ins, modern lounges and smart eating areas. With each new launch, ships have become larger and many now are so-called 'jumbo' ferries, carrying over 1,000 passengers and 400 cars with on-board facilities and design features which resemble those of cruise ships. Indeed the Scandinavian and Dutch services offer mini-cruises and some companies offer short break package tour programmes. The Hovercraft, a British invention, was introduced on the short sea cross channel routes, cutting journey times by 50%. In the late eighties the Seacat Catamaran, a twin hulled high speed ferry, followed the hovercraft into service. Although both types of vessel experienced teething problems and are very susceptible to sea conditions they did stimulate great interest among the travelling public.

The arrival of the Channel Tunnel poses a tremendous challenge for ferry operators as it provides a fast and frequent car-carrying rail connection between the U.K. and France. Already the major ferry operators are combining forces to meet this threat and are rationalising services, introducing a very competitive fare structure and marketing the new 'super ferry'. The ferry operators anticipate that there will still be a considerable number of passengers who will prefer to cross by ferry with its freedom to move about on board, its amenities and duty free shops. Furthermore the tunnel has cost considerably more to build than was originally anticipated and this will mean that tunnel fares are not low as planned. Although this may still leave the ferry operators with something of a price advantage, by 1996, just before the disastrous tunnel fire, the market share captured by the tunnel services had risen to 40%.

Table 13 shows that in 1994, 6.3 million accompanied cars were carried by Ferry and Hovercraft services nearly four times greater than in 1970, reflecting both the growth in motoring holidays abroad and the increase in day trip visits.

Table 13. Ferry/Hovercraft traffic, accompanied passenger cars 1970-1994

Year	Vehicles (m)
1970	1.6
1974	2.0
1978	3.1
1982	3.4
1987	4.0
1991	5.2
1994	6.3

Source: Social Trends, CSO

Today then, the travel agent has the opportunity to sell a very high quality, high revenue earning cruise product plus a comprehensive network of ferry routes with ships that provide the very last word in comfort and facilities. As both the cruise lines and the ferry companies have marketing and reservations systems aimed at travel agents it is probable that they will remain the primary distribution channel.

(iii) Road

From the point of view of the travel agent passenger road transport divides into two major markets:

(a)   coach services including tours and express services;

(b)   car hire.

The coach business is a long established industry and even in the 1950s, express services, tours and excursions existed much as we know them today. Coach operators have been offering package tours at home and abroad since the 1920s. The 1950s and early 60s saw a rapid growth in foreign holiday coaching and companies such as Blue Cars and Global flourished. By the middle of the 1960s inclusive tours using charter aircraft, flying deep into Europe at a comparatively low cost, virtually ended this type of operation. Coach operators were forced to turn their attention to the domestic market offering four, seven and ten coach tours, primarily to the South West of England and to Scotland. One company, Wallace Arnold of Leeds, were successful in building up a sound and loyal client base, the majority of whom were over forty years of age. Except for coaching, however, the U.K. domestic market has tended to comprise mainly non-inclusive tours and therefore little of this business has actually been generated through the high street travel agent.

With the opening of Britain's first motorway, the M1 between Birmingham and London in 1960, there was a marked change in the U.K. express coach industry. Up until that time the coach industry had been fighting a losing battle against rail and air competition. The major problem facing the coach operators before the opening of the motorways was the comparatively long coach journey times between major cities. For example before the motorway was opened the trip from Manchester to London was covered by coach in 9hrs 50mins yet by 1965 the 198 miles could be covered by coach in 5hrs 30mins using the M6 and M1. Journey times were further improved by advances in engine technology and passengers were also attracted by better interior coach design. As the motorway network grew so too did the inter-city express services and by the 1980s well appointed, highly expensive vehicles, such as the 72 seater double-decker offering reclining seats, air conditioning, video, toilet and hostess service, were introduced.

One of the major factors constraining growth in this sector, however, has been regulation. Prior to 1980 the National Bus Company had a virtual monopoly on express inter-city services but this was swept away by the Transport Act of that year which allowed independent operators to compete on equal terms. There was an immediate dramatic increase in additional services bringing thousands of extra vehicles onto the already over-stretched motorways. Newcastle to London for example had three major operators, all using double deckers and together providing a virtual hourly non-stop service for prices from as little as £15 return. However stiff competition has now reduced this service to two and this has been reflected across the country as a whole. National Express, the country's leading express coach operator, serves over 1,200 UK destinations daily while Eurolines now covers 380 European destinations using the Channel Tunnel.

The types of coaches being built by the 1980s were ideal for the European holiday market as they were able to transport holiday makers to the Spanish resorts in just over twenty four hours. When linked to lower graded hotels, camping or caravan sites they offered an extremely competitive product. For example, in the mid 1980s the thrifty tourist could get two weeks on the Costa Brava for under £100. Coaches were also a popular form of transport to the European ski centres competing favourably on price with packages by air. These developments brought something of a renaissance for European coach holidays with big name tour operators such as Harry Goodman's International Leisure Group entering the market. ILG formed 'Coach Europe', supplying the latest long distance coaches to a variety of tour operators including its own NAT Holidays. Unfortunately both Coach Europe and NAT holidays were wound up with the collapse of Air Europe in 1991. In 1997, one of the largest operators in this market valued at some £31m, is Siesta Travel Europe of Middlesbrough which enjoys a market share of approximately 25% followed by Shearings (Sunshine Express) and Ferris Holidays both on approximately 16% each and Club Cantabrica, 13%.

Although a much superior and more modern product with the introduction of new and highly technical vehicles, the inclusive coach tour is still regarded by travel agents as a low grade, low revenue earning product. However in the first major independent research into the coaching industry Mintel found that between 1992 and 1996, UK expenditure on coach holidays rose by 27% from £1.3bn to £1.65bn, representing a total of 8.3m holidays. Whilst coach holidays had an 8% share of the overseas market it was estimated that they account for just 2% of the multiple agents business. Similarly less than half of UK travel agents, mainly small independents, will offer to sell the National Express Service.

(iv) Rail

In the early 1950s the majority of Britons travelled by train and the sale of railway tickets was therefore a very important part of the travel agent's business. This was the era, when under the auspices of the Creative Travel Agents Conference (CTAC) led by the Thomas Cook group, major agencies chartered special holiday trains to European destinations. Holiday brochures such as those displayed in the offices of Thomas Cook were primarily rail inclusive offers. Behind the counter of such agents could also be found racks of rail tickets just like those found in stations. The travel agency staff we refer to today as sales consultants were then known as 'booking clerks', carrying out a similar function to those employed in the railway stations.

Despite a massive investment by British Railways from 1955 to convert the system from steam to electric and diesel traction, overall railway traffic declined. Holiday makers increasingly turned to the private motor car and long distance business travellers to air. In 1961 in an effort to curb losses, the Government briefed Dr Richard Beeching of I.C.I. to cut out the 'dead wood'. Beeching cut back the system to some 12,000 miles of route, half its pre-war length. Throughout the last twenty five years total passenger journeys have declined by some 15%, although recovery began in the late 1980s as can be seen in Table 14.

The reasons for this recovery include the introduction of new high speed rail stock, the electrification of parts of the system and improved marketing techniques. The 'Inter-City' concept, for example has gone from strength to strength and is now the prime revenue earning sector for the railways. It is, however, expensive to operate and therefore its main market is the business traveller. Apart from Germany and Japan, Britain carries the highest proportion of business travellers on its rail network. Travel agents are particularly interested in handling this type of business as the average executive ticket on prime routes is well over £100, thus providing the agent with a reasonable return in commission.

Table 14. Rail passenger journeys, 1967-1995

Year	Total Passenger Journeys *(m)*
1967	837
1972	754
1977	702
1982	630
1987	727
1992	745
1995	738

Source: CSO

As already stated, one of British Rail's success stories has been the introduction of the Inter-City 125 and 225 trains offering new high standards of comfort and speed. Newcastle to London can be covered in under three hours in air-conditioned, double-glazed, air-suspension coaches with restaurant and buffet facilities. Pullmans are making a comeback with executive lounges at main-line terminals. The channel tunnel is reviving the travel agent's interest in rail travel with the introduction of through Eurostar services from U.K. provincial cities to major European capitals and resort areas. In 1996 the Government started a programme of privatisation which has resulted in some 25 operating companies taking over from British Rail. Each company is expected to up-grade its coaching stock and improve services thus attracting more travellers back to rail.

Tour Operators

The growth of the package tour industry has mirrored that of the aviation business. As aircraft became more economic to operate, the airline companies were able to pass on their savings to passengers through lower prices. This opened up air travel to a wider market. Yet the original concept of the inclusive tour was developed well before the birth of jet air travel. It was established as long ago as the middle of the nineteenth century when the pioneers of the industry began to offer inclusive tours. For instance, it is sometimes said that it was Thomas Cook and his son, who chartered a train to run from Leicester to Loughborough in 1841, who were the first entrepreneurs in the tour operation business.

In the early twentieth century travel tended to be restricted to the rich and educated and it was not until after the second world war that the package tour as we know it today was born and developed. In the following section we will follow the development of the package holiday market.

The 1950s - The Early Years

In l950, while companies like Cooks, Frames, Pickfords and Poly continued to promote holidays by rail, a young journalist called Vladimir Raitz launched the first holiday charter flight to Corsica for an all inclusive price of £32.10s, which included transfers and accommodation. Over the following years the package holiday business began to establish its foundations. It was able to do so because at this time the world's aircraft manufacturers were engaged in a non-stop battle to produce the next generation of more efficient aircraft. As each new model was sold to scheduled airlines they in turn sold older aircraft to a host of independent operators eager to establish themselves as the second force of British aviation.

In the 1950s, however, train travel still reigned supreme. Prices were still relatively cheap with, for example, one of the most popular destinations being St. Augulf on the French Riviera, to which CTAC members offered fully inclusive ten day holidays from only £22. When Raitz developed his new 'Horizon Holidays' using charter flights as the means of transport, CTAC members responded by using cheaper air seats on the scheduled services of the national carrier, British European Airways.

By 1958 a company called Blue Cars had become a very significant name in travel. It was formed by a Captain Ted Langton, who became known as the 'father' of today's inclusive tours. He was one of the first people to see the economies that existed in combining air and coach transport. He went on to form 'Universal Sky Tours', which was later to become Thomson Holidays.

As the decade came to a close the number of operators was increasing fast and included Global, Sir Henry Lunn, Milbank, Flair, Poly Travel and Swans. Global, the largest coach operator, offered seven day inclusive tours to Europe from 29 guineas while Horizon provided two week skiing trips to Zermatt for only 44 guineas. (A guinea had a value in today's money of £1.05.)

The 1960s - The Market Expands

Things started to go wrong for the tour operators in the early 1960s, mainly due to a number of failures of airline operators. Companies such as Overseas Aviation and Pegasus went under leaving tour operators to seek alternative means of getting stranded holiday makers home from abroad. Tour operators recognised that they had to be more selective in their choice of airline and the authorities needed to be more careful when granting licences. There were far too many independent airlines, flying out-dated aircraft on over optimistic schedules. In 1961 the Sales Manager of Sir Henry Lunn said:

> *"It was a season of disaster, not a week passed without reports of stranded passengers and poor hotel accommodation. It is the shabbiest story of inadequacy, inefficiency and sometimes downright dishonesty."*
>
> *(TTG)*

There were calls for ABTA to act as a clearing house by which only approved members could sell their tours through ABTA travel agents. In turn the operators were told to stop selling through "hole in the corner" addresses. It was suggested that unless this was done, public opinion would force the Government to legislate against such shoddy practices.

The early 1960s saw some significant developments. John Bloom, who had brought the automatic washing machine to Britain's housewives, now turned his attention to the travel business with cheap operations to the Black Sea resorts. Millions of trading stamps were printed bearing his head and these were given away in their thousands to purchasers of washing machines to offset holiday costs. A mini revolution in the business resulted from the arrival of a South African, Max Wilson, who set up a travel savings club. He chartered ships and engineered a complete reshaping and re-styling of the cruise holiday market and its brochures. It is interesting to note that today's multiple travel agents, with the exception of Thomas Cook, were then still in their infancy. The major activities of Lunn Poly, for example, were in tour operation. In fact Cooks, Lunn Poly, Global, Swans and Horizon were the top five operators during the early 1960s.

As the market expanded, quality became a major issue, a set of circumstances very similar to that which occurred in the mid 1980s when major operators went for volume and market share at the expense of quality. In December 1962 a TTG editorial announced that the prices of holidays during the following summer would be lower than in the previous year and this would bring travel within easier reach of the man in the street. It was only the big companies, however, who could do this as they were able to benefit from the economies of scale which their larger volumes generated. This pushed smaller organisations into using inferior accommodation and offering facilities which fell short of that expected by the customer. The consequence of such lowering of standards by many tour operators was public disappointment and a general condemnation of the whole industry. Criticism was particularly strong against supplementary charges and inadequate brochure information with the claim that "an elegant brochure with pretty coloured pictures is no measure of efficiency".

The long running sequence of major tour operator failures, exemplified by the demise of the International Leisure Group (ILG) in March, 1991, started back in 1964 when a non-ABTA operator called 'Fiesta Tours' ceased trading. ABTA had to step in to rescue customers who were stranded abroad and following this, there were calls for statutory controls and financial guarantees. ABTA responded with a voluntary agreement between operators and agents known as the 'Stabilizer Resolution' and this is discussed in some detail later in this chapter. This agreement required members to deal solely with each other if they wished to remain in ABTA.

The fight to remove the restrictive conditions of 'Provision One' (which was discussed earlier in the chapter) continued, with tour operators pointing out that short stay winter holidays to Majorca in 1965 cost more than a fifteen day holiday to the same destination in summer because of the higher winter fare structure. Breaks began to appear in 'Provision One' and saw prices for a one week holiday to Majorca fell as low as £26. The Tour Operators Study Group (TOSG) argued the case for the complete freedom of tour operators to a Government enquiry into Civil Air Transport and they were supported by consumer groups including the Consumer Council. 'Provision One' was finally removed in 1973 and its abolition opened up a new era of expansion for tour operators and travel agents.

In 1965 the 'March of the Mass Tour Operators' began when Lord Thomson of Fleet, needing to diversify from newspapers to maintain cash flows at difficult times of the year, decided that the booming travel business could provide much needed funds. He bought Universal Sky Tours, Riviera Holidays and integrated vertically from the tour operation business by purchasing Britannia Airways. His policy of vertical integration was copied by Cosmos who set up their own airline, Monarch. Such ownership of charter airlines provided tour operators with an opportunity to streamline their operations and produce low cost holidays while controlling both travel and ground arrangements. During the summer of 1965 Thomsons had around 100,000 holidays on offer and a year later Gaytours and Luxitours were added to the Thomson empire.

As the decade came to a close the package holiday had become well established. It was estimated that around 80% of all inclusive tour charter flights were now flown on jet or jet propeller aircraft. 'Provision One' was breaking down and companies such as Clarksons were beginning to become major forces in the market. Significantly, the first stirrings of the power struggle between suppliers, operators and agents were beginning to be noted, with British European Airways seeking to sell its own Silver Wing Holidays through its own airline retail outlets.

The 1970s - The First Great Price Wars

As competition in tour operating became more intense the lack of controls on the way in which operators conducted their business led to increasing problems. For example, one of the most damaging issues was that of brochure descriptions. Again and again operators misled the public about facilities at resorts. One operator was fined by ABTA over an unfinished property: the picture in the brochure showed the hotel as an artist's impression, the swimming pool was just *"a hole in the ground"*, the lift did not work, there was wet paint, windows were not set in and some rooms on the top floors were not complete and did not have doors (TTG).

Clarksons had entered the cruise market by chartering small foreign owned ships. Customers complained of poor cabin accommodation and service, poor meals with no choice of menu, no doctor on board and a general lack of facilities. These ships frequently broke down and on one it was reported in the press that "mutiny had broken out". Such incidents combined to create a very bad image for the industry with the travelling public.

These problems were partly offset by fantastic bargain offers. Sky Tours, for example, offered three night, all-in inclusive holidays to Majorca for £18 and, not surprisingly, over four thousand bookings were confirmed within two days of the holiday going on sale. The lowest recorded price was from Lord Brothers in 1971 - three days in Spain in May for £9.99. Operators denied that these low prices meant low standards. Tom Gullick of Clarksons said:

> *"If ten million people are to travel abroad by 1980 prices must be low and highly competitive, but let's explode the myth once and for all that low prices must mean low standards. Low prices must be achieved by more sophisticated handling resulting in lower overheads per person, better utilisation of aircraft, high load factors, spreading of investment and fixed costs over long periods, in fact the economies of scale."*

> *Source:TTG*

Unfortunately Clarksons were losing money, some £2 million in 1971, and were taken over by the Court Line Group two years later. The group also owned Owner Services and Halcyon Holidays and had invested heavily in new jet aircraft to support its tour operations. Parallels can be drawn with the situation of ILG (International Leisure Group) in the late 1980s. Further takeovers followed with the acquisition of Horizon Holidays and 4S Travel. Unfortunately the oil crisis in 1973, the worst economic recession that the West's economies had faced in the period since the Second World War. A financial crisis developed within the Court Line group and in June 1974 it sought Government aid. The company was baled out temporarily but eventually collapsed on August 15th 1974 throwing the industry into confusion. Until the ILG collapse of 1991 it was the largest failure the industry had faced and resulted in the company leaving debts running into millions, redundancy for 3,000 staff, a Government enquiry and new legislation - the Air Travel Reserve Fund Act 1975 - designed to protect customers. The fund actually did repay Clarksons' customers and then provided a safety net for future failures.

The 1980s - The Halcyon Days

As the tour operating business moved into the 1980s the leading thirty tour operators were riding high and making record profits of some £43.8 million on a turnover of £906.9 million. (Illustrated in Table 15) Increasing competition, however, was beginning to take its toll and from 1985 massive discounting was introduced led by the two giants, Thomson and ILG operators of Intasun Holidays. Despite an increase from 6.2 million licensed air holidays in 1980 to 12.5 million in 1987, the top thirty operators in that year turned in a net loss of £24.8 million on a turnover of £2.7 billion. This price war could not continue for long and by 1990, with a return to realistic pricing, results recovered.

Table 15. Profitability of top 30 tour operators, 1980-1995

Year	Profits	(Losses)	Net result	Net result as % of turnover
	£m	£m	£m	%
1975	13.7	(0.8)	12.9	4.6
1980	47.2	(3.4)	43.8	4.8
1985	79.9	(19.0)	60.9	3.3
1987	23.5	(48.3)	(24.8)	(0.9)
1990	41.9	(1.6)	40.3	1.5
1991	110.9	(6.1)	104.8	3.8
1992	102.2	(1.6)	100.6	2.8
1993	130.6	(31.6)	99.1	2.6
1994	136.5	(50.9)	86.6	1.9
1995	85.9	(95.8)	(9.9)	(0.2)

Source: CAA

During the second half of the decade mergers and takeovers gathered momentum as the industry struggled for survival and companies fought for market dominance. Outside conglomerates moved in and then left after being disappointed at the low returns which the travel business generated. For example in 1987, Horizon Holidays, then owned by Bass, the brewing giant, took over Wings Holidays who were controlled by the Rank Organisation. Subsequently Bass decided to move out of the tour operating business and this led to the largest take-over of all time when Thomson bought the Horizon group including its airline, Orion for £75 million. This move created much concern in the industry and was referred to the Monopolies and Mergers Commission but in December 1988 the Commission ruled that the merger was acceptable and could proceed. Thomson instantly captured a massive 32% of the inclusive tour market (which can be seen in Table 16) and with the demise of the International Leisure Group (ILG) in 1991, owners of Intasun, their share was increased yet again.

Another significant merger was that of British Airways Holidays and Sunmed to form Redwing Holidays. British Airways still held a controlling interest in Redwing but in 1990, after only two years of Redwing's operation, the airline decided to shed some of its holiday package interests by selling off Redwing to the newly emerging giant, Owners Abroad, who also owned Falcon Leisure, direct sell operators Tjaereborg and an airline, Air 2000. As the eighties came to a close, storm clouds were once again gathering as the industry faced up to a declining market with substantial over capacity. It appeared that for some operators the lessons of the previous decades had not been learnt.

Table 16. Top tour operators by market share (%), 1987-1995

Operator	1987	1988	1991	1993	1995
Thomson	25	26	32	25	24
Horizon	7	6-merged with Thomsom			-
Airtours	3	4	13	15	16
Owners/First Choice	3	5	17	14	12
ILG/Intasun	13	17	Liquidation	-	-

Source: Industry

The 1990s - Retrenchment and Consolidation

Undoubtedly for tour operators the period leading up to 1997 has been one of reflection, careful review of market needs and a more cautious approach to capacity. Although the battle for market share had not abated, up to 1994 the top 30 tour operators managed to turn in net profits, see Table 15. Major operators have disappeared whilst others have expanded and some have been re-branded. Vertical integration has been "in vogue" with the majors expanding or their own "in-house" travel agency distribution networks.

The decade got off to a very shaky start for tour operators who were still engaged in vicious discounting, the leading companies fighting for market share rather than increased profits. After the invasion of Kuwait by Iraq a War broke out in the Gulf area of the Middle East, this had a devastating effect on International Travel and for UK Tour Operators and Travel Agents business virtually dried up resulting in short-time working and lay-offs. Fortunately the War only lasted weeks but following hard on its heals was the collapse of the UK's number two operator ILG/Intasun and associated companies such as Global, Club 18-30 and NAT Holidays. This left a massive gap in capacity which was quickly filled by Thomson, the newly emerging Airtours and Owners Abroad. These three quickly acquired over 50% of the market for foreign inclusive package holidays.

For Thomson the last few years have seen the consolidation of their number one position as a vertically integrated company with their airline Britannia constantly voted by the travel agents as the best Charter Airline and Lunn Poly holding the top spot for the number of agency outlets with 799 in February 1997. The biggest challenge for the number one operator has come from Airtours who have engaged in a massive expansion strategy both horizontally and vertically. From a start in the late eighties the Chairman, David Crossland, has lead his company into the number two position concentrating first on low-cost holiday flights provided with its own "in-house " airline, Airtours International, the acquisition of budget brand Aspro Holidays and long haul operator Tradewinds in 1993. However its biggest coup was to provide its tour operating division with an extensive travel agency network through the purchase of Pickfords and Hogg Robinson Leisure Travel to form Going Places. More recently Late Escapes, one of the countries leading late telesales units was acquired. This brought the company into line with Thomson as a vertically integrated company. Since then Airtours have moved into Hotels and Cruising as illustrated in Figure 3. Finally the third in the trio Owners Abroad having fought off a take-over bid by Airtours in 1993 completely re-branded by changing its name to First Choice Holidays in 1994. Although operating its own "in-house" airline Air 2000 First Choice lacks a travel agency distribution network having failed to cement a relationship with Thomas Cook.

Figure 3. Airtours Plc

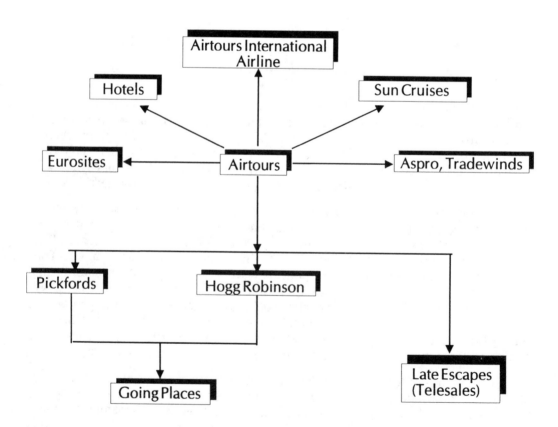

In 1996 Thomas Cook, long known as the "sleeping giant", joined in the move towards full vertical integration by purchasing Sunworld and its airline Airworld. However, disturbed by complaints from the smaller independent tour operators and consumer groups the whole question of vertical integration was referred by the Office of Fair Trading to the Monopolies and Mergers Commission. The issue being whether travel agents sell their own "in-house" holidays in preference to those of other operators or use their dominance to control supply and fix prices. The Commission is expected to report at the end of 1997.

Direct Sell

Before leaving the historical development of the tour operators we should point out that throughout the period under review the major channel of distribution for their holidays has been the high street travel agent. Towards the end of the 1970s, however, direct sell operators began to emerge, much to the concern of travel agents who saw them as a major threat.

In the period leading up to the late 1970s there were few direct sell operators. But some were known for direct sell e.g. the Travel Club of Upminster, run by Harry Chandler, and the tour operator, Martin Rooks. Each built up a reputation for value for money matched by a quality product. There were other attempts to break into this market, all of which were to fail. One such operation was started by a Captain Langton. Called the Hughie Green (after a TV quizmaster) Happy Travellers' Club, it offered up to 20% discounts on package holidays. There were predictable protests from agents, some of whom retaliated by withdrawing Langton's Skytours brochures, despite the fact that Skytours denied any involvement in the Happy Travellers' Club. In 1965 the Freemans Mail Order company made a bid to break into the direct sell market by using its own home agency system, which primarily involved housewives acting as selling agents. This broke all the ABTA rules in respect of qualified staffing, thereby putting all tour operators who sold through Freemans in a difficult position. Fortunately for travel agents the idea did not catch on with other catalogue firms and was subsequently dropped by Freemans three years later. The Readers Digest also tried direct sell through its large mailing list of subscribers but failed, primarily due to the postal strike of 1971.

It was not until 1978, however, that the direct sell revolution began to be felt with the entry into the British market of the Danish direct sell giant, Tjaereborg. This company, which had been hugely successful in Scandinavia, launched its first programme in the U.K. and backed it with very aggressive advertising which denigrated the role of the agent. There was a flood of complaints from agents to ABTA who took up their case with the Advertising Standards Office. This resulted in a number of adverts being reworded to be less critical of the agents' role. Tjaereborg's prices were was still extremely competitive, however, with savings of around 10% made by cutting out the agent's commission. Their initial success with a programme of 30,000 holidays soon attracted a Swedish operator, Vingressor, and subsequently an off-shoot of the Thomson empire, Portland Holidays. This move by Thomson greatly angered the travel agents who were responsible for around 90% of Thomson Holiday sales. Thomson countered the argument by saying that it was unwise to allow outsiders like Tjaereborg and Vingressor to dominate the market and, by providing competition, it would check their progress. Agents were not convinced, however, fearing other major operators would follow suit, but were powerless to act as most depended on Thomson sales for a substantial part of their turnover.

By the end of the seventies these three companies, by then joined by Martin Rooks, who had been taken over by British Airways, were carrying 250,000 passengers out of a total of about 4.2 million. It was estimated at that time that by the mid 1980s direct sell could account for as much as 50% of the package tour market. Such predictions proved grossly exaggerated and even by the late 1980s only around 15% of all inclusive tours were being sold by direct means. One of the major problems that those seeking to develop direct sell faced was the very high initial start-up and marketing costs. For example, it was estimated that Tjaereborg spent around £83,000 in 1978 on advertising to bring their new product to the attention of the public and keep it there without the support of the travel agency network. (A tour operator launching its product through the travel agency channel would have been faced with comparable costs of around £5,000). High costs were suggested as the cause of the early demise of Vingressor which was forced to sell out to Portland only a year after it was launched in the U.K. The major problem faced by direct sell operators, however, arose in the mid eighties when travel agents were given the go-ahead to offer cash discounts on the sale of package holidays. This undermined the major selling point of the direct sell operators, that they could save the customer 10% by not having to pay commission to agents. Travel agents were now giving some of their 10% back to customers as a marketing incentive.

Table 17. Direct sell tour operators by market share (%), 1988-1995

Operator	1988	1991	1993	1995	Parent
Portland	9	10	6	5	Thomson
Eclipse	-	-	7	5	First Choice
Tjaereborg	4	4-rebranded to Eclipse			
Martin Rooks	4	4-rebranded to Eclipse			
Club Med	6	6	n/a	n/a	
Saga	6	6	n/a	n/a	
Direct Holidays	-	-	-	3	

Source: Industry estimates (revised)

The leading direct sell tour operators and their market shares for 1988 to 1995 are shown in Table 17. It is interesting to note that the two leading companies are in fact part of the top two mass tour operators, who also support the agency channel of distribution. For agents this is always a worry and a constant source of irritation in their business relationships with these two organisations. It remains to be seen if the total share of the inclusive tour market held by direct sell operators will increase in the next decade, but to date it would appear that the tradition of the British public in preferring to use agents, combined with aggressive agency price discounting will dampen any further progress.

Travel Agencies

1950 to 1980 - The early years

Originally the public's need for a travel agent arose from the expanding air and sea business rather than from demand for package holidays. Transport suppliers needed a means of distribution for their products and the costs involved in developing their own network of booking offices were prohibitive. The early agencies such as Thomas Cook, Dean and Dawson and Frames, were given licences by long haul shipping companies and international airlines. They also traded as tour operators in their own right so that the distinction between supplier and agent was often far from clear. It was not until after the Second World War that the agents emerged as a significant independent sector increasing in size from a mere 97 ABTA members in 1950 to 1896 member companies, operating 2,305 branches by 1979 (ABTA, see Appendix F).

As we noted in the previous chapter the agency industry has developed a number of specific sub-sectors ranging from the mainly single shop independents to the giant multiples. We have mentioned that in the 1950s all the large agents and operators were linked together in an organisation called the Creative Travel Agents Conference (CTAC) which was to develop into ABTA. The major members of CTAC were:

- The Polytechnic Touring Association
- Frames
- Sir Henry Lunn (later to become Lunn Poly)
- Wayfarers
- Thomas Cook
- Co-operative Travel
- Pickfords
- Dean and Dawson
- Workers Travel Association

During the early 1960s many unlicensed agencies were set up. It was easy to set up in the agency business at this time, all that was needed were premises, some furniture, a telephone and little else. There were no controls, no compulsory membership of ABTA, no bonding or consumer protection schemes and no requirements regarding premises or qualified staff. Travel agents often started up in back street offices, basements or within the businesses of existing shops such as newsagents or green grocers. Operators were wary of 'barrow-boy agents' who were looking for appointments from them. But the severity of competition in the agency market was beginning to be reflected in the poor standards shown by some agencies in the handling of tour bookings. A number of agents simply disappeared overnight, causing a storm of protest from their unfortunate customers, the media and subsequently the Government.

In 1964 Sir Henry Lunn and Poly Travel combined their branches to start what was to become the country's largest travel agency chain. A. T. Mays opened their seventh office and even then the now familiar cry that "there are too many travel agents" was heard. This charge has continued to be voiced throughout the past years and yet until recently growth has continued. Calls for improved commission rates have been constant and yet, over the period under review, they have moved only slightly (see Table 18) reflecting the ever increasing squeeze on profit margins in travel retailing. In a survey carried out in 1968, Harry Chandler, (Travel Club of Upminster) concluded that only 67% of his business was only making money whilst 33% was losing it. Today most agents rely on extra income earned from overide and incentive commissions paid over the base rates to remain profitable, see Chapter 5.

Table 18. Comparison of commission base rates 1968-1996

Product	1968 %	1990 %	1996 %
Inclusive Tours	9.4	10.0	11.4
Air (International)	7.0	9.0	9.0
Air (Domestic)	6.8	75	7.5
Rail	7.0	5.0	9.0
Ferries	7.3	10.0	10.0
Cruises	10.0	10.0	11.6

Source: Industry

The battle between the agents and the direct sell operators is also not a new phenomenon. At the 1968 ABTA convention many suppliers were criticised for their policies on direct bookings. The airlines, for example, were introducing new aircraft such as the Boeing 747 'Jumbo Jet' and were accused by the agents of being concerned only with filling their planes irrespective of the way in which the tickets were sold. They were also accused of trying to cut out the agent by building their own new hotels around the world and in so doing creating their own complete travel package which could be booked directly through their own computer reservations systems.

In 1971 Thomas Cook, at the time the world's largest travel group, was put up for sale by the British Government, who were then its owners. While Cooks pushed ahead with expansion plans for an additional sixty sites, the company was bought for £22.5 million by a consortium of the Midland Bank, Trust House Forte and the Automobile Association. The sale sent shock waves through the travel agency sector as they contemplated the thought that travel and holidays would soon be available through banks, restaurants, garages and hotels. This fear was, however, unfounded as the Midland became the sole owner and did not wish to confuse its customers by converting their high street banks partly into travel agencies. The bank considered that such a move would be detrimental to both its businesses.

The period of the early 1970s can, with hindsight, be seen as the beginning of the 'March of the Multiples', perhaps the most significant change to the structure of the sector since its inception. Because it was a potentially profitable sector requiring relatively little financial outlay, several organisations outside the travel business, as we have noted, were keen to become involved. W.H Smith, the high street newsagent and bookseller, for example, decided to apply for ABTA membership with a proposal to convert parts of their existing shops into travel agencies. The National Bus Company announced plans to set up one of the largest chains of agencies in the country, capitalising on its already existing 500 regionally owned bus ticket outlets. These regional operations would be co-ordinated under a corporate sales and marketing policy and all offices would be fully licensed.

To counter such threats a group of small independent travel agents in the North West of England came together to form one of the first U.K. consortia called Group 20. Their aim was to make special arrangements with travel suppliers and operators on such things as insurance cover for customers, joint advertising and marketing. In addition they would collectively buy in bulk for their day to day needs for such things as stationery. Other groups of agents followed suit with schemes very similar to the formula adopted by independent retail grocers such as the Mace and Spar groups, who were faced with competition from multi-outlet supermarkets. Two large consortia have emerged over the last twenty years NAITA, the National Association of Independent Travel Agents now trading as Advantage Travel Centres and ARTAC, the Alliance of Retail Travel Agents Consortia trading as ARTAC Worldchoice. The latter entered into an alliance with the multiple A.T.Mays at the beginning of 1997 to form the largest grouping with over 1,000 travel agency outlets knocking Lunn Poly off its top spot. See Chapter 5.

After the collapse of Clarksons in 1974 Thomas Cook launched a twenty four hour money back guarantee scheme which caught the whole trade by surprise. Other agents and ABTA were extremely annoyed by the scheme which was advertised in such a way as to give the impression that customers were only safe against loss if they booked through Cooks. Some agents who bought their travellers cheques and foreign currency through Cooks threatened to switch to other suppliers and a number of formal complaints were made to ABTA on the grounds of unfair practice. After investigation, however, ABTA considered that the scheme did not contravene its codes of conduct on unfair trading practices but Cooks nevertheless agreed to reword the advertising so that it did not give such an impression. ABTA, clearly forced to act as a result of the publicity surrounding the Cook's scheme, responded by announcing a similar twenty four hour compensation scheme which applied to all its members.

The March of the Multiples

The next decade, the 1980s and beyond, has been dominated by the 'March of the Multiples'. We shall discuss the development of this phenomenon here in this chapter but we shall examine its rationale, causes and effects in more detail in Chapter 5.

Figure 4. Travel agency takeovers/mergers in the 1980s

Blue Sky   }
Frames   } Thomas Cook
Four Corners   }

James Hill (Yorkshire)   }
Norman Richardson (North East)   } Pickfords Travel
Lunn Poly Business Travel   }

Ellerman Travel (North)   }
Renwicks Travel (South West)   } Lunn Poly
Plantravel   }

                    } Wakefield Fortune   }
Blue Star   } Exchange Travel (39 shops) } Hogg Robinson
                    } Pendle Travel   }

Hunting Lambert Travel   }
Nairn Travel   } A. T. Mays
Abroad   }

Ian Allen Travel   } W. H. Smith

Kenning Travel   } A.A. Travel
Ashdown Travel   }

Source: Author

After years of being able to dominate the market, old established firms like Thomas Cook and Frames were to be challenged by new and revitalised organisations. In 1983 the Chairman of Hogg Robinson Travel, Brian Perry, predicted that the following five years would see an increasing number of mergers among multiples when he said:

> *"Costs will force them to come together. Many will come together by merger or association with a view to pooling central costs."*

The truth of his prediction can be seen in Figure 4.

Hogg Robinson was one of a number of companies which were involved in a series of spectacular takeovers. It took over the 93 branches of Wakefield Fortune, a company which itself had only recently taken over Blue Star Travel. Today's giant, Lunn Poly, identified regions in which it had little or no presence for its takeovers which included the 53 branch chain of Renwicks based in Exeter and Ellerman with 63 branches in the North of England and Scotland. As the business moved into the mid 1980s the multiples, led by Lunn Poly and Thomas Cook, changed their emphasis from acquisition to new openings on 'green field' sites. Lunn Poly's expansion was the most dramatic, increasing from a base of 180 branches in 1984 to over 500 by 1989. The company introduced its 'Holiday Shop' concept in 1986 when it sold its business travel interests to the expanding multiple, Pickfords. With the backing of the Thomson travel group Lunn Poly became the largest agent chain in terms of branches in the space of just five years. The rapid concentration of the sector over this period resulted in the top five multiples controlling nearly 25% of all travel agency outlets by 1990 (see Table 19). The ninties saw still more expansion and the merger of two of the largest agencies, Pickfords and Hogg Robinson to form Going Places. In total Going Places parent company Airtours spent around £40 million aquiring 546 shops to put them into the number two position. By 1997 the top four were controlling approximately 33% of all outlets.

Table 19. March of the Multiples - top agents outlet shares (%) 1984-1996

Company	1984	1988	1992	1996
Lunn Poly	3.1	6.1	7.7	11.5
Going Places	-	-	-	10.4
(Pickfords)	3.6	5.1	4.7-rebranded Going Places	
(Hogg Robinson)	3.1	3.4	3.6-rebranded Going Places	
A.T.Mays	2.5	3.4	4.5	5.6
Thomas Cook	4.8	4.9	5.7	5.5
Top agents	17%	23%	26%	33%
Other agents	83%	77%	74%	67%

Source: Industry ABTA

These takeovers, mergers and openings illustrate the 'snowball' effect of the March with the smaller chains and some independents getting picked up and absorbed as the multiples roll forward. The small chains and the independents found it increasingly difficult to compete in terms of discounting, special deals with suppliers or investment in new technology. As the sector moved into the late 1980s and early 1990s the economy slowed down and this left not only the independents feeling the squeeze. A major multiple, Exchange Travel, failed leaving debts estimated at over £2 million and with many of their small independent agency franchisees (see Chapter 5) facing ruin. Many independents decided they had had enough and offered their businesses to multiples, some of whom, however, realised too late that they had over estimated the market. Even so, despite dire predictions in the travel press of over 2,000 agencies likely to go out of business, the actual number of agencies remained relatively static during 1990s.

Along with the expansion of their branch network the multiples increased their market share, putting further pressure on the independent agents. By 1983 the top five multiples accounted for about 27% of sales of the £1.8 billion inclusive tour market and this rose to about 44% of a £3.2 billion market by 1988. The most consistent performer over the later part of the 1980s was Lunn Poly who increased its share of IT sales from only 6% in 1983 to a remarkable 22% in 1990. (This is illustrated in Table 20) By the mid-ninties the top four were estimated to be taking over 50% of a £7.8 billion market.

Table 20. March of the multiples - top agents I.T. shares (%), 1983-1996

Company	*1983*	*1988*	*1992*	*1996*
Lunn Poly	6	15	21	23
Going Places	-	-	-	14
(Pickfords)	6	9	6-rebranded Going Places	
(Hogg Robinson)	4	4	4-rebranded Going Places	
Thomas Cook	9	12	10	10
A.T.Mays	2	5	5	5
Top agents	27%	45%	46%	52%
Other agents	73%	55%	54%	48%

Source: Industry/Keynote

The 1980s produced mixed financial fortunes for travel agents and while some have prospered, others found life very difficult. In addition to the increasing market concentration, another cause of concern for agents was the introduction of discounting. When the original ABTA Codes of Conduct were produced, travel agents were not allowed to offer individual inducements to customers, as it was thought that this practice could destabilise the industry. These rules, however, were later lifted as they were thought to be against the public interest under the Restrictive Practices Act, 1956.

In addition agents were not allowed to undercut the prices advertised in tour operators' brochures. This agreement between agents and operators was deemed to be against the public interest in a case between ABTA and the Office of Fair Trading in 1982. Every tour operator, however, remained free to insist on the travel agent selling at the specified brochure prices. After this ruling the relationship between operators and agents remained virtually the same except that agents were free to offer incentives to customers, providing they did not give the impression that the customer was purchasing a reduced rate holiday.

The growing competition between the multiples produced new incentives for customers such as free travel insurance and free transfers to the airport. A system of redeemable vouchers, introduced by the Ilkeston Co-op travel agency, caused a further investigation by the Office of Fair Trading into the issue of discounting in 1986. Customers were given vouchers on the purchase of holidays which could be spent against other goods and services within the store. A number of leading tour operators took the view that this was tantamount to reducing the price of the holiday and in so doing the agency was undermining the agreed price controls. As some operators refused to allow the Co-op to sell their holidays the agency decided to take the matter to the Monopolies and Mergers Commission who investigate amongst other things, restrictive practices. At that enquiry the Leicester based agent Page & Moy gave evidence that they had actually obtained written agreements from suppliers giving permission to give cash discounts although their contracts called for retail price maintenance. The Commission's decision, reached in the Autumn of 1986, was that as long as agents charged people the holiday price decided by the operator they could then offer whatever 'pecuniary inducements' they wished. In other words the agents could offer any other form of monetary inducement they wished as long as the holiday price itself was not affected. As a result of this ABTA had to amend its rules which led to an explosion of discounting in the winter of 1986/7 with all the major multiples advertising money-off deals. One of the most radical deals was the introduction of low deposit or no deposit incentives. Instead of collecting a standard deposit of £40 per person which usually amounted to 10% of the holiday price, the agents asked for a minimal deposit of only £5 or, in some cases, no deposit at all if the customer booked early. This move seriously affected the agents' cash flows as they still had to pay the full deposits to the operators.

This activity severely reduced agents' net margins and profits to the point where they are probably the lowest in any comparable service industry and has weakened the agents' financial stability to such an extent that many small independents have decided to sell out or close. In 1988, for example, 971 ABTA travel agents, which is about 34% of the membership, had a turnover of no more than £400,000. (We will discuss this in more detail in Chapter 5.)

The Association of British Travel Agents (ABTA)

Any examination of the development and effectiveness of the travel agent as a distributive system would be incomplete without an analysis of the role played by the Association of British Travel Agents. ABTA was created by the travel agents and the tour operators themselves and became a powerful self regulatory body which not only had influence in the corridors of power but was a model for other similar associations throughout the world. Its most significant contribution to the development of the travel industry has been in the field of consumer protection in providing the British public with one of the most comprehensive systems available anywhere in the world.

As the Association comprises both travel agents and tour operators it has influenced the pattern of distribution for the inclusive tour product in favour of the agent. The management's of leading organisations within both sectors meet in the Councils of ABTA (see Appendix G) to discuss issues of mutual concern. Critics of the Association argue, however, that it operates a closed shop or cartel, allowing little room for individual freedom to make decisions either by operators or agents. Nevertheless there are still sound historic reasons why the Association has the blessing of Government in its regulatory role.

The Early Development of ABTA

The Association came into existence in 1950 when it was created by the leading travel agents and members of the Institute of Travel Agents (ITA). Its first offices were in fact within the premises of Thomas Cook in Mayfair Place London, and it was Cooks who also provided its first Chairman, James Maxwell. In his inaugural speech he said:

> *"the expansion that has taken place in the last ten years in the travel industry is greater than that which normally takes place in half a century. In recognition of this, we in Cooks are ready to throw the whole weight of our organisation into this new body. The machine will creak, there will be lots of difficulties and lots of problems to get over, but the great thing is to find a body which is going to represent us and stand up to the changed conditions now upon us."*
>
> (TTG, 1950)

By 1954 ABTA had 200 members with 580 travel offices and a year later merged with the ITA. Its early regulatory rules stated that members must have been in business for a minimum of five years and hold at least two of the requisite licences such as those from British Rail, the British Shipping Passenger Agency Conference or the International Air Transport Association (IATA). Alternatively the agency could hold only one licence but must have been in business for no fewer than seven years. A major problem was that it was not compulsory for the newly emerging tour operators and travel agents to join ABTA. Consequently some chose not to join. Unfortunately many of these 'outsiders' did not live up to the higher standards being imposed on ABTA members and many argued that there was a need to introduce some form of control whereby the public could at least distinguish between legitimate ABTA members and others.

By the late fifties ABTA had drawn up its first Code of Ethics to guide members in their dealings with the public, principals and with each other. These were later to become the ABTA Codes of Conduct. Compared to today's more liberal approach to trading, however, these Codes contained some very tight restrictive practices. Examples of such restrictive practices included regulations which specified that:

- agents should offer no special inducements such as free insurance or money discounts;

- sales could only be made at authorised prices;

- the travel agent's office should be properly equipped and have qualified and experienced staff;

- agents were forbidden from selling products from tour operators who offered discounts or free goods such as luggage or free travel to airports as these were regarded as 'gimmicks' and would undermine the status of the agent.

Until 1964 tour operators had no separate official standing within ABTA and many of its members believed that there was no sharp division between operators and agents. The problems facing the industry were thought to be common to all and one statement in the press at the time said ABTA was an Association of travel agents, all were retailers and that tour operating was just part of the travel agency business, a statement which is quite unthinkable today. Pressure continued to mount, however, for a separate body within the Association and this resulted in the formation of a so-called 'Committee of Tour Operators', which was the forerunner of today's Tour Operators' Council, formed in 1972. At the same time the agents got their own Travel Agents' Council.

As we noted earlier in this chapter, during the early 1960s the expanding industry was in turmoil with a number of notable failures and reports of poor quality products being sold to the public. The situation attracted the attention of a Labour MP, Eddie Milne, who was determined to establish Government control over tour operators and travel agents. This led him to present his registration bill to Parliament in 1964. ABTA responded with further measures of its own to protect the public. These included:

- the creation of a 'Common Fund' to help package tour customers stranded abroad as the result of the failure of an ABTA member;

- the requirement of members to submit annual audited accounts;

- a precondition that new members should take out insurance or a banker's bond;

- an arbitration scheme to settle disputes between operators and the public.

The government decided against introducing a system of registration, with its attendant bureaucracy, preferring ABTA to continue its self regulatory role. Despite these safe-guards, however, it was the failure of non-ABTA members that was doing the most harm to the industry and its reputation with the Government and the general public. The Association was forced to use its own funds to rescue holiday makers who were travelling with failed non-ABTA operators, as many were booked through ABTA travel agents. Prompted by a number of major failures including that of Fiesta Tours in 1964 the general public, the media and the Government demanded action from ABTA.

Stabiliser

ABTA responded by introducing what was to became known as 'Operation Stabiliser' or the 'Stabiliser Resolution' which created in effect a virtual closed shop. From 1st November 1966 no ABTA tour operator would be allowed to sell its foreign inclusive tours through a non-ABTA agent. Similarly from 1st January 1967 no ABTA travel agent would be able to sell foreign inclusive tours organised by a non-ABTA tour operator. This rule was incorporated into ABTA's Articles of Association and all existing and new members would have to accept it. This historic development laid the foundation upon which the Association would develop. It would provide the means by which ABTA could impose further consumer protection schemes on its members, including financial guaran-tees, controls on members, form of operation and attempts to further enhance the service provided by ABTA members to the public. It is important to note however that 'Stabiliser' did not apply to domestic inclusive holidays, to other forms of travel such as air, rail and sea transport.

The effects of the Stabiliser Resolution were dramatic, as overnight it became virtually impossible to trade without being a member of the Association. Membership rocketed from 715 to 1334 within 12 months (see Appendix F). It dramatically affected the pattern of distribution of travel products by cutting off both those operators who were selling direct to the public and those agencies who sold foreign coach tours but who were not members of ABTA. It bound together those operators and agencies who were members of the Association "as to belong meant trading exclusively together". Due to the introduction of the EC Directive on Package Travel Stabiliser was removed by ABTA in 1993, see end of this chapter.

Bonding

Unfortunately the introduction of Stabiliser did not mean an end to failures. For example, four air charter tour firms collapsed within the space of two days in September 1967, requiring ABTA to pay out £40,000 to rescue customers. It quickly became obvious that the only source of funds, the 'Common Fund', could not cope with too many similar events. A bonding scheme was therefore introduced by a number of leading tour operators who had formed themselves into a Tour Operators Study Group (TOSG). A bond is defined as:

"a financial guarantee arranged by a third party, e.g. Bank, Insurance Company or Finance House, to be used in the event of financial failure".

Each tour operator pays an annual premium based on projected turnover for this facility. Bonding for all ABTA tour operators took effect from July 1972 and it was believed to be, at that time, the biggest single advance in consumer protection in any service industry, affecting as it did more than two million British holiday makers. A similar arrangement applies to ABTA's travel agency members who must provide a bond as part of their application for membership. This requirement did not apply, however, to existing members at the time of its introduction and this fact was not fully appreciated until the collapse of Exchange Travel in 1990. Exchange travel agencies were not covered by a bond and rescue funds had to come out of other resources, which resulted in a levy being imposed by ABTA on its other members.

As the industry moved into the 1970s and the power of the operators grew, it became clear that they could no longer sit easily around the same council table as the agents. The split came in 1971 when each sector was given its own Council to discuss objectives, issues and problems. The ruling body, known as the National Council, comprised nominees from each of the sector Councils (see Appendix G). Since then critics argue that there has been a lack of communication between operators and agents, problems which are often aired in the trade press rather than within the Association itself.

The acid test for bonding and consumer protection came in August 1974 when the Secretary of State said that Court Line, and with it Clarksons and Horizon Holidays, must go into liquidation. The TOSG trust fund directors organised a programme of flights to repatriate some 100,000 Clarksons passengers stranded abroad. The Clarksons and Horizons bonds, however, fell far short of the amount required to fund this operation. ABTA were able to 'sell' the idea of an 'Air Travel Reserve Fund' to the Government who provided a £15m interest free loan to enable the repayment of all moneys lost by clients. The Air Travel Reserve Fund Act 1975, also introduced a 1% levy on all inclusive tour departures from 1st September of that year. This money was used to build up the reserve fund and repay the Government loan. Two years later funds were sufficient to allow the levy to be stopped but the Act remains to this day, thereby allowing a further line of defence should bonds prove inadequate. So out of the tragedy of the Clarksons collapse ABTA was able to enhance its credibility and increase its standing with both Government and consumer watchdogs.

Restrictive Practices

ABTA faced a potential difficulty with the introduction of the Restrictive Practices Act (Services) Order, 1976 which suggested that 'Stabiliser' and other rules and regulations which ABTA had developed might not be in the public interest and therefore illegal. Both its Articles of Association and Tour Operators and Retail Codes contained restrictive practices and so ABTA were obliged to register them if they were seeking to continue to operate them legally until the matter came to court.

The crux of the case revolved around the following question: "would the public be better served by allowing ABTA tour operators to sell their foreign package holidays through whichever channel they so desired, for example any retail outlet, newsagents, supermarket, garage and the like and for travel agents to sell any tour operator's package irrespective of whether or not they belonged to ABTA".

It was not until the end of 1982, after lengthy proceedings, that the Restrictive Practices Court delivered its first judgement relating to 'Stabiliser'. It decided that the restriction of exclusive trading arrangements between operators and agents should be retained, the rationale being that:

> "on balance it was in the public interest because it enabled ABTA to effectively enforce its membership requirements".

These included:

- financial protection for customers of operators who fail financially (primarily through ABTA's bonding system but also through "second lines of defence" in the shape of industry-wide funds and insurance schemes);

- compliance with comprehensive Codes of Conduct governing business practices of its members vis-à-vis their customers;

- participation in a free conciliation service and low cost arbitration scheme for the resolution of complaints.

> *Source: Elton, M. A., UK tour operators and retail travel agents: ABTA and the public interest. Tourism Management, 223-228, Sept 84.*

One important rule that ABTA decided could not be defended was that relating to the price maintenance operated by retail agents which prohibited discounting. Consequently it was removed in 1978 and in its place ABTA imposed provisions requiring agents to sell at the prices specified by their principals. This was not a distinction without a difference. It was one thing for ABTA to have prohibited discounting by agents, which was clearly indefensible under the Act, but quite another to state that it was for tour operators or other principals to decide the price at which their own holidays should be sold by their agents to customers. This was neither more nor less than the principal's prerogative under the general rules of agency. ABTA were later criticised by the Court for their action, although it was not legally challenged and it was left to individual principals to enforce this rule if they so wished.

This issue soon hit the headlines again when, as we described before, a number of tour operators tried to prevent Ilkeston Co-op Travel from selling their holidays with vouchers that could be redeemed in other parts of the store. Throughout the hearing called by the Monopolies and Mergers Commission, ABTA spared no effort to persuade the Commission that tour operators should not be deprived of the right to decide at what price their holidays should be sold to customers by their agents. The MMC upheld this view, although it also decided to make it illegal for a principal to prevent an agent from offering inducements, including 'pecuniary' (or monetary) inducements. In effect the practice of price maintenance for inclusive tours by which the operator could control the final price a customer paid was now dead and buried. Agents were now free to offer financial inducements and the result was the explosion of discounting which followed.

EC Directive on Package Travel

Whilst ABTA had been successfully operating its own consumer protection schemes this was not necessarily the case in other European Union Member States. Therefore in an effort to harmonise regulations concerning inclusive package travel the EU introduced a Directive on Package Travel which had to be put into law by member countries by the 31st of December, 1992. The major requirement was exactly what ABTA already had in place for its own members, that was to provide financial protection for customers in the event of failure. In practice this is to rescue those who may be stranded abroad, refund deposits and balances or provide alternative holidays. For those operators who were not members of ABTA they were now bound by law to provide protection. Failure to do so **is a criminal offence punishable by fines or even imprisonment. For ABTA this meant that there was no longer a need for the "Stabiliser" rule and it was removed in October 1993.**

Many thought that would be the end for the Association as all tour operators could choose any channel of distribution to sell their products and likewise all travel agents were free to sell tours produced by any operator. Because of other rules which still apply for membership such as financial stability, staff qualifications and premises most members have decided to remain within ABTA and new companies are still joining. This is because ABTA membership offers a way of automatically vetting both operators and agents. For example, a new travel agent will probably not be given an appointment to sell holidays by a tour operator unless it has joined ABTA. Likewise a new tour operator may have difficulty in getting travel agents to sell its holidays unless it is an ABTA member. By looking at the ABTA Membership statistics in Appendix F it can be seen that numbers have remain relatively static. Other reasons for membership include:

- Use of the ABTA logo signifying quality and financial reliability.

- Financial protection schemes at low cost.

- Independent arbitration to settle disputes between members and customers.

- Representation with Government and International Tourism Organisations.

- A legal advisory service.

Chapter 3

Travel Product Distribution

Travel Industry Distribution Channels

In his book *Marketing in Travel and Tourism* Victor Middleton suggests the following definition of distribution in travel and tourism:

> *"A distribution channel is any organised and serviced system, created or utilised to provide convenient points of sale and/or access away from the location of production and consumption, and paid from out of marketing budget."*

In layman's terms this means getting the product to the customer by the most efficient means possible at the minimum cost.

In Chapter 1 we explained that the travel industry has a distribution framework which is similar in many respects to that of other manufacturing industries. Travel principals, as the suppliers of the product, and travel agents, as the retailers, are both part of the chain of distribution which is used to get the product to the consumer. As we noted in Chapter 1 principals can chose either to sell through a travel agent or can sell directly to the ultimate consumer. In the following diagram we illustrate these two basic channels of distribution in travel and tourism.

Figure 5. Basic channels of distribution in travel

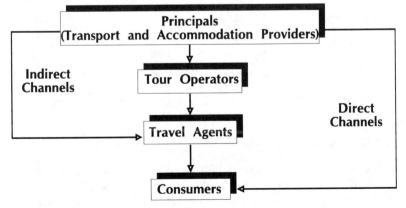

Our diagram is somewhat over-simplified as it does not take account of the individual nature of travel and tourism products and their potential markets. For example, the air travel market is divided into a number of different segments including business travel and holiday travel. Because of this and the differing customers for each market segment, the airlines must use a variety of distribution methods to sell their seats. We shall see later in this chapter that this includes sales through travel agents, sales direct to the public through the airlines' own offices and sales to specific customer groups through a 'consolidator'. Other examples of principals selling their products through differing means of distribution include cruise operators who try to reach their customers directly through newspaper and magazine advertising and car hire firms who sell franchises to others allowing them to rent out cars under the main company's brand name. In the next section of this chapter we shall examine the main distribution methods used in the major sectors of the travel and tourism industry.

The Travel and Tourism Industry's Channels of Distribution

In this part of the chapter we shall consider the following sectors.

1.   Air Travel

2.   Surface Transport

3.   Accommodation

4.   Inclusive Tours

1. Air travel

As the air travel market is quite complex we will sub-divide it into its two main sectors:

(a)   scheduled services;

(b)   non-scheduled services.

(a) Scheduled Services

These are services which operate to a published timetable, irrespective of the number of passengers to be carried on any one flight. On international routes the service will operate as a result of an agreement between the Governments of the originating and destination countries, and the air travel authorities in each country will issue licences which determine the frequency of services.

The Scheduled Business and Leisure markets

The British scheduled airline market divides roughly into two parts, with 20% of the market made up of business travellers and the remaining 80% catering for holiday and leisure travellers. Most airlines adopt what is known as a 'total market' strategy to exploit both segments and, to enable them to capitalise on the total market, they have to employ a complex distribution system. This is illustrated in Figure 6.

Figure 6. Airline distribution channels - scheduled - business/leisure

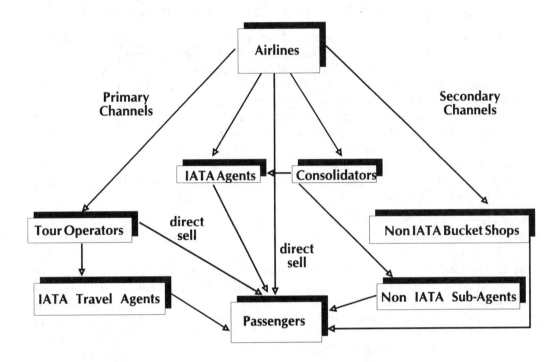

On the left of the figure are what could be termed the primary channels with business passing through the traditional high street travel agents and seats bought by tour operators to be combined into a package with accommodation. On the right are the secondary channels, still of crucial importance to some carriers, whose business is generated by consolidators using non-licensed sub-agents or through non-licensed 'bucket shops'. Taken together both of these channels account for some 80% of all airline ticket sales in the U.K. with the remainder being bought directly by passengers.

We will now examine each channel more closely to explain its method of operation and the role and activities of each of the participants in the channel of distribution.

Primary Distribution Channels

(i)   The Airline sells through an IATA Agent directly to the Passenger

This is the major channel of sales for airlines throughout the world. It accounts for some 75% to 80% of indirect sales using intermediaries. Basically airlines have the freedom to appoint agents as their distributors and the criteria used by the airlines are normally that the agent must be an ABTA member for domestic flight sales and an IATA member for international flight sales. Airlines are particularly supportive of those agents which service business travellers as this is normally a highly profitable market. As you can see from the figure, however, a certain amount of scheduled business is processed through the secondary channel using a consolidator who will offer tickets often at below published rates. (We shall explain this method in some detail a little later in the chapter.)

With an estimated 80% to 90% of all scheduled air sales coming through agencies it is not surprising to find the airlines concentrating their main marketing effort in this direction. Airlines in general are firmly and fully committed to the IATA distribution system. Apart from new technology based self ticketing, the prospect of airlines concentrating their marketing efforts to generate direct sales does not seem to be a possibility in the near future. One prime reason is the costs incurred by the airlines both in time and money when dealing directly with the general public. This would entail setting up reservation centres, having the staff to take the volume of telephone calls from the public wishing to make reservations and the time taken to explain fare structures and schedules - it is a prohibitive expense. This is especially true for the smaller U.K. domestic airlines and for all foreign carriers.

The primary holders of IATA licences to whom the airlines concentrate most of their marketing efforts upon are the business travel agents giants such as Carlson Wagonlit, Hogg Robinson and American Express. Other high street leisure agents are sometimes criticised by airlines for the service they give but of course they have to mix leisure and business travel products side by side. This makes the job of the sales consultant very complex indeed and therefore some of these agents have now separate flight booking centres. The smaller independent IATA agent has to cope with finding the money for investment in the latest technology to keep up with the rest and therefore may be viewed by airlines as being at the bottom of the pile when marketing support is required.

Like other retailers travel agents need to have a specific market position, with the right image and the right products but such a strategy needs investment. Some airlines are also concerned that agents are seeking to generate volume sales rather than provide a quality service and such a policy has lead to discounting and a lowering of the image of the product. This in turn reflects on the airlines. In the 1980s British Airways, with its up-market, long-haul business, set up its own network of agencies, Four Corners, to reverse this trend. However, the development angered many of agents and its concept, involving a completely different design of office and way of selling, did not succeed. In a cost cutting, streamlining exercise, the Four Corners chain was sold off to Thomas Cook in 1990.

*(ii)   The Airline sells through a Tour Operator who then sells either through an
        ABTA Agent or directly to the Customer*

Special rates, known as ITX fares (Inclusive Tour Fares), are available to tour operators who take allocations of seats on scheduled services. Generally such ITX fares are restricted to long haul flights, as short haul flights are dominated by the charter carriers.

Tour Operators such as Kuoni, Thomas Cook and Thomson take allocations of seats and package them together with accommodation. British Airways has its own tour operation, originally known as Speedbird, is now part of British Airways Holidays, and as such BA acts as a tour operator in its own right.

A number of operators specialise in 'seat-only' sales. This involves them in either selling seats to customers who can make their own accommodation arrangements abroad or alternatively selling seats to destinations where the accommodation element is not required to qualify for a cheaper rate. Such operators include Jetsave and Unijet.

As mentioned earlier there are also some 'direct sell' tour operators who market directly to the customer rather than through an agent and these operators are considered later.

Secondary Channels of Distribution

*(iii)   The Airline sells seats through a Consolidator who then re-sells through
        Sub-Agents or directly to the passenger*

The role of the consolidator is rather like that of the wholesaler. The consolidator negotiates on behalf of a host of retailers, in this case sub-travel agents, to obtain a better deal on price from the airline in return for bulk purchase. The consolidator uses a completely separate distribution structure from that of the travel agency, often based around the variety of tightly knit ethnic communities that exist in the U.K. The consolidator's role is essentially one of gathering together passengers who wish to go to a common destination and, in making up a group, qualifying for a discount. The areas the consolidators serve are primarily the Indian sub-continent, the Far East and Latin America. For this reason they are usually tied to specific airlines who, in return for their loyalty, will give preferred group rates and incentive commissions. Such commissions vary from the standard 9% to 30% and in some cases even as high as 50%. Consolidators are fully licensed by IATA and therefore should not be confused with non-licensed sub-agents or 'bucket shops'.

Consolidators need to reach members of a specific community and they achieve this through a network of non-licensed sub-agents. They are often owned and operated by members of the community which they serve and are often operated in tandem with other businesses such as insurance broking, electrical goods retailing or the fashion trade.

Bookings are normally placed with the consolidator who will issue tickets by return. Consolidators work on very high rates of commission and usually have few overheads. As the members of ethnic communities often prefer to use their own sub-agents rather than normal travel agents, airlines have little choice but to sell their seats in this way. Approximately 85% of the consolidators' business goes through sub-agents, with the remaining 15% being bought directly by individual passengers.

Many consolidators were originally established by the airlines themselves to shift excess capacity, but some now regret this, as consolidators have become very powerful and are dictating fare levels and commissions. Consolidators have in the past caused friction between the airlines and established high street agencies as they were given preferential fares which the agencies could not match. More recently, however, agents, especially the multiples, have set up special fares units similar in their operation to consolidators and they are now being offered prices below published rates on specific flights by the airlines. Within their own ethnic market sector, however, consolidators cannot be matched by U.K. agents and therefore airlines cannot afford to ignore them.

(iv)   The Airline sells seats to a 'bucket shop'

The difference between a sub-agent and a bucket shop is the way in which each obtains airline tickets. Whereas the sub-agent uses the consolidator, the bucket shop is supplied directly by the airlines. The bucket shop's operation is technically against the law as no scheduled airline is allowed to sell tickets at below the advertised published fare agreed by the respective governments of the origination and destination countries. In theory therefore airlines could be prosecuted for this but in practice this is highly unlikely to happen as it would cause substantial embarrassment and political difficulty between the governments concerned. There have been many attempts by airlines to 'clean up' this channel of distribution but bucket shops still exist today, although they are fewer in number than they were some years ago.

(v)   Alternative channels

Over recent years and despite repeated media reports to the contrary, there has been little evidence of enthusiasm from scheduled carriers for the development of alternative distribution channels such as telephone sales or self ticketing. A major problem perceived by the airlines is that customers probably think that if they contact an airline directly they will be offered a restricted choice of routes, times and fares, whereas an agent should offer an unbiased choice. As scheduled prices are no longer fixed and schedules can be complicated, there is an increasing need for an intermediary who can sort out such problems.

Self ticketing poses a similar problem. Customers using an automatic ticketing machine would still want to select from a wide range of choices, yet airlines would, for obvious commercial reasons, only want to offer their own services. It is more likely therefore that, apart from routes such as domestic shuttle services, automatic self ticketing machines may be supplied by intermediaries, such as travel agents who are not tied to a particular airline. These self ticketing machines could be placed in airports or hotels or, as is already happening, within the premises of large business customers. The issue of self ticketing is now being overtaken by ticketless travel using smart cards (We will discuss the development of such technology in Chapter 6.)

Airlines do, however, sell a considerable number of seats over the telephone to customers using credit cards and the airlines are responding to this demand. For simple uncompli-cated ticket sales it is very convenient, but when the customer also wants to buy additional services such as accommodation, car hire or insurance, many airlines prefer that the customer deals with a travel agent.

The Charter/Leisure Market

Non-scheduled services, usually referred to as 'charter flights' work in conjunction with tour operators. Although they fly to a specific timetable this is not published except in the tour operator's brochure and the decision whether or not the flight should take place is often subject to a satisfactory number of passengers being booked. Unlike a scheduled service a charter flight can be cancelled if there is insufficient demand. Alternatively the passengers of two flights can be put together on a single flight, a process which is known as 'consolidation'.

Normally origination and destination countries have agreed in advance to permit charter flights and therefore the difficulty of having to obtain a licence is avoided. The distinction between scheduled and non-scheduled has become blurred in recent years with a gradual relaxation of rules, a process which is often referred to as 'liberalisation'. This has allowed charter-only airlines to fly scheduled routes and visa versa.

This sector is much simpler than the scheduled market and we illustrate it in Figure 7 on the following page.

Airlines charter their aircraft to inclusive tour operators who in turn sell packages to the public, primarily through travel agents. Around 80% of air charter business is carried out in this way although as the previous figure shows, some tour operators such as Portland, Eclipse and Direct Holidays do cut out the agent and sell directly to the customer.

Whole plane charters are usually negotiated directly between the airline and tour operator, however, in some cases, the services of an airline broker are used, especially for part charters where a number of operators share seats on the same flight. The broker acts as a clearing house and adviser, organising deals between the airlines and the operators.

In recent years seat-only operators have become more common, dealing with excess capacity on charter flights. Such organisations operate in much the same way as conventional tour operators, but they do not provide accommodation, relying on customers to arrange their own hotel, villa or apartment. In some cases, as a condition of flying to certain destinations, seat-only operators may provide some basic accommodation which the customer may or may not use.

Figure 7. Airline distribution channels - Charter/Leisure

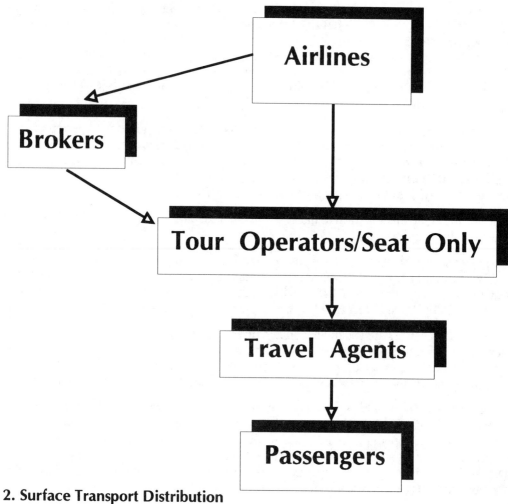

2. Surface Transport Distribution

(a) Coach Tour Operators

We can divide the coach operator market into two categories:

    (i)   those specialising in domestic and foreign tours;

    (ii)   those operating inter-city express services.

Both types of operator have always had a problem in how they should best sell their seats. Coach travel in general is seen by travel agents as a low revenue earner and therefore of low priority. As a consequence the coach operators have, in many cases, been forced to concentrate their marketing efforts on selling their seats directly to the customer.

(i) Domestic and Foreign Coach Tour Operators

of the U.K. bus industry in the early 1980s hundreds of small private operators have set up to sell directly to the public through newspaper advertising or through small non-travel retail shops. One problem facing customers who buy coach holidays in this way is their lack of consumer protection should the operator fail. Some operators are members of the Bus and Coach Council and, as a condition of membership, must provide a financial guarantee. Yet many coach operators are extremely small, working from back street garages with profit margins which could not support the commission costs of selling through a travel agent.

Coach operators specialising in the home tour market need not be members of ABTA to sell through ABTA agents. The problem in this case, however, is that consumers often do not see the necessity of booking domestic holidays through a travel agent, believing that agents are really only necessary for booking foreign holidays. Consequently bus operators frequently sell domestic holidays directly to the customer or through other types of retailers such as newsagents, sweet shops and general dealers. Another popular method is to hold joint promotions with local and regional newspapers.

Many coach operators regard travel agents as having a negative attitude towards their product. Their major concerns revolve around the effectiveness of travel agents. Coach operators feel that agents often demonstrate a lack of product knowledge especially in relation to U.K. holidays and this is compounded by the fact that many agency sales consultants are perceived by coach operators as having little understanding of the basic geography of the British Isles. Coach operators would prefer to see an expert in UK domestic products in each agency. They question the level of service on offer despite the bright and shiny high-tech offices. Poor salaries in the agencies are blamed for a high staff turnover, resulting in too many young, inexperienced sales staff. Another problem perceived by coach operators is that many agents see themselves as the customer's agents rather than that of the suppliers so that when it comes to settling complaints there seems to be an unfair bias against the supplier. Finally coach operators feel that there are too many agents and if the number could be significantly reduced then those left could specialise more and operators in turn could afford to support them with rewards and training.

Many coach operators feel that direct selling is probably their most effective method of distribution. The problem, however, is achieving this most effectively. One possible 'half-way house' open to operators is to have their own network of travel shops; however, this is extremely costly. Direct advertising is another alternative. For example the commission paid to agents on a £40m turnover would be £4m. Such a sum could buy a great deal of advertising. In addition the agents must be serviced by representatives and the operators may have to offer incentives, increasing the cost to around £6 m. Coach operators also find that, through agencies, they convert only about one in every forty brochures into a sale, whereas with direct sell this brochure/conversion ratio would probably be as high as one sale for every three brochures issued. Although the coach operator would need a large reservation centre and staff would have to spend a much longer time on each direct call, this alternative to agency sales is tempting to coach operators. Nevertheless travel agents are well established and the British public are stuck in their ways. To go direct would be a very expensive and a risky process for most coach tour operators.

The major means of reaching their customers for most coach tour operators is through TV and newspaper advertising. They do this because they have so much trouble in getting brochures placed on the racks in agencies. As brochures are the coach operators' only way of getting their product to the attention of the public they must be able to put them into the hands of potential customers. If they cannot do this through the agencies then they must use direct advertising. Nevertheless most operators' advertising is geared to 'push' the customer towards the agents. We examined the three objectives of the 'push theory' in Chapter 1 and restate them now.

The first objective is to get the customer to recognise the supplier and product, the second is to get the customer to send for the brochure and the third is to persuade the customer to go into an agent to book. This approach contrasts with direct response marketing, which seeks to 'pull' the customer into booking directly with the supplier.

One radical alternative open to a coach operator should the agencies fail to deliver sufficient bookings is to open up its own chain of retailers. This would achieve the twin objectives of gaining exposure for its products and raising the company's profile. Although an expensive option, it could be achieved by some of the larger coach operators through a combination of buying existing agencies and opening new locations. The operator does risk alienating its existing agency outlets however.

(ii) Express Coach Operators

Of the estimated £86 million in revenue generated in 1989 by some 14.5 million passengers on National Express coach services, only about £35 million came through traditional high street travel agencies. The balance of £51 million was split between sales at coach stations such as London Victoria, which accounted for £12 million, and through the offices of regional bus operators. By 1996 the revenue had risen to £158m including European services and if we assume that travel agencies still have around a 40% share then their income is approximately £63m with £95m going direct through the coach and bus operators.

Undoubtedly it is the public's perception of bus travel that determines how it is sold. Most people do not feel that they need to use the services of a travel agent for what they regard as a fairly uncomplicated transaction. Similarly many agents feel it is not worth the cost of training staff or the expense of servicing a product with an average commission return of only £1 or £2 per passenger.

National Express as the only major scheduled coach operator in the U.K. has a strategy which seeks to maximise sales both by selling directly to the public and through intermediaries. Unlike the Train Operating Companys, National Express is in fact a marketing organisation and acts on behalf of many regional bus operators. Surprisingly it does not own any coaches but hires them from these regional operators who also, more often than not, own the major coach stations within their area. This is a problem for National Express as it has to pay a commission on every passenger departure from a coach station which it does not own. Until the early nineties National Express pursued a policy of trying to buy out the major bus stations in order to save millions in commission payments. Although this strategy no longer exists National Express currently own four coach stations in Birmingham, Leeds, Liverpool, Manchester and has 19 retail outlets. It no longer owns the country's largest at Victoria, London.

Coach customers can use the telephone to make bookings directly and pay by credit card. There are a number of self ticketing machines at some coach stations but again they are operated by the bus company owners rather by than National Express itself. It would be virtually impossible for National Express to site its own machines in every bus station as the station operators would not welcome a move that would reduce their 'departure fees'. As each express coach sale is of relatively low value it is not worth National Express's while to engage in direct response marketing and so it relies on television and newspaper advertising.

Having had its own travel agency chain, National Travelworld, sold off through privatisation in the early 1980s the company appear to have no desire to return to the high street unless it sees its major supporters, the small independents, frozen out by the march of the multiples. If this were to occur, National Express have to seek alternative channels of distribution, possibly through the re-establishment of its own chain of agencies. The problem the company would face would be similar to when it owned National Travelworld - a public perception that these offices were only coach booking offices. Unfortunately, using an entirely different name, not associated with coach travel, would present the agency chain with an identity problem. One possibility is that National Express offices could offer a specialised British tourism service including domestic travel, accommodation and tours. At the present time, however, the company has made no such move.

National Express views its network of around 3,000 agents as of great importance and is offering an "agents hotline" plus a state of the art CRS called "SMART". This system includes timetable, reservations and ticketing facilities. However in some cases it still has to cope with a poor attitude of both management and staff toward its product. As mentioned previously express coach travel is a low revenue earner for the agent, it is of low priority and often left to junior members of staff to sell. Routing, schedules and ticketing, however, can be fairly complex and therefore service standards are jeopardised. The smaller independent agencies, looking to get all the business they can, often provide the best service and coach operators will provide support and a vital source of income for such agents.

(b) Car hire

The car hire business can be split into two categories:

(i) the major international car hire firms such as Hertz, Avis and Eurodollar, who depend to a great extent on the agency distribution system;

(ii) the many hundreds of small regional and local firms who generate business directly.

The major car hire firms often complain that travel agents are missing out on a very lucrative market which is worth millions despite the fact that agencies are estimated to be handling some 60% of all car hire business. This business is divided 70/30 between business travellers and those who hire cars for leisure purposes. Virtually all car hire for the business traveller, and especially business car hire overseas, is channelled through agents because of their specialisation in this sector of the market. It is in the leisure market where agents may be accused of not following up each holiday booking with a suggestion that the client also take out car hire. As a consequence the majority of customers do not see car hire as one of the travel agency's services and hire their car directly from a car hire firm after they have made their holiday arrangements.

Car hire firms use a number of direct methods to secure business. All the leading operators have offices in most major centres of population as well as a presence at most airports. They also have overseas offices, licensees and agencies. In Britain there is a network of 'licensees' who are independently owned and hire out their own cars, but trade under a nationally recognised brand. Additionally there are 'agencies', again independently owned, but this time hiring out cars owned by the national operator.

For the small regional or locally based car hire firm the position is entirely different. They cannot support the agency network and therefore rely on generating business from advertising and bookings received directly.

All the leading car hire firms such as Hertz, Avis and Eurodollar have targeted the travel agent as a potential source of revenue in recent years although this was not always the case in the past. Strenuous efforts have been made to encourage agents to sell car hire although this effort has, up to now, met with limited success. Partnership deals have been agreed with major multiples and with suppliers such as the Train Operating Companys and British Airways.

The car hire operators have identified major potential growth, especially in the area of business travel, where agents have become far more competent and specialised. In the past many commercial organisations had their own travel managers and car hire companies tended to deal directly with them. In recent years, however, many large organisations have felt it less essential to have their own travel managers, preferring to deal with an agent.

A major concern for all large car hire firms is that travel agency sales consultants regard their product not as low revenue, low priority, but as complicated. Sales consultants have tended to shy away from car hire because of the variety of tariffs, rules and regulations and complex payment vouchers, especially when dealing with overseas car hire. The car hire operators have made some efforts to simplify this, and they have offered computerised reservation systems, free sales training and certification to encourage management's to push the product, however, the problem seems to persist.

Car hire is sometimes seen very much as an ancillary product and therefore left as an after-thought by sales consultants. Even the payment of high commission and incentives seems to do little to improve the picture. But there seems to be little attraction to the car hire firms to sell directly to the public, the major reason being the lack of resources at their headquarters to meet the demands of telephone or written enquiries and bookings. If the agents continue to avoid this sales opportunity, however, then the situation could change. Already new technology is providing touch screen car hire reservation computers sited in U.K. airport domestic 'shuttle' lounges (a shuttle being a regular guaranteed seat service such as that between London and Glasgow) enabling the customer to make an instant reservation and pay on the spot. Such machines are currently supplied by a third party who is paid a commission, so such transactions are not actually a direct sale by the car hire firm.

Car hire companies tend to use advertising to 'push' customers to travel agents rather than to sell them the product directly. As direct response marketing requires a sophisticated and up-to-date database most car hire firms find this to be time consuming and costly to set up and administer. Nevertheless many customers do use the telephone to contact firms directly, either through their Head Office or their many car hire pick up points.

(c) Rail Transport

By its very nature the railway industry has a national distribution network using its own railway station booking and enquiry offices and around 80% of its sales come through these outlets. For the Train Operating Companies (TOC's) there may be little point in licensing numerous travel agents close to a railway station as this simply reduces its revenue by having to make commission payments. The general public also have the perception that buying a rail ticket is not something to be done at a travel agent and some agents in turn do not think it is worth their time and trouble to undertake rail bookings as it distracts staff from selling high revenue products like inclusive tours.

The TOC's, however, may still regard the 20% of sales passing through agency hands as a very important part of their business. You can judge its importance when you realise that about 40% of all first class tickets are bought through business travel agents. The relationship between the former British Rail and the travel agents was always an uneasy one, with agents accusing BR management of attempting to undermine their business in a number of ways, such as the promotion of direct sell initiatives, the opening of BR's own business travel centres and the aborted attempt to convert all mainline enquiry offices into mini-travel agencies selling a wide variety of non-rail products. Similarly British Rail has in the past accused the agents of a lack of interest in its products. It remains to be seen how this relationship will now develop between 25 TOC's and the travel agency industry.

Another means of selling seats for the TOC's involves inclusive tour operators selling tickets at reduced rates. Such sales can be divided in the following way. First, there is the U.K. domestic market which consists primarily of short breaks, where operators combine accommodation and rail travel and second, there is the international market where TOC's provides special reduced fare tickets to airports and other departure points. These sales, while amounting to around £15 million in 1988, only represented about 1% to 2% of BR's total revenue.

Before privatisation British Rail introduced self ticketing, using machines placed at stations but so far this has only been successful for short suburban journeys where transactions are simple and of low cost. BR also made self ticketing facilities available to some large commercial and public organisations, e.g. local authorities, who generate a great deal of business. Such organisations were linked to their local station, which supplied them with a stock of travel warrants or ticket books, thereby cutting out the need to use an agent and this was seen by some organisations as a quick and convenient alternative to using an agent.

The railway industry is the only major principal in the travel business to have an 'in-house' distribution system through its stations, and its policy is strongly influenced by this. It only needs a limited supplementary distribution system to cover geographical areas where it does not have a station or where this is in an inconvenient location for the public. It sees no point in having its product sold through various travel shops with different branding all in the same street while there is a station nearby. However BR did regard the agency system as the most cost-effective way of getting to the customer if the business did not come to it directly through the station sales office and this applied especially to business travel.

Travel agents attitudes' towards the sale of rail tickets reflect the changes in the nature of agency business during the last fifteen years. Once dominated by the 'all-services' agent, who believed rail was an essential product to sell, the sector is now split between leisure and business travel, each with its own sales objectives. On the leisure side many agents have decided that rail ticket sales do not provide them with a sufficient profit and have withdrawn their sale. Business travel, however, has to provide rail as part of its 'complete' service to customers and in this sector it remains important.

Because of this BR was concerned about the low level of rail product knowledge in leisure agencies and the general lack of interest in the promotion and selling of rail travel. Of course, such a situation can become a vicious circle, for if the agencies cease to promote rail travel they will have fewer sales and as a consequence their sales consultants' knowledge of the product and the quality of service will decline. There are many weak retail outlets providing a poor quality service, presentation and advertising for rail travel although there are some notable exceptions. In a concerted effort to reverse this BR launched a massive 'quality service' campaign in 1990 requiring all licensed outlets to have at least one sales consultant who holds a certificate of rail competence backed by the Travel Training Company a subsidiary company of ABTA charged with the training and education of travel staff and Management. This 'quality service' has since been adopted by the new TOC's. Now that the channel tunnel is fully operational it is expected that interest in selling rail travel will revive and leisure agents will no longer be able to ignore it as it grows in importance on the international scene.

BR was generally satisfied with the quality of service given to business clients. Most business agents have sophisticated computer reservations systems, such as Galileo, which allow automatic reservations and ticketing to be carried out. Within this sector of the market the biggest problem for the TOC's is the barrier which the agents create between themselves and the customer. Throughout the industry agents tend to resist bringing the supplier and the customer together as they see a risk of a direct sell operation developing.

A few years ago the biggest threat to agents appeared to be the prospect of BR developing its station booking offices, especially in the major cities, into full scale travel centres. The idea was to increase the services available to include such products as mini-breaks, car ferry bookings and even package holidays. BR dropped this policy, however, as it found that core rail travellers were being delayed at counters by the increasing number of enquiries and bookings for non-rail products. As rail business was increasing in the late 1980s, the pressures on enquiry offices prevented them from expanding their business product range. This was a fortunate development for travel agents who potentially could have lost a great deal of business.

However, until privatisation, British Rail still continued to offer a business travel service where there was a local demand. Some business travellers prefer the train operator to look after all of their rail travel requirements but this places the new TOC's in something of a dilemma as, on the one hand they wish to support business travel agents, yet they are competing with them by offering the service directly to customers.

Experiments with self ticketing machines which take credit cards have been tried with limited success. As an experiment Barclaycard machines were placed in the forecourts of selected mainline termini such as Euston and Kings Cross. They were not popular with customers and were later withdrawn. BR believed the machines would have to become more 'user friendly' before they became more widely accepted. For the longer journeys it would appear that customers want the security of dealing with a station clerk rather than entrusting the transaction to a machine. For local journeys automatic self ticketing is much more popular and machines have appeared in most mainline stations. It does save the customer from having to queue up for a low purchase transaction and the machines are quite simple to operate. Such local business is also not normally booked through travel agents.

(d) Sea Transport

Sea transport can be divided into two major categories:

    (i)   cruise ships;

    (ii)   ferries.

Regular long distance passenger sea routes known as 'line services' have now declined to a point where the business is relatively insignificant. For example, Cunard's QE II is now the only regular passenger service between the U.K. and U.S.A. and even that is only in the summer season.

(i) Cruise ships

The sale of cruises is split between agency sales which account for 85% of the market and direct sales which constitute the remaining 15%. The growth of the cruise market has to some degree mirrored that of travel agencies as it was not until the 1960s that both were to benefit from consumers' increasing wealth and leisure time. The sale of cruises has always been a lucrative business for travel agents as it is a high cost product which produces a relatively high commission. Furthermore cruises provide an ideal 'niche market' for those agencies wishing to specialise.

A very popular way of stimulating the sales of cruises is the use of newspaper promotion. For example, a travel agent will strike a deal with the local paper and then approach the cruise operator with a proposal. Obviously in return for such a promotion the agent will expect the cruise operator to offer an attractive price to boost sales and will also be seeking a good return in terms of commission.

Alternatively cruise operators often strike deals directly with newspapers. Local agents are then invited to join in by placing adverts in a special feature. Usually such a feature is tied to one specific cruise departure with the operator providing transport to the port and the services of a cruise escort. The attraction of such a promotion is that it will have some degree of local identity and there will hopefully be some relationship between reader and paper. The newspaper is seen as offering security, a local departure point and a good price. For the agent it provides good advertising at a cheap rate with a wide circulation within its catchment area.

We noted earlier that only about 15% of cruise business comes from direct sales and of this 10% comes straight from customers who telephone or call in to the cruise operator's office. Such customers are very independent people, not specifically looking for price discounts and not wishing to deal with agents. Unlike air, coach and rail operators, cruise operators cannot afford to maintain a network of sales outlets and therefore this limits their opportunity to attract direct customers.

The remaining 5% of sales come through outside organisations which take large blocks of accommodation to be used as part of an incentive scheme. For example, a car manufacturer, such as Ford, may have a marketing scheme whereby its top salespeople or dealers are rewarded with a free cruise if they meet their sales targets. Direct sell tour operators such as Saga Holidays will also take large blocks of accommodation and sell places off as special deals to their own customer base.

In the cruise market it is travel agents who are the prime means of distribution. For P & O, the U.K.'s largest cruise operator, the travel agent is a key element in its marketing operations. It is regarded as the most cost effective and efficient means of distributing its products. Rather than being critical of travel agents P & O appreciate the opportunity of having such a wide network of sales points in exchange for a commission rate of only 10%. It compares the travel agency's basic 10% commission charge with the mark-up made by retailers of other products such as jewellery (50%) and furniture (33%). To have over 7,000 agents prepared to put its cruises on display at this rate is seen by P & O as good business. Whilst accepting that in many cases agents are not particularly good at selling cruises, P & O recognises that in selling in this way it is able to get its product into every high street in the country, something which it could never do without the use of agents. Unlike many other travel product suppliers, cruise operators are generally against the idea of reducing the network of agencies as they fear that a concentration of outlets into fewer hands would lead to demand for higher commission rates backed by the threat of refusal to rack brochures.

Yet the travel agents' position is constantly under threat because of their failure to capitalise on such a lucrative market:

> *"Responsibility for direct selling cannot be solely at the feet of operators. After all can you blame people whose job it is to sell a product in a tough market for using all the tools at their disposal?"*

(Brown, TTG, 1990)

This statement from a cruise operator which strongly supports the agents clearly shows the dilemma facing cruise operators.

As with other principals the problem for cruise operators of selling directly to the public is the cost of back-up services and reservations facilities. P & O, for example, would not contemplate the expansion needed in its London based reservation centre because of the costs involved in space and staff. Its computerised reservations system is geared up for sales through agents not for direct bookings. P & O feels that, like the coach tour operators, its client base is within the older generation who do not book from videos or inter-active TV using credit cards. It is customers who drive the business not the industry, it is their needs that matter and how they want to buy the product that is the issue.

(ii) Ferries

The nature of the ferry business is such that people often book at the last minute, making a spur of the moment decision to travel. Therefore although the ratio between agency and direct sales is narrower than that for cruising, it is still estimated as being 60/40 in favour of the agent.

Although not quite as low a priority as express coach business, ferry bookings are still regarded as being of relatively minor importance for some travel agencies. Ferry sales are perceived as being low cost and low revenue and were, until the opening of the channel tunnel, considered to be potentially the largest single growth segment in travel. In 1989 the business was worth around £26 million a year rising to £34 million in 1996 and was split fairly evenly between the multiple agents and independents. Of the two categories of agent it was the latter group which regarded ferry sales as being a more significant part of their business.

A high proportion of direct sales, for example 40% in the case of P & O North Sea Ferries, comes from group bookings. Ferry operators therefore target their marketing on coach operators, clubs and societies to fill their ships, especially in the off-season periods. There is an element of direct sell using television and press advertising, but always in conjunction with the travel trade. The major effect is still to 'push' the potential customer towards the agent by urging them to "see your local travel agent".

Ferry operators are generally in favour of travel agencies. If a passenger contacts the ferry operator directly for a brochure then the accompanying letter will usually 'push' the client towards an agency. The ferry company will not refuse a direct booking, however, as it will save the commission payment, although the passenger will receive no financial benefit.

As with the other transport suppliers a major concern for the ferry operators is the perception by travel agents of their business being low value and therefore of low priority. Ferry operators regard agency staff as having limited geographical knowledge and while some motorists may turn to agents for advice on the best road routes to continental destinations, this is often not forthcoming. There have been some recent improvements in agency staff training on ferry services but it is clear that ferry operators need to raise the profile of their products, especially with the advent of the channel tunnel which, on short sea routes is seriously undermining their business.

Ferry operators sometimes feel that agents do not make sufficient use of new technology which can save both time and money. All major car ferry operators are linked via viewdata networks, yet most agents still pick up a telephone to make a booking. One feature of travel agency operation which tends to annoy some ferry operators is that the agents seem reluctant to stock sufficient of their brochures. Agents often feel that customers are using them as a free brochure collection point and then booking directly with the operator and so tend to stock many more inclusive tour brochures than ferry brochures. Yet the ferry operators argue that this is self-defeating as without brochures there will probably be no sale.

There appear to be no plans in the near future for the major ferry operators to move onto a direct sell basis. Nonetheless, in order to survive, ferry operators target group travel organisers who are, in the main, small independent coach operators. This cuts out the agent in most cases but is essential to fill ships in the off-season.

Many ferry operators now generate new business through newspaper advertising using telephone response. Those who respond can be included on a computer database, together with passengers who have recently sailed with the company. Operators then send a ferry brochure direct to potential customers with a personalised letter inviting them to book, although they will often encourage the customer to use a travel agent. An example of this is P & O North Sea Ferries who, whilst mailing clients direct will always highlight the opportunity to book through a travel agent. Operators are anxious not to alienate a system producing between 60% and 70% of their total business.

3. Accommodation

Second perhaps only to the airline business in its complexity of distribution is the accommodation industry. Such is the diverse nature of the accommodation sector, ranging from small independently owned guest houses to de luxe hotels owned by multinationals, from private villas to holiday centres, that many different means of reaching the customer have developed. We illustrate this in Figure 8.

Most accommodation business is generated by direct contact between the hotelier and the customer and probably up to 80% of all accommodation sold in the U.K. for non-inclusive deals uses this approach. The smaller types of accommodation such as small hotels and guest houses, especially those at U.K. seaside resorts, generate their business through 'off the street' booking or by placing adverts in the local resort or regional brochure. Some of these providers and some of the larger hotels, however, join a 'consortium' which will act on their behalf by providing marketing facilities, centralised reservations and accounting. Examples of leading consortia in the U.K. are Best Western and Consort. Such consortia sell directly or through a travel agent or, although not shown in the figure, through other alternative channels.

Leading national and multi-national hotel chains such as Forte, Holiday Inns, Hilton and Hyatt have their own centralised reservations systems. Most will offer special inclusive packages especially short break deals. These are sold directly to the consumer or through travel agents.

Figure 8. Alternative channels for accommodation providers

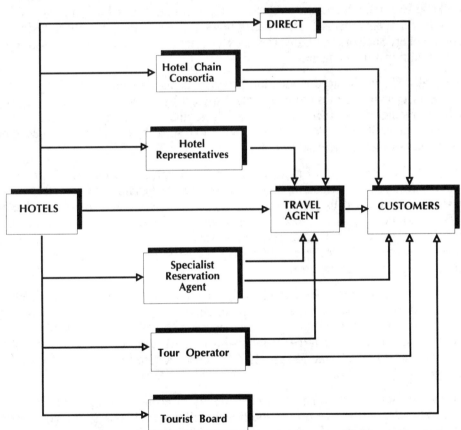

For those hotels, both independent and chains, who do not wish, or do not have the resources to provide their own centralised reservation service, there are the hotel representatives such as The Leading Hotels of the World. In contrast to the chains these are independent organisations, who, in return for a commission, represent hotels in the same way. They provide services such as a reservation service, business promotion and advertising. Their prime means of distribution is through travel agents.

There has always been an uneasy peace between the hotelier and the travel agent. Historically hotels resisted using agencies because of their commission costs. Agents often found making individual bookings with hotels difficult because of the communication problems involved. Arguments between hoteliers and agents over the acceptance of pre-paid vouchers and the payment of commission have been commonplace. As the larger chains have developed, however, especially those catering to business travellers, special arrangements have been made to encourage booking through travel agencies. Examples of such arrangements include centralised reservations units linked by new technology, coupled with fast and efficient payment systems based on vouchers and business travel agencies which often offer corporate rates to their customers, making it cheaper to use them rather than booking directly.

A more recent phenomenon has been the emergence of specialist reservation agents such as Utell and Expotel, which cater exclusively for accommodation bookings and, although used by travel agents themselves, actually market and sell directly to the business and leisure traveller. Such organisations are, in effect, another form of middleman competing with the traditional travel agent.

Figure 8 also shows the accommodation provider using tour operators. These fall into two primary categories, those tour operators owned by hotel chains which incorporate their accommodation into inclusive tour packages, and other independent domestic tour operators such as Superbreak, Wallace Arnold and Shearings, which buy in accommodation as part of their packages.

Finally, the U.K.'s network of national and regional tourist boards provides a valuable source of information on accommodation for tourists. For example, a tourist board may maintain a computerised list of all registered accommodation and that which has been inspected may be given an official classification. As public authorities, however, the boards do not provide a full scale reservation service, only limited 'book-a-bed-ahead' schemes for which they make a small service charge to defray expenses, while the customer pays directly at the hotel.

The hotel sector is sceptical about the benefits of relying on any one means of selling its beds, therefore it adopts a diverse approach. Hoteliers use all available means to maximise their sales and will sell both through an agency and directly to the general public. Of course it is far easier for the larger hotel chains to market through agencies than for the independent hotel keeper, who has to rely on a consortium to sell effectively through the travel agent.

Hoteliers often target the business traveller directly offering a variety of incentives such as corporate rates or the free use of additional facilities such as a sports complex, and potential business customers can be quite easily identified by hotel representatives visiting industrial estates or looking through industrial journals. Individual travellers are much more difficult to target so extensive advertising is often used by the large chains, especially in respect of their short break programmes. Although such advertising may suggest booking through an agent, any direct responses will be accepted and potential client information put onto a database. Previous short break customers will be mailed directly and, for some hotel chains, such a strategy has produced a loyal core market.

Such policies reflect the uneasy relationship which has existed over the years between hotels and travel agents. A familiar story from hotel groups is that of lack of product knowledge and geography, especially by travel agency staff in respect of the U.K. domestic market. Travel consultants are also often unsure about how to book a hotel bedroom.

Small independent hotels have to rely on direct sales as it would be impossible for them to service the travel agency sector as a whole. Competition between hoteliers also means that room rates have to be low and so there is a tendency to try and cut out the commission costs of agency bookings. Such hoteliers have to depend on advertising in local newspapers, travel magazines and resort brochures. For the large hotel chains, however, even though it may be more cost effective, concentrating on direct bookings would create problems, particularly in selling short break holidays.

Holiday Centres

Before leaving this sector we should mention the holiday centre business, encompassing such companies as Butlins, Pontins and Haven. Despite strong attempts by these companies to get agents to take a greater interest in their business they still only sell about 30% of their holidays through agents, with the remainder sold directly to the public. Agents have, in the past, been reluctant to give this market substantial attention, possibly because of its old fashioned 'Hi-di-Hi' image. However as these companies have made, and are continuing to make, multi-million pound investments into their centres, agents do show more interest than previously.

As with so many travel principals, the holiday centre operators tend to be guided by the demands of their customers, which they have come to know through research and an examination of booking patterns. Such operators do encourage customers to use travel agents by providing promotions and incentives, but around 70% of their business comes from direct bookings. As one marketing manager of a holiday centre operator remarked, "we don't sell through agents because we like them, we market our products through them because there are customers who wish to purchase that way, so as long as that preference remains we will support them".

Often holiday centre operators perceive travel agents as having poor selling skills when it comes to their products despite being very good at displaying the product and having premises in prime positions. This failing has been highlighted by various surveys which confirm a lack of selling technique, the most important aspect being the inability to convert an enquiry into a booking. Agents' rather negative attitude towards holiday centres has changed only marginally over the last ten years although a number of major travel agency chains now appreciate there is potential for the sale of holiday centre holidays, despite their continued bias in favour of the overseas package tour. It has been difficult for the holiday centres to chip away at these attitudes, even though agents can earn more money from the sale of their holidays compared to cheap overseas packages. Unfortunately agents tend to view the profitability of a product on the basis of income per head, despite the fact that it is not this which is important but the income per booking. Agents can earn an average of £43 per holiday centre booking because holiday centres tend to have four people per booking form, whereas overseas holiday operators only have an average of 2.2 per booking form. Taking a cheap overseas budget holiday of £150 per person that only gives the agent about £30 in commission.

Holiday centre operators are somewhat negative in their view of travel agents, who are not seen as good professional retailers like some of their high street counterparts. The fact that agents provide advice when it is asked for rather than being pro-active retailers is seen as a disadvantage and holiday centre operators would prefer that agents used the same techniques as other retailers to make customers come into the shop. Agents should use bright interiors, an effective presentation of the product and well trained sales staff who may not know everything, but know how to establish a relationship with the customer. Agents must identify customer needs and know how to go about satisfying them. This problem was underlined in a survey undertaken by one holiday centre organisation of agency customers who had booked a short break. The found that only 10% had gone back to the agent to re-book, with the two key reasons given that when they went to the agency the brochure was not available and that when it was displayed the staff showed no interest in wanting to sell it. The ultimate responsibility for this must rest with an agency's senior management team who must act and lead as professional retailers.

Most holiday centre operators still sell about 70% of their holidays either through direct sales (45%) or through group bookings (25%). Such group bookings can be sub-divided into categories such as tour operators, private parties from senior citizens or groups from sports and social clubs. The key marketing area for most leading holiday centre operators is direct marketing with up to 70% of their client base re-booking. The advantage of this method is the operator's ability to communicate its message directly. Using direct response marketing techniques centre operators have built up large databases and brochures, personalised letters and special offers can be mailed directly to all previous customers or targeted at special interest groups.

4. Inclusive Tours

Operators selling inclusive tours have two means by which they can sell their products: through travel agents or by selling directly to the customer. Currently agency sales account for some 85% of this business. The choice of whether to sell through agents or sell directly to the public has always been a contentious issue in the relationship between operators and agents. Nevertheless because of the impact of the now defunct ABTA 'Stabilizer' resolution (which we discussed earlier in Chapter 2) suppliers and agents have been locked together in the interests of consumer protection.

It is often assumed that ABTA tour operators must sell through ABTA agents but this is not so as they still have the choice to sell directly to the public. It was the use of non-ABTA agents to sell foreign inclusive holidays that was previously prohibited by ABTA regulations. Consequently market leaders such as Thomson Holidays and First Choice use both means and have special brands for direct sales, Portland in the case of Thomson and Eclipse in the case of First Choice.

Figure 9. Distribution channels for U.K. tour operators

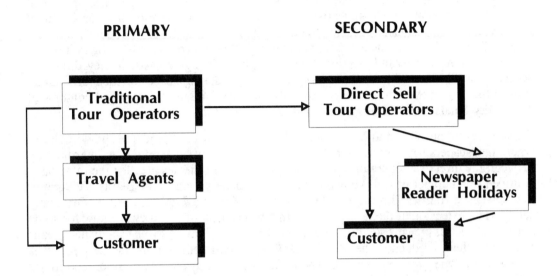

The most usual method of sales is through the travel agent who will be rewarded by a commission on each sale. This commission, however, has to be built into the cost of the package therefore making it, in theory, more expensive. As a result of discounting and other incentives offered by agents, however, this increase in price is often not passed on to the customer. (We discussed this in some detail earlier).

When customers decide to contact the operator directly, the operator will either accept the reservation or advise customers to contact their nearest agent. If the operator does accept the booking directly it is important to realise that the customer does not make any saving as the packages sold in this way already have a price which is inclusive of the agent's commission. If there is a discount on offer at the travel agents then it would be uneconomic for the customer to use this alternative.

The secondary channel of distribution consists of either those operators who have made the decision to sell all their products directly or those operators (such as Thomson/Portland, First Choice/Eclipse) who produce special brands for that market, (see Table 17.) The dilemma facing this latter group is the conflict inherent in trying to maximise both means of distribution. Whilst on the one hand seeming to support travel agents, they also promote other products which effectively cut travel agents out. Naturally agents become somewhat frustrated and fearful of direct sell products despite assurances from the operators that they are not out to destroy them. The agents' main weapon, that of refusing to rack offending operators' brochures, has not been used as agents rely too heavily on the two leading brands, Thomson and First Choice. To carryout such a threat would be akin to 'shooting oneself in the foot'.

Apart from the big two brands (Portland and Eclipse) the other direct sell operators are far smaller and for the most part specialists. Many, such as Saga who have built up a very strong presence in providing holidays for the elderly, concentrate on 'niche markets'.

Saga, for instance, decided to 'go direct' in 1987 as only 2% or 3% of business was coming through agents. Saga, like others, relies on direct marketing, using direct mail and press advertising to build up its lists of customers. Even more important for the direct sell operator is repeat business generated through loyalty and word-of-mouth recommendation. The smaller the niche the more operators must rely on direct marketing as it would not be economically feasible to distribute through 7,000 agents and, if they did, such operators would be unable to find sufficient, if any, racking space for their brochures. Instead they target their market very precisely by advertising in the classified columns of the quality Sunday newspapers and in magazines.

Another recent phenomenon has been the development of the 'Reader Holiday' concept where newspapers have assumed the role of the travel agent by acting as an intermediary between the direct sell operator and the customer. Such schemes are, for the most part, confined to a number of well known regional newspapers such as the Belfast Telegraph, the Newcastle Journal/Chronicle and the Western Mail and Echo in Cardiff. Originally set up as an extension of the newspaper's promotions department, they are now for some operators, such as Newmarket Promotions and Blue Chip Travel, a well established means of selling their products. The Reader Holiday department within the newspaper is effectively a type of travel agent to whom the operator pays a commission. The major difference, however, is that the department does not have consider the possibility of being a member of ABTA as there is no financial transaction between the customer and newspaper. Therefore all deposits and balances have to be made payable to the tour operator with the newspaper merely passing on the correspondence. If there was a financial transaction then of course there would be a financial risk, and those operators who were members of ABTA, but who dealt through newspapers, may require them as their agent, to join the Association as a sign of security. You will appreciate that the high street agents are against this form of trading as the newspapers avoid all the complications, responsibilities and costs of being an ABTA member. The agents have attempted on numerous occasions to have the practice stopped, but ABTA have admitted there is little that they can do to prevent it.

In Chapter 1, we highlighted some of the benefits gained by operators and other suppliers of selling through an agency. In deciding whether or not to use agencies a number of negative aspects can be identified. These include:

(a)   some agencies provide a low standard of service and poor selling skills;

(b)   certain agents, and particularly the independents, demonstrate a lack of investment generally and specifically in the use of technology;

(c)   most agents seem to concentrate on volume and price rather than quality;

(d)   there is discrimination by some agents against certain products;

(e)   a low level of product knowledge may be shown by agency staff;

(f)   poor salaries for agency staff result in high staff turnover and hence inexperienced staff;

(g)   agents tend to regard themselves as the 'customer's agent';

(h)   agents do not act as professional retailers.

Direct Sell in Tour Operating

In this section of the chapter we will examine the issue of direct sell in tour operating. Once predicted as a potential calamity for retail travel and the death knell for travel agents, the direct selling of inclusive package holidays seems to have gained only a small foothold in the market. We shall now attempt to determine why this has been the case and what evidence the tour operators themselves present as possible reasons.

(a) Mass Tour Operators

The track record of the U.K.'s direct sell operators shows that they have not penetrated the mass market. Considering the massive increase in the number of holidays taken over the last decade, direct sell has not posed a serious threat to agents. In a period of tremendous growth, when low prices have been a key factor, we could have expected a substantial breakthrough in direct selling but this has not happened as it has on the Continent. Operators estimate that in 1989 direct sell accounted for only about 10% of the mass market and this percentage has been generally static. The attraction to customers of direct sell is the saving they gain of the 10% travel agent's commission. However, agents are now giving some of this away in the form of discounts and other incentives, therefore trumping the direct sell operators' ace card.

Direct sell could be seen as an ideal means of selling a restricted, specialist product, yet for a mass tour operator it is not considered a realistic proposition. There is a high cost of entry into this sector as it is necessary to advertise heavily initially to get the company's name known by the public and then to build up and maintain a mailing list. Major direct sell operators have to invest substantial sums in the early stages of operation to get their message across. There then comes a point at which the operator has built up business sufficiently to "milk the brand" with a good percentage of repeat clients and lower marketing costs. At this stage the problem is to make the next leap to higher capacity in order to bring down operating costs.

Few operators believe that direct sell is lower in distribution costs than selling through an agent, especially once the costs of selling late stock are considered. If a conventional operator has a special late offer this can be brought to the public's notice quite quickly by using viewdata technology through its agents. Conversely the cost of selling last minute stock on a direct sell basis is high because the operator has to advertise it to an ever decreasing market. As the holiday season progresses the potential market declines yet advertising costs remain the same, so as the year proceeds it becomes more and more expensive to reach each potential customer. One operator is quoted as saying that "in a sense the direct sell versus agent argument is a slightly irrelevant one, what we are actually looking at now is a very different scenario and that is methods of booking through agents, for example credit cards or telephone centres, it's about agents themselves marketing more directly". Such statements from operators underline the fact that the industry no longer believes that direct response marketing will seriously undermine the role of the travel agent, rather it is a question of how suppliers can work with agents to market their products more effectively.

The suppliers themselves tend not to have mailing lists as their customers' names and addresses are held by their agents and not written onto booking forms or tickets, consequently unless operators purchase lists they cannot market directly. Most mass operators do not wish to sell direct, but rather seek to push agents into adopting a variety of ways of distribution. Nevertheless they are keeping their options open and if, for example, agents became too greedy by demanding higher override commissions, then other options such as direct sell will become more attractive. The future development of direct selling in the mass market seems to lie partly in the hands of the agents themselves.

(b) Independent Tour Operators

Outside the mass tour operators there are hundreds of smaller independents. A representative from their trade body, the Association of Independent Tour Operators (AITO) is quoted as saying that distribution channel choice depends very much on the size of the organisation in terms of the number of passengers carried. Most new small independent tour operators start by using direct means, placing adverts in the classified columns of daily and Sunday newspapers, or specialist journals/magazines if in they are in a niche market. The build up of their business will then rely on repeat sales and further advertising until they reach a point where it is both difficult and costly to generate any further increases from such sources. It is at this stage that they must consider a change to using agencies.

A major factor in this is the size of their brochure print run. For example, an operator carrying around 20,000 customers would probably print about 60-80,000 brochures for direct sales, assuming a conversion ratio of about four brochures to every sale. For the operator to sell through agents it would need a print run of five times that figure, some 300-400,000 brochures, to generate the same level of business, as the booking/conversion ratio of agents is something like 20 to 1. Some small independents selling via agents print up to one million brochures yet still carry only 20-30,000 passengers. As brochures are expensive to produce, up to £2 each, especially if they cater for an exclusive up market niche, this calculation is critical. In the end the choice of whether or not to leave direct channels for agencies will depend on the operator's ability to keep on bringing in the business from direct sources, such as repeats, recommendations and advertising, as well as increasing sales through the agencies. The question often faced by independent operators is whether they will be able to achieve their estimated optimum level of business without resorting to agencies.

If they decide to 'go agency' the most serious problem facing small independent operators is that of' racking'. In other words can they persuade the agents to display their brochures? Because of the wide variety and scale of operators many agents are now much more selective about which brochures they will rack and base such decisions on popularity, quality and commission return. (We will discuss this in more detail in Chapter 5). There is no point in an operator using agencies if its brochure is not going to be available. Some of the smaller operators, especially those belonging to AITO, have consequently 'turned the tables' and devised their own 'preferred agents' list. Those agents which are selected guarantee racking and endeavour to produce a high level of business. In return AITO members offer as much sales support as possible, for example by ensuring adequate brochure supplies and providing joint advertising and training for agency staff. Most of the preferred agents are independents themselves and need to offer the widest possible range of products to compete with the multiples. Brochure racking remains, however a 'thorn in the side' of the relationship between small operators and the agents, with independent operators complaining regularly to ABTA that as members they are expected to use the agency network yet cannot get their brochure displayed.

(c) Short Break Operators

The most successful of the independent operators in exploiting the agency distribution channel have been the short break specialists. This is thanks to the nature of their product which is often an impulse purchase. For example, one short break operator is quoted as selling a third of its product, within the two weeks prior to departure, leaving little time for direct mailing or advertising. If it were to try to sell such holidays directly it would have to have monthly mail shots and almost continuous advertising to be effective and this would be very costly. All the leading short break operators, with the exception of the hotel groups, state that they find travel agents to be the most cost effective and efficient means of distribution and some have a policy of selling exclusively through agents. Unlike the hotel groups, who have direct access to existing clients through their chains, short break operators have to reach their potential customers in other ways. One operator which tried direct response marketing mailed 60,000 carefully selected and targeted addresses with a special package and yet had very poor results. This same company has also carried out research to find out the effectiveness of each means of distribution in terms of its brochure/booking conversion. The results as shown in Table 21 make interesting reading for those advocating direct channels.

Table 21. Brochure/booking conversion - short break operator

Channel	Brochures to booking conversion
Travel agents	8 to 1
British Rail stations	16 to 1
Direct mail	16 to 1
Coupon response	80 to 1
Promotional activities	250 to 1

Source: Industry

This operator concluded that, even allowing for the 10% commission, agents were far and away the most cost effective method of distribution. Yet many short break operators do try to use direct selling, although it is perhaps only by selling a high value product to a loyal and existing client base with a high repeat purchase ratio that it can be really cost effective.

In the future the market for short breaks will continue to be extremely competitive with very slim margins and it is clear that agents are now demanding more to ensure the visibility of the product, a factor which is vital for an impulse purchase.

(d) Seat Only Operators

Most of the leading seat only brochures found in travel agents are in fact part of the mass tour operators' product range. Therefore it can be assumed that the companies' policy on seat only business is similar to that for their other brands, i.e. one of agency support rather than direct sell.

One independent seat only operator is quoted as saying that it did not have a fixed long-term distribution policy as the industry changes so fast it needed flexibility. Traditionally it had put 99% of its efforts into selling through agencies and although it did not have much direct sell activity at present, this could change within the next five years. It saw other direct operators such as Portland and Eclipse being successful and direct mail as being a useful marketing aid. The problem such independent operators face, like many other suppliers, is ensuring the balance between upsetting agents and satisfying their shareholders.

(e) Direct Sell Operators

An example of one of the most successful direct sell operators is Saga Holidays of Folkestone who, after some 35 years of using agencies, decided to drop them in 1986. Being very much a U.K. domestic operator, specialising in value for money holidays aimed at the elderly market, Saga's holidays tended to generate little commission for the agents. Consequently only about half of the 6,000 agents accepted Saga bookings and even these were producing fewer and fewer customers. Coupled with higher brochure, distribution and sales support costs, it became prohibitively expensive for Saga to continue to support its agency sales when these only amounted to around 10% of its total turnover. Saga also suspected agents of 'switch selling', turning the customers away from a Saga holiday to a higher value product with another operator. In addition it was finding it impossible to get all its brochures racked. It also felt that it was unrealistic to expect agents to know the details of all its products and that this could be done better by its own telephone staff. Although Saga was not so much dissatisfied with the service the agents were providing, it was faced with the constant dilemma of never being able to say it was selling direct because of the aggressive reaction of agents. Customers had to be told that they should either book directly or use an agent, and this, in the opinion of Saga, was a confusing message and was producing an unsatisfactory position in the market for the company.

Thus a combination of factors led to Saga's decision to go direct. It introduced a free telephone and postal service funded by its savings in commission payments to agents. Saga's whole operation is now run with the aid of a very sophisticated computerised database holding details of clients which have been built up over years of trading. It is now fully committed to direct response marketing, creating a special relationship between the company and its customers. The customer profiles it holds allow potential buyers to be targeted through personalised letters with special offers. Highly trained telesales people then act as the customers' advisers in the booking process. Because of such sophisticated targeting Saga claims that the movement of late stock is not a problem. For Saga then there is no myth about direct selling being more cost effective – it is!

Figure 10. Tour operators' conventional selling process

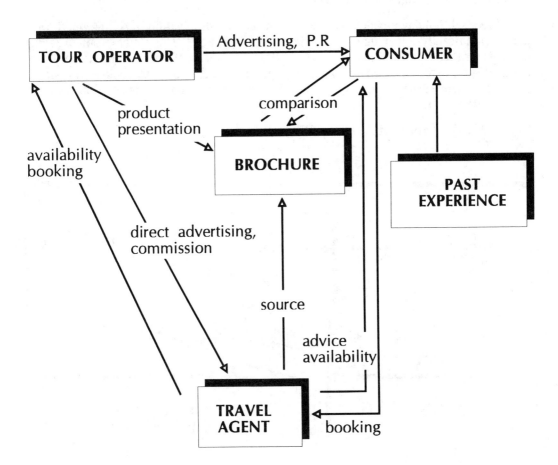

Aspects of Channel Economics

The Costs Involved in Selling Travel and Tourism Products

In the previous section we noted the many factors which influence a supplier in deciding which way to sell its products. One of the key elements is the cost involved in selling to the public and in this section we shall examine some aspects of this from the point of view of both the tour operator and the customer.

The direct sell holiday business is based on the simple proposition of selling holidays at prices significantly lower than conventional tour operators. The major problem facing direct sell organisations is that of marketing their product, of both placing it, or rather the brochure, before the consumer and then getting the consumer to book it without the aid of an intermediary. The basic difference between the two channels is illustrated in Figures 10 and 11

Figure 11. Tour operators' direct selling process

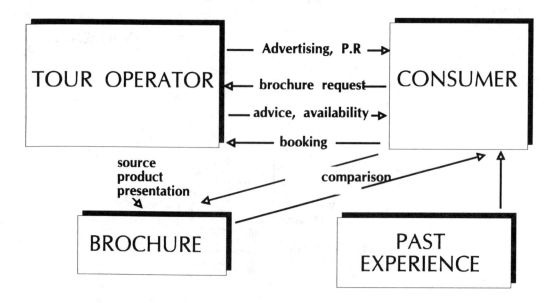

Conventional tour operators use travel agents to distribute their brochures and rely on them to recommend their holidays to consumers when asked for advice. Travel agents also take the bookings and collect the money for conventional tour operators. An operator's advertising in this case is simply to aimed at persuading the consumer to consider that operator rather than another when choosing a holiday. It is not necessary for the advertising to inform consumers how to go about booking their holiday.

In the case of a direct sell holiday purchase the consumer must first know of the existence of the operator in order to get a brochure, and then make direct contact for advice, information and to make the booking. Advertising is therefore much more important as it has a dual role in both creating demand and telling the consumer how to satisfy that demand.

It is not surprising therefore to find that the cost of advertising is considerably higher for direct sell operators than it is for conventional operators, both during the launch of a business and in its subsequent growth. This is illustrated in Table 22 which is based on the launch of Tjaereborg in 1978. The payment of agents' commission by conventional operators and the provision of agency support services could, however, more than outweigh the benefits gained from a low advertising budget. As you can see from the table, the overall saving in costs enjoyed by a direct operator is something in the region of 6.5%.

Since these figures were published industry experts believe that the cost differential between direct and conventional selling could be even wider than 6%, as today most established direct operators have been able to reduce their advertising budget as product loyalty has built up and led to repeat business. In addition the production and brochure costs faced by conventional operators are now estimated to be nearer 5% as a result of an increase in both the number of agencies and the costs of brochure production. This illustration, however, was based on an operator with a relatively limited capacity, in this case 29,000 holidays, and clearly the differences would be greater as the direct operator's capacity increased.

Table 22. Comparison of direct sell costs with conventional costs

	% share of turnover	
	Direct	**Conventional**
Advertising	2.7	0.14
Production	1.94	0.06
Brochures	1.63	2.23
Postage and packing	0.91	–
Ansaphone/handling	0.31	–
Sales force	–	1.00
Launch	–	0.29
Travel agents commission	–	10.00
Total selling costs	7.16	13.72

Source: The launch of Tjaereborg Rejser, Advertising Works, Holt,
Rinehart & Winston, 1981

In fact there are two crucial economic issues to be considered in this context-the capacity of the programme and the unit value of each holiday:

(a) The Capacity of the Programme

Operators whose capacity is small, say up to 30,000 holidays, have a real problem in servicing over 7,000 travel agents with brochures and sales support. There is a capacity level, however, where the economic benefits of conventional selling begin to outweigh those of direct selling. As the company grows and capacity increases so it becomes more difficult to sell its holidays without using travel agents. To continue to sell directly it will find that a greater burden is put on central services such as reservations and administration, its brochure print run and distribution costs rise, and the advertising costs involved in selling late stock increase. While direct marketing in the mass inclusive tour market is fundamentally weak, once below a certain capacity, it becomes the only efficient method of shifting brochures. If a company is working on a brochure conversion rate of 10 to 1 and is selling 10,000 holidays, it must produce 100,000 brochures. Even if it produced 300,000 brochures this would still not be enough to service all the agents.

(b) The Unit Value of each Holiday

If the holiday is low cost as with a short break, or has a low profit margin as the result of excessive competition, then there is little left for the operator to spend on direct marketing. If, on the other hand, the holiday is high cost with a high profit margin, as for instance with long-haul holidays, the operator will have much more to invest in direct distribution. Any holiday costing above £400 lends itself to direct marketing while under £400 this is more doubtful, unless there is high repeat business and the operator does not need to mail out brochures as frequently.

Customers' buying habits are also important. Ten years ago most people booked their holidays much earlier, for example before or immediately after Christmas for the following Summer. Direct operators could therefore manage with a single brochure mailing. Today, however, it is estimated that only 50% of holidays are sold at this time. Therefore direct operators must have at least two mailings a year and considerably more advertising throughout the year. These extra costs are now eating into the operators' savings from not having to pay the agent commission.

Chapter 4

The Importance of Distribution and Retailing to the Travel Agent

In this chapter we shall examine aspects of distribution, retailing and consumer behaviour and relate them to the operation of travel agents. By seeing retail travel in a wider context we will go some way to explaining the way it has developed and the way in which it operates, as a means of distribution.

It is only in recent years that the travel industry has begun to concentrate on the role of distribution in a competitive market. As Michael East said:

> *"Distribution will be a key factor influencing the development of the travel industry over the next decade"*

> *(East, Travelnews, 1986)*

East went on to say that one trend that should not, and must not, be ignored by anyone who wants a future in travel is the revolution that is taking place in what is known as distribution.

Yet the study of distribution has in the past tended to concentrate on tangible goods. It has been concerned with

> *"...the process of transferring goods from producers to final buyers and users. It includes physical activities such as transporting and storing goods, and the legal, promotional and financial activities performed during the transfer of ownership."*

> *(Cundiff/Still/Govoni, 1985)*

Distribution is seen as one part of an overall marketing strategy and the formulation of that strategy consists of a series of clearly defined steps which are shown in Figure 12. (We will discuss these in some detail later in the chapter.)

We need to determine whether distribution in the travel business is different from that in the traditional manufacturing industries because clearly in travel we are selling a service rather than a tangible product. In his book *The Tourism System*, Mill (1985) states:

Figure 12. Distribution strategies as part of an overall marketing plan

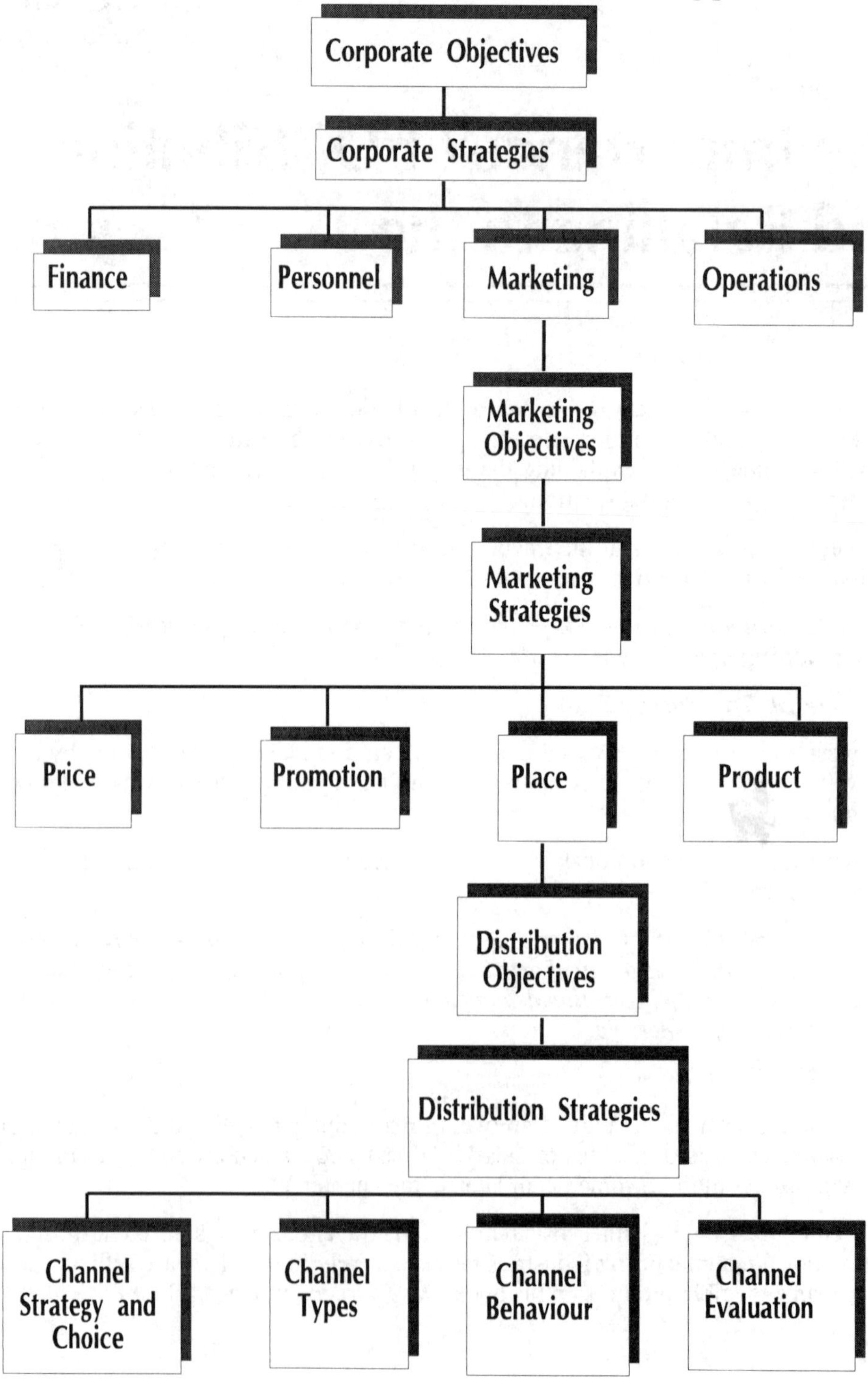

> *"that the purpose of distribution is to establish a link between supply, demand, producer and consumer. It is the system of distribution that makes the product available."*

If, as Mill has done, we relate this to the travel business then distribution is about the process of transferring the travel products produced by principals, such as transport, accommodation and inclusive tours, to the consumer. There are none of the physical activities involved in other forms of distribution such as the purchase, transport and holding of goods, and, apart from the distribution of brochures, the only physical things which are delivered into the hands of the traveller are pieces of paper, such as tickets or vouchers. There is no need for the travel agent to store actual products for they only become tangible when the customer uses them, for instance when the ticket is handed in on boarding a plane or the voucher exchanged for accommodation. A travel agent cannot store unsold seats for tomorrow's flight or unsold holidays leaving today. As Mill says *"...for this reason they must be sold each and every day or the sale is lost forever".*

There are many similarities, however, between the distribution process of tangible goods and that for travel and holidays. In both cases ownership passes from supplier to customer and therefore similar legal, promotional and financial activities must take place. All principals enter into legal contracts with their customers and only provide the service when they are paid. It is the role of distribution to get the information from the supplier to the customer so that a sale can be made. As Michael East goes on to say in the article quoted earlier:

"Distribution in travel is how information about the product is sent to the agent or customer; it is how he or she makes the purchase, i.e. makes the booking; it is how the physical 'goods' (the confirmation, the ticket etc.) are delivered; and it is how the principal is paid."

Channels of Distribution in Travel and Tourism

In any industry a channel of distribution is the way in which the ownership of a product is transferred from its original owner, normally a manufacturer, to the ultimate owner, usually a consumer. It quite often involves 'middlemen' who may for a time purchase the goods themselves before reselling them or, as in the case of the travel industry, middlemen, such as travel agents, who never actually own the product yet are responsible for ensuring the effective transfer of its ownership from the supplier to the consumer.

In any industry a channel of distribution can be simple or complex. In travel, for example, it could be based on a handshake agreement between a supplier, such as a hotelier, and a travel agent. It may require a detailed written contract. Alternatively, as we have already mentioned in Chapter 1, some suppliers prefer to deal directly with customers and choose not to use agents as middlemen.

Yet in travel and tourism the 'middlemen' often provide more than just a means of transferring ownership from principals to consumers, they also provide help and information. Mill notes that the role of distribution in travel "...implies a two-fold purpose, ensuring that potential travellers can obtain the information they need to make a vacation or trip choice and, having made that choice, that they can make the necessary reservations". In other words in the travel business those organisations acting as the channel of distribution must get sufficient information to the right person at the right time and in the right place to allow the consumer to make the right purchase decision. In addition such organisations must provide a suitable mechanism so that the consumer can make, and pay for, the necessary purchase. This is nicely expressed by Middleton (1988), who refers to a channel of distribution as:

> "*any organised and serviced system, created or utilised to provide conven-ient points of sale and/or access to consumers, away from the location of production and consumption, and paid for out of marketing budgets*".

Clearly the choice of marketing channels is a crucial decision in a supplier's marketing strategy. Getting the product or service from the supplier to the consumer has to be done in a way which is fast, efficient and well managed. As we shall see in Chapter 6 new technology is improving the way in which this can be done, often to the benefit of the travel agent.

By delivering both the product or service itself and the ownership of the product or service to the consumer at the right place, time and in the right amounts, marketing channels also perform an important service to the consumer.

The Choice of Distribution Channel

There is a tendency among suppliers in the travel and tourism industry to be concerned more with their plans for product development, promotion and pricing and to neglect somewhat the important decision of which means of distribution to use. In such a highly competitive market, however, there is a crucial need to carefully select the most appropriate means of distribution. In the travel industry as in many industries the means of distribution are constantly changing with new organisations entering the market and customer demands and needs altering as to how they wish to buy the product. Suppliers' overall success in marketing their products depends on their ability to anticipate such changes and to adapt to them. In the long term such success is also affected by the supplier's ability to make such changes profitably and by offering customers new combinations of product and service.

There are a number of reasons why travel suppliers should not see their choice of distribution method in isolation from the rest of their marketing strategy:

(i)   The means of distributing products or services should be integrated with all other marketing plans and should be seen as part of a single process if it is to achieve maximum impact at the point of contact with the consumer.

(ii)   Travel suppliers should regard their total marketing and distribution process as part of their competitive strategy with their rivals.

Suppliers must recognise that it is the method which best suits the consumer which is the right means of distributing their product rather than the method which best suits them. In establishing a strategy for distributing their products and services, travel suppliers should begin with the needs of the consumer and plan upwards from the final selling stage rather than downwards from production. It is the consumers' needs which are paramount, and having established those needs, the process is to provide the most convenient channel by working backwards towards the supply.

Often the choice of how to sell a product or service is the most important step a supplier will take, especially for those entering the market for the first time. It will take a long time to develop good relationships with agents or to build up a direct sell customer database. Where other suppliers already have well established channels of distribution, it is often difficult for a new company to enter the market. A good example of this is when a new and unknown tour operator tries to launch its product for the first time.

Once a supplier has generated a good relationship with distributors, then it is easier to sell new products. In many industries the means of distribution tend to be traditional and well recognised and the travel business in the UK is no exception. The travel agency network is wide-spread and strongly based with a high degree of public awareness. Therefore the temptation for a supplier to follow the traditional routes is very compelling.

Supplier's costs as well as profits are affected by the decision on which means of distribution to use. As we have already noted a company which chooses to sell directly to the consumer must undertake, and pay for, all its own marketing and distribution; in return, it reaps whatever profits there are. On the other hand a supplier which chooses to use agents reduces its per-unit distribution costs but obviously also reduces its per-unit profit because the agents will take their commission. It is evident that each supplier should use that channel or combination of channels of distribution which will provide it with the optimum profit and a supplier must analyse its costs in relation to its sales revenue as a basis for its choice. It has to be said that there is little available evidence of detailed comparative costs between the alternative channels of distribution within the travel business. Furthermore the problem is not helped by the fact that many of the figures derived for comparison are merely estimates.

Davidson (1982) lists six key factors which a supplier should consider when deciding on the most appropriate means of distributing its products. These are as follows:

- exposure to target markets;
- performance requirements;
- influence;
- flexibility;
- supplier's profit;
- channel needs.

We shall now examine each of these and try to apply them to a travel industry context.

(a) Exposure to Target Markets

From a supplier's point of view, the primary purpose of distribution is to make its products or services available and visible to its target customers. A good product may fail to sell because it is being distributed in the wrong way or is not being exposed to the people most likely to buy it. In travel and tourism suppliers usually try to make their product visible to consumers by using media advertising, brochures, leaflets or timetables. The important question facing suppliers is which means of distribution can best put their products before the right customers. For transport operators the most efficient method may be to use media advertising first and then to sell both directly to the consumer and through agents. For tour operators, where the brochure is their key selling tool, agencies can offer immediate exposure to potential buyers in the high street. Alternatively they must use direct advertising to persuade consumers to ask for their brochures.

(b) Performance Requirements

As travel suppliers have no tangible products to display, they need a means of selling their products which provides a combination of selling skills and customer advice about such things as destination, climate, entry requirements, health and foreign exchange. If they are selling directly operators must provide this information themselves whereas, by using indirect methods, such services will be performed by the agents. As well as booking a holiday the customer is required to pay for it. If a travel agency has taken the booking then it is the agent who must collect the money. With direct sell operations suppliers will have to collect the money themselves and this could cause difficulty if the customer should cancel, change the booking, or for some reason simply refuse to pay.

(c) Influence

A supplier's influence over how its products are distributed and sold often depends on its power, size and market share. In some retailing sectors suppliers are extremely powerful with manufacturers such as Ford, Coca-Cola or McDonalds having considerable influence through their own network of dealerships and franchisees. Suppliers in the travel business tend not to have the same sort of power and influence, with the exceptions of the direct sell operators and organisations, such as Thomson with their own travel agency chain. Suppliers must rely to a great extent on independent distributors. At the very least, suppliers need sufficient bargaining power to get their products exposed to the right potential customers, to maintain a sufficient quality of service and still be profitable. In contrast to selling through thousands of independent agents, by selling directly, suppliers are able to maintain complete control over this aspect of their business.

(d) Flexibility

In deciding which method to use to sell their products, suppliers are often making a long-term commitment, yet it is sensible for them to try to retain the greatest degree of flexibility to alter their methods of distribution in such a dynamic industry as travel and tourism. For example, when the Danish direct sell operator, Tjaereborg, entered the UK market in the late seventies, Thomson were flexible enough to be able to compete with them almost immediately by introducing their own direct sell subsidiary, Portland Holidays.

Most operators, while supporting the agencies, keep their options open and do not see such a policy as necessarily permanent or irreversible. Similarly there have been many examples in recent years where established direct sell suppliers have decided it would be in their best interests to open up distribution to the agency network.

(e) Supplier's Profit

It is important to a supplier that the means of distribution it chooses provides it with the maximum revenue at the minimum cost. Consequently some suppliers argue that if agents keep pressing for higher commission and override payments they could end up making themselves an uneconomic means of distribution. On the other hand, direct sell operators are increasingly faced with higher advertising costs as they must repeat adverts because of the trend towards late booking and the need to move late stock. When such rising costs are combined with increasingly fierce price competition from agency discounting, the profit advantage of the direct sell operator can be minimised.

(f) Channel Needs

One important factor in deciding on the most effective means is the cost of servicing the distribution process which the supplier chooses. For example, if the supplier decides to sell through agencies it must provide computer reservations support, sales representatives and an increased brochure print run. For direct sell suppliers there are the costs of running a sophisticated computer database, of direct advertising and the need to provide an enhanced level of customer service and back-up as a substitute for that which would have been supplied by the agent.

Different Forms of Distribution

Earlier in the book we examined the distinction between direct and indirect means of distributing products in the travel and tourism industry. In this next section we will try to take this analysis one stage further by examining different characteristics of each type of distribution channel.

(a) Channel Length and Width

We will now consider the concepts of channel 'length' and 'width'. By the channel's length we mean the different levels of intermediaries or middlemen that exist between supplier and customer. For example, if an airline is selling seats as part of inclusive holidays there are two intermediaries, the tour operator and the agent.

By 'width' we mean the number of intermediaries involved at any one level. In a 'narrow channel' the airline only sells through a limited number of tour operators, whereas in a wide channel it deals with many operators.

Figure 13. Distribution channel types

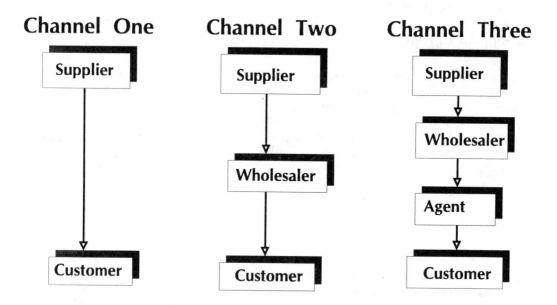

Christopher Holloway (1988) developed this concept further in relation to the travel and tourism industry by placing distribution channels into three categories:

- intensive;
- selective; and
- exclusive

(a) Intensive Distribution

When a supplier uses an intensive distribution policy it attempts to use as many outlets as possible. This is the most common policy in travel with many suppliers using all 7,000 ABTA appointed travel agents. It involves the supplier in considerable cost in relation to the number of brochures it must print and the level of sales support. The supplier must weigh the benefits gained in terms of maximising the visibility of its product with consumers against these considerable costs. In some cases a supplier may have a product which is so specialised or geographically targeted that an intensive approach is economically inappropriate.

(b) Selective Distribution

In this case the supplier selects a limited range of retail outlets through which to sell its product. In the travel business an example of such a policy would be in airline ticket distribution, where airlines select agents on the basis that they have satisfied the requirements of the International Air Transport Association (IATA). A further example is the case where the operator sets a minimum turnover which the agent must meet before being allowed to continue as a distributor. Other minimum criteria for selection include such factors as financial guarantees, staffing qualifications, security and business development potential.

(c) Exclusive Distribution

A further refinement of selective distribution occurs when a supplier grants exclusive rights to an agent to sell its products. An example in travel would be where a tour operator has prepared an exclusive product for, and on behalf of, an agent. We discuss this practice, known as 'own-branding' in some detail in Chapter 5. As the product is then exclusive to one agent it can only be bought through its own branches. From time to time certain brands of Thomas Cook Holidays have only been available through its own branches and there have been fears expressed that Thomson Holidays may one day make its products available only through its subsidiary, Lunn Poly.

Table 23 shows the characteristics and intensity of the channel types mentioned above.

Controlling the Channels of Distribution

Mill (1985) approached the classification of distribution channels in a different way. He tried to examine them in terms of how they are controlled. Under this heading he identified three types of distribution:

- consensus distribution;
- vertically integrated distribution; and
- vertically co-ordinated distribution.

Table 23: Intensity of channel coverage

Characteristics	Exclusive Distribution	Selective Distribution	Intensive Distribution
Objectives.	Prestige, image, channel control and loyalty price stability.	Moderate market coverage, solid image, some channel control and loyalty.	Widespread market coverage, channel acceptance, will accept some distortion to product image.
Channel Members.	Few in number, well established, enthusiastic to promote product.	Moderate in number, well established, high volume.	Many in number, all types of outlets, minimum requirements usually ABTA membership.
Customers.	Few in number or high socio-economic income groups. Business travellers. Willing to travel to agent. Brand loyalty.	Moderate in number, brand conscious, somewhat willing to travel to agent.	Many in number, price and convenience orientated.
Marketing Emphasis.	Exclusively, highly specialised product requiring highly trained and professional staff.	Wide choice of outlets. Joint advertising, good level of service.	Mass advertising, nearby locations.
Major Disadvantage.	Inconvenient locations, limited sales potential.	May be difficult to carve out a niche.	Limited channel control. Distortion of product image. Lack of expertise.
Examples.	Virtually non-existent in U.K.	Moderate application in U.K. Agents supported because they meet sales targets. Car hire agents, IATA appointed agents.	The most popular choice in U.K. Most tour operators use this form. Car ferry operators etc.

Source: Adapted from Evans/Berman, *Marketing* 3rd Edition, Macmillan, 1987.

(a) Consensus Distribution

Mill suggested that in most instances no single company in the chain of distribution controls the whole process and that organisations at each stage of distribution work together because they see it as in their mutual interest to do so. Although this is generally the case it is important to recognise that some very large organisations, such as Thomson and British Airways, do exercise considerable control over other levels of distribution by virtue of their size, buying power and reputation.

(b) Vertically Integrated Distribution

As we saw in Chapter 1 some organisations have taken control of some or all of the stages of distribution. We referred to this as 'vertical integration'. For example, Thomson Travel own Britannia Airways and Lunn Poly. Thomas Cook, primarily known as a travel agent, is also a tour operator selling its own Thomas Cook Holidays, Sunworld and Time Off brands. Vertical integration is particularly common in the German travel and tourism industry where tour operators often control their own chain of agencies, which deal exclusively with the products of the one operator.

Figure 14. Vertically integrated distribution in travel

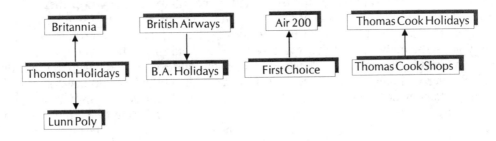

(c) Vertically Co-ordinated Distribution

While a supplier may not own all the stages of the distribution process it may be able to control them. This is referred to as 'vertically co-ordinated distribution'. An example in travel is where a tour operator can control distribution through contractual or financial commitments from travel agents. Franchising is another obvious example of such a system and we will discuss it in Chapter 5. In Germany, franchising plays an important part in travel distribution and suppliers sell a franchise to agents and then agree to sell only through such franchised outlets. At present this type of arrangement has not yet entered the UK market. Here it has been the multiple travel agent who has acted as franchiser selling the franchise to trade under a particular brand name to other small independents. The ill-fated Exchange Travel was the market leader in franchising until its collapse in late 1990. Preferred operator schemes are to some extent an example of vertical co-ordination although very few products, and usually only own-branded or own-label products, are available solely through specific agents.

Travel Distribution as a System

(a) The Respective Roles of Different Organisations within the Distribution System

One way of looking at distribution is to see it as an overall system in which each of the organisations has a role, which they generally accept, and each acts in a way which contributes to the smooth running of the system as a whole.

So if the travel industry is to operate as a co-ordinated system it is essential that suppliers are confident that travel agents will perform their part of the process efficiently and effectively. Suppliers would also like to be able to anticipate the actions of travel agents in terms of their likely marketing and pricing policies. For example, suppliers would not like it if a major multiple agency chain varied its policy on discounting their holidays on a day-to-day, ad hoc basis.

For the system to work suppliers must also 'play the game', even if this means missing out on lucrative opportunities or not exercising to the full extent the power they hold as a result of their financial strength or market position. Thomson Holidays is again a prime example. They could, if they so wished, decide to sell all of their holidays directly to the consumer and simply cut out the travel agent. This would lead, however, to Thomson being shunned by the agency sector and other major competitors would step in to fill the void. Similarly Thomas Cook, once owned by the Midland Bank, could have opened up travel counters in the bank's branches, but this again would have gone against the accepted norm of trading and might have resulted in other agents retaliating by taking sanctions such as refusing to sell Thomas Cook travellers cheques. Clearly one of the most important aspect of such examples is that in order for the system to work, the most powerful organisations must curb the use of their market power.

Many of the routine transactions, such as booking arrangements and commission payments, are made possible only because there is a general consensus within the industry about how these should take place. If each transaction had to be negotiated individually the system could not function. So both principals and retailers accept that each has a job to do and that each must make a sufficient profit to remain financially viable. Conflict arises when this consensus about each other's role breaks down, for example when a travel agent demands more commission without increasing sales or a tour operator decides to have the best of both worlds and begins to try to sell directly to the public as well as trading through agencies. To some extent there is a need for some degree of conflict as it sharpens the entrepreneurial edge. Each company is trying to come up with new creative ideas which will increase its profit and power. If, however, such behaviour upsets all the traditional and accepted working patterns it could seriously hamper the system's efficient operation and ultimately lead to a complete breakdown of the system as a whole. For example, if Thomson were to go direct, others might follow suit leading to a complete collapse of the agency system. There is, at present, no evidence to suggest that this is likely to happen in the foreseeable future. Furthermore if the actions of one company or a group of companies are seen to be a potential threat to the system then it is more likely that other organisations will react against them to protect it. A good example of this, which, although in a non-travel sector, mirrors the potential reaction of the travel business, involves the decision of the Pentos Bookshop group, trading as 'Dillons', to break the Net Book Agreement. This is an agreement between book-sellers and book publishers to fix the retail price of books. Pentos argue that such a restriction limits their ability to cut prices, attract more buyers and compete more aggressively. The publishers' case is that by allowing the large book-shops to undercut the small independents, many small shops will close and the system as it is today will collapse. Interestingly W.H.Smith, the other major bookshop chain, supports the publishers' case and wishes to maintain the status quo within the system.

In a distribution system the respective positions of each organisation are often distinguished by the marketing functions associated with them. So traditionally it was the operator who advertised on national television while the agent tended to use local marketing methods. Although these marketing roles do change, for instance as the retail chains increasingly play a larger part in TV marketing, there is still a degree of conservatism. New marketing methods, often developed outside the established channel of distribution are often rejected at first. This was the case when mass direct selling first came to the U.K. inclusive tour market. It was introduced from outside by the Danish company, Tjaereborg, and was initially rejected by the major U.K. tour operators.

(b) The Use of Power in the System

As we have already noted, within any system of distribution some organisations tend to be more powerful than others. Such organisations are sometimes referred to as 'channel commanders' or 'channel captains'. Their dominance can derive from either financial power (for instance the ability of tour operators to buy racking space through incentive payments) or from market-position, often the result of customer loyalty to a particular company or brand (for example British Airways which claims to be the world's 'favourite airline'). If customer loyalty to a supplier's brand is strong enough to persuade a customer to buy only its product, as with B.A., then all travel agents will want to be able to offer that brand. This gives the supplier considerable power. If customers are relatively indifferent in their choice of brands, for instance in the case of package holidays, then it is the agency which may have the power, for it will be the tour operators who will wish to have their brand distributed through the preferred agency. In the travel trade, there has been a swing from supplier dominance to agency dominance over recent years created by the wide choice and relative similarity of inclusive tour products and the expansion of the multiple agency network.

Another source of power stems from the information and communication networks used in the distribution system. Suppliers are often dependent on retailers for information about factors influencing consumer demand. Retailers occupy a key position because of their close relationship with the consumer. Thus suppliers might attempt to reduce their dependency for information on the retailer by conducting their own consumer research. For example, Thomson have an extremely sophisticated customer survey system which samples the satisfaction levels of homebound Thomson holiday makers. Such techniques improve the supplier's power in relation to the retailer.

It is true to say, however, that generally in the travel business the suppliers are not as dependent on agents for information concerning consumer demand as manufacturers in other industries. Like Thomson most suppliers spend a great deal of money on research and also use their sales figures as a measure of success. They do not appear to use agents as a primary source of information, which is something of a wasted opportunity.

A further aspect of power in the distribution system is 'channel leadership' which you should recognise as being distinct from 'channel dominance', although both are often exercised by the same organisation, with Thomson Travel as a case in point. A channel leader is an organisation which initiates change and helps to structure the distribution relationship. Leadership, unlike dominance, need not derive from financial or marketing power. A company which has market power, however, will find it easier to have new initiatives accepted and, conversely, an organisation which is successful in introducing new initiatives may become powerful as a result. Again using Thomson as an example we find that, not only does it dominate the inclusive tour market, especially because of its vertical integration with Britannia and Lunn Poly, but it also provides leadership in such ways as its introduction of new products, sophisticated computer reservations systems and automatic banking. Many other operators follow Thomson's lead, waiting for its brochure launches and looking at its prices before deciding on their own. By the mid nineties however, this dominance was being challenged by Airtours

(c) Co-operation and Competition

It is clear that for a system to survive and operate successfully co-operation is as important a factor as competition. The stability of the system depends on co-operation and on the agreement of both principals and retailer to maintain not only their broad trading relationships but also the details of them, such as the agreement to maintain continuous trading relationships and other agreements of a more detailed nature which are conditions of trading.

For some small independent agents their only chance of survival is co-operation with those fellow channel members in a similar position. This of course is the rationale of the voluntary groups such as the agency consortia, Advantage (ex-NAITA), ARTAC Worldchoice etc. They seek vertical co-operation between themselves and suppliers to fend off competition from multiples.

The effectiveness of each travel supplier in competition will depend not only on his own efficiency, but on his ability to induce agents to co-operate with him. Such are the benefits of vertical co-operation that the drive to organise the market has far greater dynamic effect than the horizontal competition taking place at any one level. This powerful drive naturally leads to tensions between strong agents and strong suppliers, as was seen in an argument between Airtours and Lunn Poly (1990) when the agent accused the operator of poor quality service but was probably worried about incentive commission levels. Ultimately, however, it is customers who drive the need for co-operation and it is their needs which have to be met.

To summarise, the implication of the behaviour systems approach may be stated as follows: decisions are made by both leader and non-leader, dominant and non-dominant institutions; and it is desirable that these decisions should be consistent and mutually supporting; the plans of individual channel members should link; there should be provision for consistent growth and change; standards of performance must be established and maintained through a mix of rewards and penalties; good two-way communications are essential.

Retailing Theory and Practice

As was discussed in Chapter 1, it is debatable whether or not travel agents should be regarded as retailers. There are many who say that they are not because they do not take risk by buying stock; their role is that of an agent, no more and no less. Others, however, take the view that it is simply a play on words and in the real world they play a part in the high street like their other retailing neighbours. They must therefore adopt the policies and marketing strategies as others do to compete and survive. It is useful therefore, in this context, to look at retailing theory and practice and to apply it to the travel agency business. This is exactly what a number of leading multiple agencies have done over the last twenty years to bring 'professionalism' to their businesses.

It must be pointed out that this is a very extensive area of study and readers may wish to refer to other leading texts and journals on retailing.

Aspects of Retailing Theory and Practice

(a) Role and Function of Retailing

Retailing is the final link in the chain of distribution of consumer products and services. The functions retailers perform are the consequence of the separation of distance, time and information between producers and consumers (Giles, 1978). In travel, however, the tasks of overcoming distance and time have been largely overcome with the advances made in information technology. Rather than assisting in the physical movement of goods travel agents are involved in effecting a change of temporary ownership.

The function of the retailer in the modern pattern of distribution has become increasingly complex. Essentially his role is that of a local supplier of merchandise, offering a direct service to the public. Davidson (1988) brings it down to one simple statement: "a retailer distributes products and service in the consumer market". He goes on to say, however, that society expects retailers to accomplish the classic distribution functions required by consumers in an advanced economy. These include:

(i)   creating product and service assortments that anticipate and fulfil consumer/family needs and wants;

(ii)   offering products and services in quantities small enough for individual or family consumption;

(iii) providing for the ready exchange of value through:

- efficient handling of transactions;

- convenient hours and location;

- information that is useful in making choices;

- competitive prices.

Travel agents do seem to fulfil all these functions thereby supporting the argument to regard them as retailers. For example, they provide for the consumer a wide range of travel products (assortments), even allowing for a measure of product preference through incentive commission payments. There is usually enough choice to fulfil consumer needs and wants. Each item of travel is purchased separately, usually on an individual or family basis. Unlike some forms of retailing there is no necessity to buy in bulk to gain a discount. The question of efficient handling of course depends on what the customer perceives as 'efficient'. Certainly travel suppliers have been concerned about the levels of service but it is probable that travel agents are, overall, no better or no worse than other high street retailers.

One of the prime reasons for the existence of the agent as a distributive channel is its ability to provide a convenient location. In general office hours are the same as other shops and in some cases are longer with late opening and Sunday trading etc. For example where agents have moved into new out-of-town shopping developments such as the Metro Centre near Newcastle and Meadowhall just outside Sheffield they stay open until 8p.m. The new telesales units provide all day trading plus weekend opening. Provided training and service levels are high, useful and accurate information is given. This should of course be unbiased allowing a customer to make a well informed choice. There is no doubt that thanks to discounting (see Chapter 5) the customer does have the opportunity to pay an extremely competitive price.

So on all counts then, in respect of the so-called "classic functions of retailing", the travel agent appears to meet the criteria.

(b) Institutional Change

Modern retail managers must be aware of changes that are likely to take place in the nature of the institution within which they work and plan accordingly. A number of important theories have been expounded to account for these changes.

The Wheel of Retailing

This theory was presented by Professor McNair some thirty years ago. It suggested that new retail outlets always enter the market as low status, low margin, low price operators. They are financially able to do so by reducing services, shop status and sometimes quality of merchandise. Over time, competition pressures from their own kind forces them to add services to gain a differential advantage. Eventually the wheel turns upward and as the institution matures, costs increase and there is room again for a new institution to enter at the bottom. For travel retailing, however, the hypothesis is suspect in that as new agencies mature, although their costs may increase, the price to consumers is usually more competitive thanks to better incentive deals gained from suppliers. However, it is a true reflection on the trade that new entrants are low status in the eyes of suppliers and are thus unable to secure incentive commission payments. They cannot, however, afford to be low on price as they will generally not have not the financial capacity to discount.

The Retail Life Cycle

In a similar way that products have a life cycle, so does the retailer. Davidson (1988) identifies four stages in the cycle:

(i) Innovation

Usually represents a sharp departure from existing norms. An example is Lunn Poly, the first major multiple to introduce discounting in 1985 and its decision to concentrate its marketing efforts towards the 'holiday shop' concept. Other examples are Page & Moy, the Leicester based tour operators and agent launching the Holiday Club credit card concept and Thomas Cook taking its tour operation in-house and introducing the phonecentre (see Chapter 5). The advent of "off-the-street" telesales units using teletext television advertising is another example of innovation.

(ii) Accelerated development

This is characterised by growth in geographic expansion, number of units, sales and profits. This can be dramatically illustrated by Lunn Poly between 1984 and 1990 when its shops grew from only 180 to over 500. It took over as the largest UK travel agent, taking with it the highest proportion of inclusive tour sales. It is said that the Page & Moy credit card scheme brought in an additional 10,000 or more new customers. In the nineties Airtours shot into the top multiple travel agent league table with its purchase of Pickfords and Hogg Robinson.

(iii) Maturity

This is said to be the most significant stage in the cycle, since the competition is at its most intense. Market saturation, over-expansion, intense discounting, administrative problems can and often do occur. In recent years multiple travel agents could be said to have 'shot themselves in the foot' by opening too many branches and giving away money through heavy discounting, then facing near collapse when the market dived into recession. "Multiple shares in the market have 'topped out' because we are getting to the stage where we are reaching the end of a list of locations where multiples can be viable" (Lovell, TTG, 1991). Early in 1997 there were rumours that Lunn Poly was considering a rationalisation of shops especially those in close proximity to each other.

(iv) Decline

Decline can be avoided or postponed by repositioning or modifying market approaches. For example, the decision of Thomas Cook in the late 1980s to introduce the 'superstore' concept into its agencies when millions were allocated to revamp offices, which included the separation of interiors into up-to-date product areas. Unfortunately this was halted and delayed because of the recession in 1989/90. In 1991 the same company decided to re-evaluate all its suppliers, the objective being to improve the quality of the products on offer. Unless firms introduce new approaches, then decline may set in, leading to lack of confidence of investors and suppliers with an end result of take-over, merger or closure. An example would be Pickfords travel who in 1991 were suffering from intense competition, reducing market share and difficulty in positioning and as a consequence was taken over by Airtours.

(c) Natural Selection

The Darwinian notion of survival of the fittest postulates that the life form most capable of adapting to its changing environment is most likely to survive. Retail institutions may be thought of as economic life forms, some adapt to environmental change, other, like the dinosaur, become extinct. Some high street department stores, especially those in family ownership, failed to adapt to the changing needs of customers in terms of shopping environment, product range, facilities, etc., and went bankrupt. Others were innovative, remodelling interiors, introduced modern selling techniques and customer services and as a consequence survived.

Until the eighties Thomas Cook was regarded as the 'sleeping giant', held back from expansion and development by nationalisation and a succession of elderly management teams who had worked up from the 'shop floor'. They lost their 'top spot' to other multiples and were regarded as having a very limited customer base. The company was privatised, brought in new management teams who took a fresh approach to sales and marketing, turned the company around and saved it from extinction.

The retail management's of today have therefore to combine aspects of theory to economic and environmental change.

The Retail Marketing Mix

Much has been written about the marketing mix as applied to suppliers of goods and services. The essentials of the mix, referred to as the four P's - product, price, place and promotion (Middleton, 1988) have helped suppliers to meet both customer needs and corporate objectives. The same market strategy can be and is applied to retailing and is known as the 'retailing mix'. "It is a concept relating to the familiar marketing mix and differs only in those matters which distinguish manufacturers' marketing from middlemen marketing" (Davidson, 1988). The ingredients of the retailing mix are designed to meet and satisfy consumer expectations as illustrated in Figure 15 which has been adapted to a travel agency situation.

Figure 15. The retail marketing mix for travel agencies

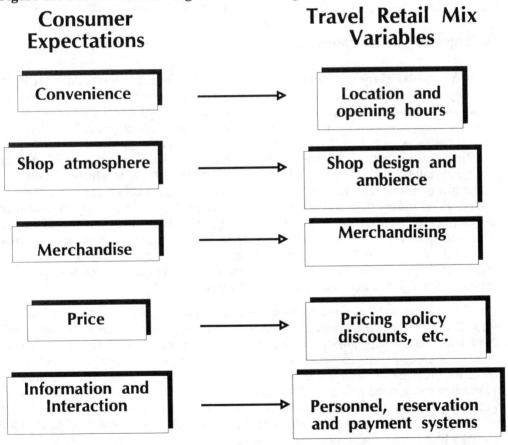

Source: Adapted from Davidson (1988), Retailing Management, 6th Ed., Wiley.

(a) Location and Opening Hours

Customers want travel shops to be convenient and easy to get to. However, as experience has shown, this does not necessarily mean that they have to be in the immediate vicinity like the street corner grocery shop. Many customers regard a major purchase like the annual holiday as necessitating a trip to the nearest town or city centre. Some local agencies have not survived or rely on low revenue earning products. There is, however, a 'middle ground', usually in urban areas which have a focal point for the community. Once the domain of the small independent travel agent, a number of multiple travel agents, in particular Lunn Poly, have taken the opportunity to exploit such positions. Opening hours have long been a 'bone of contention' with travel agents who originally saw themselves as offices rather than shops. However, intense competition and changing customer buying habits have forced them to adopt late opening- all day Saturday and in some cases on Sunday- especially in the booking season immediately following Christmas.

(b) Shop Design and Ambience

Travel agents should try to provide an appropriate atmosphere and ambience for travel shopping. The problem of appropriateness will depend on the agent's position in the market, customer type, lifestyle, and its physical location. For example, an agent dealing with relatively low cost holidays such as UK holiday centres, near-Mediterranean destinations, coach travel, etc. will probably prefer a counter-type interior for a quick and efficient throughput of customers. In contrast an agent dealing in up-market long-haul and cruise holidays would be best advised to use low level desks at which the customer can be given the time and attention needed when the purchase cost is high. A great deal of time, effort and expense has been given to this issue by agents, especially by multiples. Very expensive refurbishing programmes have been introduced such as the £3 million 'super-store' concept launched by Thomas Cook. Here separate specialist product areas have been created within the shop such as flight savers, long haul, foreign exchange, etc. Many travel agencies, however, still have uninspired frontages, out of date and drab interiors with high counters creating customer barriers.

Branches acquire ambience and branding through colour, lighting, exterior and interior fixtures and fittings and sales staff uniforms. On entering the shop the customer should feel a warm and friendly atmosphere with sales staff immediately showing an interest and smiling. If space permits decor should be supplemented by soft furnishings such as a settee for brochure browsing, a coffee machine, travel video booth, potted plants and maybe low background music. Unfortunately it would appear, according to trade paper weekly reports, that many agents fail miserably in this respect with uninspired frontages, unappealing window displays, out-of-date, drab and cold interiors with high counters behind which sit unfriendly sales staff keeping their heads down until questioned.

(c) Merchandising

Merchandising is concerned with all the marketing activities which take place at the point of sale. In traditional retailing it is therefore concerned with packaging, positioning and display in the store and on the shelf and with the provision of point of sale materials. Merchandising has also been defined as "any form of behaviour - triggering stimulus or patterns of stimuli, other than personal selling, which takes place at retail or other points of sale and is a basic tool in the promotional mix employed by businesses whose customers are exposed directly to their product offering" (Buttle, 1984).

There are distinct parallels between traditional and travel retailing and today's agency management's continue to introduce merchandising practices in a determined effort to bring a more professional approach to sales. The parallels can be seen as:

Packaging	Brochure
Positioning and display	Racking policies
Point of sale material	Posters, counter cards, neon-lit signs etc.

Whereas some of the attributes relating to the packaging of goods in shops are not as relevant to travel, e.g. product protection, physical distribution factors and costs, reuse value to customer, there are many similarities. For example, the role of the brochure: just like a tangible product its purpose is to create sales appeal and to be the main vehicle of the product concept, integrated with advertising and distribution channel requirements. The design and size has to conform with the requirements of the agency for racking and storage purposes. If there is competition for racking space and it is not specifically linked to commission incentives then good packaging, i.e. brochure cover, can stimulate the agency's interest in using the product in preference to others on the rack and for counter and window displays.

It is now established that positioning and display of products in shops greatly affects consumer reaction and sales. Stores, especially supermarkets, place great emphasis, not only on general overall layout, traffic flow patterns, etc., but also on the horizontal and vertical locations of products. Best selling products, perhaps with higher margins, new lines and so on, will be placed at eye level, perhaps on a corner or special display unit. The objective for the travel supplier is to secure, not only as much racking space as possible, but also locations which do most to catch the attention of potential customers. This can of course bring suppliers and agents into conflict where marketing objectives differ. Agents, especially multiples, now use sophisticated brochure rack 'planograms', which all branch offices must adopt, reflecting the merchandising policy of the company.

Point of sale (POS) materials may act to attract attention, as a straightforward reminder, or to recall a favourable image already created by theme advertising, or to trigger off impulse purchasing. It is important to integrate point of sale materials into the overall marketing theme, for example by co-ordinating it to media advertising. In shops point of sale materials can be a problem, they can spoil the overall image, they can be cumbersome, easily out-dated and discarded. Over the years travel agents have tended to move away from POS materials, wanting to give a 'clean image', for these materials do not sit happily alongside sophisticated computer reservations systems. Perhaps the most widely used POS are now the late offer cards present in nearly every agency window. They also highlight the agency brand rather than the operator. Critics say they spoil the image by cluttering up the window, preventing customers from seeing the style and effect of the shop interior. However, it would appear that the need to stimulate late sales through this method of merchandising outweighs the drawbacks.

(d) Pricing Policy

As far as the travel agent is concerned the product price, be it an airline ticket, package holiday or cruise is determined by the supplier. However, after a judgement by the Monopolies and Mergers Commission in 1986 agents can offer 'pecuniary inducements' i.e. money-off offers (see Chapter 5). This cash back inducement is linked to the preferential terms given by suppliers in the form of enhanced commission levels. However, it is up to each individual agent to decide on its own pricing policy. All the top multiples offer cash back on a sliding scale: the higher the holiday cost the higher the discount. However, some independents, especially those with only one shop, steadfastly refuse to join in, preferring to emphasise the quality of service on offer. Views vary widely on the issue, some saying that the public are now conditioned to buy on price and will search out the best discounts. Others say price expectations are not as important as the aspect of quality and value for money. Some agents may underestimate the price expectation of consumers which could be considerably above what the agent may consider as an optimum level on price. Therefore consumers' sophisticated perception of value is simultaneously a challenge and opportunity for the responsive agent.

(e) Personnel, Reservations and Payment Systems

Customers purchasing many types of merchandise frequently look to the retailer to provide detailed information about product appropriateness, characteristics and usage. A travel sales consultant is expected to carry out a similar function. As the range of travel products and destinations is so vast, and the ability to communicate and close a sale is also a requirement, the recruitment of quality staff is essential for the agent. The problem is that salary levels start as low as £4,500 per annum for a junior trainee and around £9,000 for a manager. It is little wonder therefore that agents have difficulty retaining their experienced staff, losing them to transport suppliers and tour operators and to other better paid industries outside travel.

Developments in new technology (see Chapter 6) are enabling agents to fulfil consumer expectations on the fast supply of information, ability to make reservations, efficient payment systems and ticket issue. Today agents have an all embracing, multi-functional systems meeting most of these requirements. It is said that technology could do away with the travel agent through the use of free standing POS computers at suitable locations. Current evidence suggests, however, that machines are at present mistrusted by the public- especially for travel purchases - open to abuse and, as they are devoid of human contact, are unable to respond to problems and complaints. Point of sale machines at airports have shown that there is a section of the market who will wish to purchase in this way but it is expected to remain small as will buying for home.

Aspects of Consumer Behaviour

An extremely important aspect in analysing the travel agent as a distributive system is the behaviour of consumers in the buying process. For both supplier and agent a thorough understanding of this behaviour is necessary for successful business practice. The changing environment in which consumers live must be followed as must their buying habits and the processes which they use. The factors which affect institutions, such as social, political, economic and technological changes also impinge on consumers. In each decade life style changes according to the environment under which consumers live and work. So far the objective has been to examine theory and practice in relation to the supplier. This section is devoted to the consumer, although it has to be said that this subject is extensive and full justice cannot be done to its importance within the limitations of this work.

External Influences on the Buying Process

The customer makes a two-part independent decision in the market place. In travel this is which product to buy and where to make the booking. It is impossible to buy a product without choosing a supplier but in most cases there is a choice of where to make the booking. It is imperative therefore to know what factors influence this choice.

(a) Social and Economic

Social and economic realities heavily influence behaviour patterns. These can include the changing structure of the family, where the working mother is now commonplace. This extra income increases the propensity to tourism. The tendency to have smaller families has also increased the possibility of holiday taking with fewer mouths to feed and clothes to buy. Of course travel has to compete with other luxuries such as the family car, household appliances, etc. In economic terms the travel manager should understand how the consumer behaves in response to the ever changing fortunes of economies both at home and in overseas destinations. Consumers are extremely susceptible to inflationary pressures as can be seen from the dramatic effects of the 1990 recession in the U.K. Inflation reached double figures, the Government kept interest rates high, the housing market collapsed and family debt increased. Little wonder that the travel industry faced a declining market.

(b) Political

Linked to, and in most cases inseparable from social and economic influences, are political factors. At home it is likely to be the way the Government is running the economy and the faith that people have in their ability to govern. Any weakening of Government credibility is likely to unsettle the travel market through recession and pressure on the currency. In the political cycle, the years just prior to a General Election are usually good as the incumbent Government tries to ease monetary pressure off the voters. After the 'honeymoon' period new Governments often use the early stages of their session to introduce their most difficult pieces of legislation, sometimes lowering consumer spending and thereby hurting the travel trade. Overseas, political influences are more likely to be those connected with internal unrest, as seen recently in Yugoslavia, or conflicts such as the invasion of Kuwait by Iraq. Tourism in the immediate vicinity is seriously affected by such events.

(c) Motivations

However, besides the obvious social, political and economic influences, a full under-standing of consumer behaviour would have to include motivations. "Motives are inner states of tension that activate human behaviour and direct it towards goals" (Davidson, 1988). Travel marketers, managers and especially staff would probably do a much better selling job if they tried to understand and interpret human motivation as it is directly linked to the needs, wants and desires which they hope to satisfy. There is a plethora of texts regarding human motivation, now a scientific subject, from authors such as Maslow, Murray and Moutinho. In relation to travel four basic motivations have been identified-physical, cultural, interpersonal and status/prestige (Robinson, 1976).

Physical - holiday makers are motivated by the thought of being able to "get away from the daily routine of life" and to do something that will improve their physical well-being. This can be either to relax in a luxury hotel or apartment or to be physically active by, e.g. climbing, golf, skiing, etc. Both types of holiday, although very different, can have the same end result.

Cultural - the desire by people to travel in order to learn about other countries, their peoples and culture. This would include visits to festivals, art exhibitions, theatres and concerts. Travel agency staff should not view the foreign holiday as just the opportunity for 'fun in the sun' but a chance for many of a real educational opportunity. They should therefore be aware of specialist operators in this market and take an interest in other cultures themselves. It is a very important motivation as it can lead to better understanding between the peoples of the world.

Interpersonal - anything to do with interaction and relationships with other people. It is more likely to be the desire to make new friends or to visit relatives abroad. However, it could be taken as the desire to escape from those whom we share our lives with at home and work! This can be linked to the physical motivation where the desire can be to 'get away from it all'. There are many examples of operators specialising in this market such as Club 18-30, 2wentys, Saga Holidays and family reunion organisations.

Status - often difficult to accept, especially by very independently prestige minded people, but this motivation is stimulated by 'what other people think'. It was prestigious to go on a package holiday to Spain in the 1960s- it was like the car, a status symbol. Today the destination has to be long haul to acquire the same response from friends and relatives. This category can include travel for business and professional interest, education, etc.

The Buying Process

Kotler (1984), provides a useful framework for the retail buying process which can be used as a basis for a comparison with travel buying.

Figure 16. Kotler's 'five stage model' of the buying process

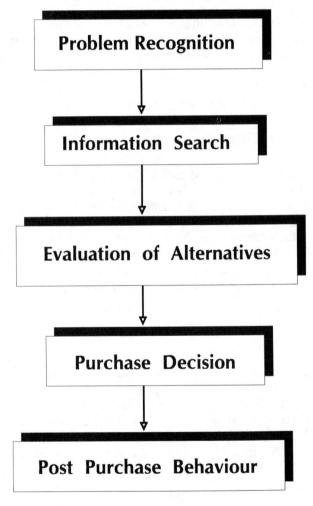

Source: Kotler, (1984)

(a) Problem Recognition

At sometime in the yearly life cycle of events most people make a decision that "they must get away from everyday pressures of life and go on holiday". The motivations for this were described in the last section, e.g. to visit friends and relatives, or on health, medical grounds, business etc. The theorists would say that this is the recognition of yet another problem to be solved. To put it more simply, it ends up on the shopping list.

(b) Information Search

Once the decision is taken to travel then the search for information begins. Here is the second problem facing the consumer: where to obtain the relevant information. It can come from a variety of sources of which the agent is only one. Adverts and articles in newspapers and magazines, advice from friends and relatives all challenge the agent for the potential customer's attention. However, it would appear at the moment that most people think of the travel agent, for foreign travel.

(c) Evaluation of Alternatives

Having once gathered together the alternative choices available, consumers have to go through a process of evaluation. Which holiday or air, rail, sea service meets their needs and wants, price range, etc. This is often done in the home, especially if the product is to be bought direct from the supplier. Where an agent is used this should be the most important aspect of their 'service' to the consumer. As an 'expert' the agent's advice should make the purchase decision much easier. If all agents offer the same levels of discount, the same product range and merchandise in the same way, then the only distinguishing feature is in fact the help in the evaluation phase given through high levels of service.

(d) Purchase Decision

The decision to purchase will be made on the basis of all the alternatives put before the consumer. The important aspect of this stage for the agent is not so much the actual decision itself but "how and where it will be purchased". There may be only one channel available such as direct or via an agent. In some cases, however, there could be a duel channel choice, for example an airline, coach or rail ticket purchase. This is the most crucial part of the buying process model for the agent, which must use all its marketing powers to persuade that customer to visit highlighting all the advantages that it could bring.

(e) Post-purchase Behaviour

There are two main aspects to post-purchase behaviour. First, when the product has proved unsatisfactory, then complaints will ensue. These must be handled just as effectively as the original booking in order to retain customer loyalty. Second, if the travel arrangements went well there is usually no contact from the customer until they decide to book again. To ensure that this is with the original agent these firms should employ direct response marketing techniques to establish a permanent relationship.

Taking Kotler's original model as a basis for consideration, Figure 17 is an attempt to translate this into a travel buying context.

Figure 17. The travel buying process

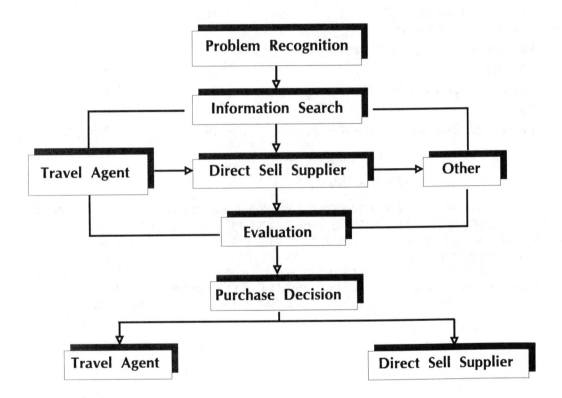

The model in Figure 17 shows the travel buying route the consumer can follow. At the information search stage many will use all three sources. Evaluation, although shown as an individual task, will be influenced by which source was used. However, there comes a critical point when the decision to buy has to be taken and one of the two choices will be available for most product types. The attributes of each channel will then come into play. These attributes were sought in a survey by Mintel and are listed in Table 24 in order of importance, together with the rating for each channel.

Table 24. Attributes affecting consumer choice of method of purchase and channel rating

Attributes	Preferred channel %	
	Agent	**Direct**
Personal service	90	11
Efficiency	58	31
Fewer mistakes	50	13
Always used this method **and found it satisfactory**	46	9
I like to be able to get information	38	12
Cheaper	25	13
Could see what I was getting	28	7
Fast	16	38
Less trouble than other methods	19	13

Base: 804 adults choosing a booking method

Source: Adapted from Mintel, (1988)

It can be seen that for most consumers the aspect of personal service is a key issue in the buying process. This is supported by both research analysts and industry suppliers. Here the travel agency has its most potent weapon to fight off competition from direct channels. Surprisingly perhaps price is not a top issue for the majority of consumers, conflicting with some of the marketing priorities that have been adopted by some agents. This factor does not bode well for direct suppliers, especially in the field of inclusive tours, whose existence depends on offering a cheaper deal than that which is available through agents.

Chapter 5

The Travel Agent and Change

This chapter considers why in the last twenty years decade there has been such a dramatic change in the structure of the travel agency sector and in the marketing activities of many travel agents. The growth of the large retail chains, known in the trade as the 'March of the Multiples' has stimulated and increased marketing by travel agents. Once it was essentially the preserve of suppliers but now the growth in agency marketing by the multiples has placed many smaller independents under increasing commercial pressure. A further consequence of the 'March of the Multiples' has been the change in the business relationship between agent and supplier. The first part of this chapter will look at the reasons for such changes, the second will consider the marketing techniques which are used, 'the multiples', the third will examine the effect of such changes on the small independent travel agent. Finally we will assess the changes in the business relationships between agent and principal.

The Reasons for Change

As we mentioned in Chapter 2, one of the major phenomena of the eighties, and which has continued into the nineties, has been the emergence and rapid growth of the large multiple travel agents. This has had a major impact on the distribution policies of suppliers and on their business relationships with agents. No longer do the suppliers have so much control and power as the multiples flex their negotiating muscle for better deals because of their extensive networks.

We shall see that the multiple chains decided to expand not just to increase profit but for a number of other reasons including:

- the desire to increase market share;

- the determination to acquire assets, expertise and goodwill;

- an attempt to benefit from economies of scale;

- the need to develop a brand image.

(a) Increase Market Share

One of the most important factors in the battle for supremacy between the multiples is a desire to increase market share. When one travel agency chain takes over another it can gain the double benefit of not only increasing its market share but also reducing the level of competition. Alternatively the company may seek to increase its size by opening new branches, and while this can be a slower process, the final objective is the same.

An increase in market share is extremely important to the retail chain because of the knock-on effects it generates, including increased status and power with suppliers, the ability to negotiate better commission deals and, as a consequence, the ability to offer customers incentives such as money discounts, low deposits and free insurance.

As the chain grows it takes an increasing percentage of a supplier's product and as such can become a virtually indispensable means of distribution. If this happens the agency can ask for special commission and override deals and the supplier will find it very hard to resist. As the agent increases its market share it will get much better deals from suppliers wanting to benefit from the enlarged network of offices. Once the agency has acquired such deals, the savings it makes can help to finance any incentive offers it wishes to make to the general public. In fact, if it were not for such deals, discounting would not exist in the form it does today. This is one major reason why smaller independents, especially one shop businesses, find it so difficult to discount their prices.

(b) Acquisition of Assets, Expertise and Goodwill

When a multiple takes over another smaller chain it will immediately acquire a valuable network of shops and possibly the smaller company's head office. Many of the newly acquired branches may be in prime high street locations and as such will be well known to local customers. The multiple then has a number of options, either to retain the branch and continue to trade, to close the office and sell it off or, if the company already has a branch in the area, to decide which to keep in operation. Similarly the company may have acquired head office premises which can be sold off with all its functions merged into the buyer's existing head office or it may wish to keep the old company's head office and use it as a subsidiary office.

In addition to the physical assets a company will secure through a take-over it will also gain people – all the sales consultants, managers and administrators of the company which it has taken over. One of the major reasons for the take-over may have been to move into an area of business in which the buyer was weak. For example, this may be the major reason for a leisure agent to buy a business travel agent. Again the buyer has a number of options, either to retain staff, re-deploy them or make them redundant. In this situation the buyer can take an overall look at the staff and perhaps retain only those considered to be the best. For example, as a result of the take-over, the newly merged company will. probably have two marketing directors and two regional managers for each area, and the buyer can then decide who to retain. Finally, like any other retailing business, the agency which has been taken over will have a customer base, that is people who are loyal to it and who return whenever they want travel services. Some long established agencies may have such a high level of 'goodwill' that, for the first few years, it may be necessary to retain the original trading name. Of course 'goodwill' is measurable in cash terms and the buyer will have to pay to acquire it.

(c) Economies of Scale

When one travel agency takes over another, or expands through the opening of new shops, the existing head office may be able to cope with the extra volume of work without having to increase staff or equipment. The company is said to benefit from 'economies of scale'. Similarly a small agency will still have to have administration systems whether it has two or ten branches. When the multiple, Thomas Cook, expanded its branches in the 1980s the extra volume of work was still handled thorough its existing systems at its head office in Peterborough. Likewise, Lunn Poly, although moving its head office from London to Leamington Spa, was still able to benefit from economies of scale. More recently Airtours closed the Pickfords Head Office in Enfield and moved to the Hogg Robinson Head Office in Woking which is now the Going Places Headquarters.

In the area of management, senior executives may have to cope with the extra pressure which expansion brings without the company having to make new appointments. For example, it may be possible for a travel agency regional manager to cope just as well with twenty branches as with ten. There will, however, come a point when the demands on management and the volume of administration become so great that the company will have to invest both in new people and equipment.

(d) Brand Image

Usually an important and valuable feature of a company's goodwill is its 'brand image'. This determines the degree of public recognition the agency enjoys and perhaps whether the general public regards it as a quality retailer or recognises it as a supplier of some particular type of product. All of the major multiple travel agents are looking to establish their names alongside other national retail household names such as Marks and Spencer, B.H.S. and Boots. Clearly the more branches the chain has, the greater is the likelihood that this objective will be achieved and of course the greater the potential for securing higher sales. Once a company has established its image it is essential to 'brand' the company throughout the whole organisation, hence the multiple will insist on similar shop designs, logos and staff uniforms.

Lunn Poly has established a very distinctive brand, as well as being recognised as a specialist in a particular product area with its holiday shop concept. Conversely, Thomas Cook, a much older and longer established agency, has a name which is widely recognised by the public but has had difficulty in establishing a distinctive brand or in being seen as a specialist in a particular market segment.

(e) Geographical Spread

A multiple agency needs to have a wide geographical spread of offices throughout the country if it is to achieve a national brand image. It needs to have a location on every major high street in the country. All of the major chains have therefore pursued a policy of either acquiring smaller regional multiples or of increasing the number of new shops they open throughout the country. An early example from the 1980s is when Lunn Poly took over Renwicks, based in Exeter, this gave the multiple an immediate presence in the South West of England where previously it had been weak. More recently A. T. Mays, the Scottish based travel agent, took over John Hilary Travel who were particularly strong in the East Anglia region. A. T. Mays also astounded the travel business in 1997 by linking with the consortium ARTAC Worldchoice, giving it an immediate presence in virtually every town and city in the UK.

The Effect of the 'March of the Multiples' on the Industry as a Whole

The 'March of the Multiples' has had a number of major consequences for the travel industry as a whole. These include:

- changing the structure of the industry and the relationship between principals and retailers;

- increasing commoditisation of the principals' product;

- parent companies whose interests are non-travel;

- the squeezing out of the independents;

- the ability of the multiples to determine which products are on offer to the general public.

(a) The Structure of the Industry and the Relationship between Principals and Retailers

To some extent the 'March of the Multiples' has been inevitable and merely reflects the process of rationalisation which every other sector of retailing has seen in the last thirty years. For example, the grocery trade has seen the decline of the small family grocer and the emergence of the supermarket chains as the major grocery suppliers. As companies such as Sainsburys and ASDA have become stronger they have been able to dictate much stricter terms to their suppliers. A similar pattern is evolving in retail travel as the agents gain market power and are able to dictate their terms to the principals. Clearly for tour operators the ideal situation is one in which the travel agents individually are relatively weak as this leaves power in the operators' hands. The gradual shift in marketing emphasis from the operators to the agents, however, is a measure of the agents' increasing influence and power and the agents' consequent demands for extra commission and discounting will continue to worry operators.

Some principals see the growth of the multiples as a good thing because of the professional management the multiples bring to the industry. For such principals it is often far easier to deal with a relatively few multiples rather than a whole host of smaller independents. Overall the tour operators regard well organised multiples favourably as they offer an effective means of selling their products. The operators gain economies of scale through brochure distribution, point of sale display materials, national joint advertising, better brochure/booking conversion rates and some tangible commitment to sell the product. As one major operator stated:

> *"We see them as our partners, they pay our wages, we find their demands are very fair, we don't fear the management although we would not want to put all our eggs into one basket".*

(b) The Increasing Commoditisation of the Principals' Product

For certain products, consumers identify more with the retailer and the retailers' brand than with the product itself or the manufacturer's brand name. The St. Michael brand is a good example. The consumer knows the product is being supplied by Marks and Spencer and trusts M & S to ensure the product's quality. Of course this means a reduction in the customer's recognition of the manufacturer's name and consequently less brand loyalty to the manufacturer. We use the term 'commoditisation' in such a situation, where the supplier's brand name becomes of less and less importance to the customer. Large household names like British Airways may be able to overcome this in the same way that Heinz, Nescafe or Kellogs have continued to be brand leaders despite being sold by Sainsburys or ASDA. Other, smaller, principals could have more of a problem when it is the travel agent's identity rather than the principal's which the customer comes to recognise and respond to.

(c) Parent Companies whose interests are Non-travel

A number of the multiples are owned by parent companies whose main interest is not in travel. For instance, at the time of writing, Thomas Cook is owned by Westdeutsche Landesbank and Travelcare by the Co-operative Wholesale Society. There is some concern that if the parent companies do not have a primary interest in travel this will be reflected in a lack of commitment to the sector. For example there is often speculation in the trade press that if profits at Thomas Cook were on a downward spiral then Westdeutsche Landesbank would quickly sell off their interests in the company.

(d) The Squeezing out of the Independents

As major multiples take over the high street the independent travel agents are increasingly being forced out into secondary positions. This has an impact on some principals, such as the smaller tour operators who depend upon independents for product visibility and scheduled coach operators whose business is low priority for multiples. Some independents find themselves in a vicious circle unable to attract higher commissions due to low volume, which in turn means an inability offer customer incentives such as low deposits, discounts and free insurance. The multiples, while competing among themselves, are wiping out competition from the smaller agents.

(e) The Ability of the Multiples to Determine which Products are on offer to the General Public

The multiples can, to a considerable degree, determine what the customer purchases through their racking policies. In this way they are able to prevent smaller suppliers reaching the general public **and in so doing they could be said to be restricting consumer choice.**

The Effects of the 'March of the Multiples' within the Agency Sector

Within the travel agency sector there have been two major effects of the 'March of the Multiples'. The first effect has been on the way in which the multiples have changed their approach to business management and marketing. The second, a consequence of the growth and increasing power of the multiples, has been the squeeze put on the small independents. In this section of the chapter we will examine each of these in turn beginning with the changes to the multiples themselves.

These include the following:

- the development of a corporate image;
- staff development;
- market segmentation;
- investment in new technology;
- product discrimination;
- customer incentives;
- own-label products;
- holiday clubs;
- direct telesales.

(a) Development of Corporate Image

All the leading multiples have been anxious to develop their own individual corporate images just like any other national retailing chain. This image can be observed in two major ways, first from the design and the decor of branch offices and secondly through external advertising. Multiples such as Lunn Poly are now quite distinct on the high street with their eye catching fascia panel above the shop window which combines the company name, logo and the 'Holiday Shop' branding all in its house colours of red and white. The window carries late offer cards, each bearing the agents name and card holder in the house colours. The window display is no longer left to the 'creativity of the manager or staff' but controlled by central marketing services from Head Office. Once inside the shop the theme is continued with brochure racks, counters and desks carefully designed and laid out to create a company ambience. All shops are identical in this respect allowing of course for differences in floor space areas. The same shop fitters will be used nationally or, if contracted on a regional basis, they will have to conform to an exact specification. To consolidate the corporate image sales staff are now required to wear the company uniform, again in house colours.

Another important aspect in creating a corporate image is through the use of advertising. Today we are used to seeing the multiples and some regional agents undertaking costly advertising campaigns on television. In addition their adverts appear in national, regional and local newspapers and magazines. All the company's advertising is co-ordinated by the head office marketing team who ensure that the branding is carried through in colours and logos to create the desired image. All this is a far cry from the days when each office had its own style and window displays, staff wore their own clothes and there was no television advertising.

(b) Staff Development

As all the leading multiples offer similar products and generally give comparable customer incentives the only thing that will separate them in the eyes of the public is 'service'. For this reason the multiples now place a great emphasis on service skills in their staff training. Whereas in the past the emphasis was on technical skills, such as the ability to read a timetable and issue a ticket, there is now much more of a balance between such technical skills and the need for a high standard of customer contact skills. The multiples tend to take this into account when they are recruiting new staff and considerable emphasis is placed at interview on the candidates' ability to show good communication skills and present themselves well. Once employed, staff are normally given a series of selling skills courses where their abilities are developed in role play situations. The multiples have also invested heavily in training videos and sales guides and in some cases a member of staff who successfully completes this training can gain a salary increase.

The growth of the multiple chains has also stimulated a general increase in salary levels, although it must be said that in many cases sales consultants are still not terribly well paid. In a survey by the Eastcastle Management Group in 1992 the average salary of travel agency managers was found to be £12,107, with senior sales consultants with at least two years' experience averaging £7,949 and juniors on only £4,610. Some of the large multiples, however, did attempt to improve the low level of pay. Thomas Cook, for example, offered in 1992 a starting salary of between £5,000 and £5,500 to counter staff, but even this was well below the salaries offered in other service industries such as banking and some sectors of retailing. By 1997 the above figures had increased between 10 to 15%. The business travel multiples however tend to recruit at a higher level and pay more, for example in 1997, a Senior Business Travel Consultant could expect to earn between £12,000 and £15,000 in a provincial city. For this reason many experienced staff regularly move between multiples and between leisure and business travel, trying to climb the pay and promotion ladder. This makes it necessary for companies to review their salary structures constantly to keep and attract the best people.

(c) Market Segmentation

The decision by Lunn Poly in the mid-eighties to shed its interests in business travel and to concentrate on the package tour market posed something of a dilemma for other expanding multiples. The problem they faced was whether or not to follow Lunn Poly's lead and reduce the number of product segments on offer or to retain a full travel service. A. T. Mays decided to go for the latter emphasising in their advertising that they were an 'all travel shop' able to deal with most enquiries. The 1992 television advert by A.T. Mays although pushing the money discount on inclusive holidays, also had the slogan 'everything a travel agent should be'. Thomas Cook reduced their product range but have been careful not to place too great an emphasis on one particular segment of the market. We discussed the advantages and disadvantages of such a move earlier when we noted that, while one of the benefits of specialisation is an improvement in product knowledge by sales staff, this can be offset by the agency's inability to satisfy all customer enquiries and a consequent loss of business to competitors who offer an all-in travel service. It is expected that this move towards greater segmentation of products will continue as suppliers become more closely linked to fewer distributors.

(d) Investment in New Technology

The high level of competition between the multiples and the need to offer the best and quickest service to customers has led to heavy investment in new technology. The multiples wish to appear as professional and as advanced as possible, therefore most modern branches have an array of computer terminals on view. The aim is to provide each sales consultant with a terminal which can be revolved to allow the customer to participate in the booking process. The most common technology in leisure shops is 'viewdata' which links agents with the suppliers' reservation computers through British Telecom telephone lines. All the multiples are engaged and paying for 'hardwiring', that is to link their shop terminals to exclusive telephone lines which, through a network provider such as Istel or Fastrak, provide access to many suppliers through one call. (We discuss this in some detail in Chapter 6.) Even this, however, is now being overtaken by global computer reservations systems (CRS) which, by using 'intelligent' personal computers, will eventually be able to link the retailers to all suppliers and provide ticketing, accountancy, management information and administration systems. Many CRS providers such as Galileo, Sabre and Worldspan are now fighting a commercial battle to win the multiple agents' business.

(e) Product Discrimination

In such a harsh competitive environment it is only natural that the multiples, like other high street retailers, wish to maximise their best selling products. It has always been and still is left to the agents and suppliers to decide on whom to do business with. However prior to the 1980s and the 'March of the Multiples' it tended to be an 'open door' policy with the agents offering anything that was going. It was left to suppliers to assess, monitor and grade their agents rather than the other way around. As the multiples became more powerful they realised that they could be increasingly selective over which suppliers they actively supported and that this could be financially beneficial as it led to higher commissions and overrides. As a result of such arrangements they had the ability to offer their customers a better deal and, in particular, better cash discounts. They also introduced the idea of 'preferred operators' whereby suppliers were categorised by the multiples according to their ability to meet a pre-determined criteria. For example, in the case of a tour operator this would include being able to offer:

- a wide range of departure points;

- a quality product where the level of complaints and problems in the branches are minimal;

- a product which will generate a considerable commission earning;

- a marketing agreement which includes joint advertising, promotions, etc.

The multiples' selection process first divides suppliers into their respective product groupings such as airlines, tour operators or car hire etc. Then, within each group, they are placed into categories. Thomas Cook for example had, until recently, 'Winners', 'Recommended', and 'Authorised' categories. Other category titles have included 'Gold', 'Silver' and 'Bronze', 'Blue Ribbon', 'Preferred' and 'Recognised' suppliers. Each category carries with it benefits and conditions and, like all league tables, it is intended to encourage and attract the players, in this case the travel suppliers, to strive for a place in the top category. Thomas Cook did this by naming those suppliers moving up the leagues as rising stars'.

Those companies being named in the top category gain such benefits as:

- guaranteed racking space for brochures with at least one or, in the case of leading tour operators, multiple facings;

- top sellers being allocated rack space at eye level with those doing less well being racked on higher or lower level facings;

- access to window displays;

- access to agency staff for training purposes;

- agency staff being encouraged to give maximum sales support;

- preferred operators being given first offers on joint ventures such as 'in-shop' promotions, advertising and trade fairs.

Those suppliers in the lower categories will receive fewer privileges on a sliding scale. Some will be able to get racking space whilst others will not. In the lowest category suppliers' products will not be displayed and will only be booked when asked for by the customer. As we mentioned previously, in return for the 'privilege' of being in the top category, suppliers will be expected to meet certain conditions specified in a written agreement. Examples of such conditions would be:

- dealing with the agent's customers efficiently and courteously in order to ensure customer satisfaction;

- standing by any promises or guarantees the supplier makes and ensuring that these are not ambiguous;

- ensuring that any amendments to travel arrangements booked by the agent are notified at once;

- ensuring that all documentation, such as confirmations, invoices and tickets are provided in plenty of time before departure date;

- ensuring that any customer complaints are dealt with promptly.

This system of 'preferred suppliers' gives considerable power to the multiples who can use it to improve product quality whilst gaining maximum commission returns. They can, if the supplier fails to meet the conditions or will not agree to commission demands, use the ultimate sanction of withdrawing support altogether. This in practice would mean the removal of the offending company's brochures from their racks. This system is clearly discriminatory and, as we discussed in Chapter 3, creates problems for the smaller supplier. Take, for example, a newly formed small tour operator which joins ABTA only to find that the multiples will not rack its brochure. Such a company will find it extremely difficult to grow when it has no product visibility through the agencies, leaving it with the only alternative of selling direct to the public.

Suppliers' views on such categorisation often depend on whether or not they are on the preferred lists. Most agree that one negative aspect of the policy is that it restricts customer choice and reduces price competition. If, for example, a multiple decides to feature only two brands from the many it could potentially offer, then price comparisons cease to be of great importance. Once the two suppliers are aware of the situation they may be tempted to keep their prices at a point which is mutually beneficial rather than reducing them to outdo their competition. Some suppliers see the preferred category system simply as a means by which the agents can gain higher commissions and overrides, with the agents deliberately and artificially limiting the number of facings on offer.

Most suppliers agree however that it is the agents' right to sell the products they chose, and provided it is a fair system, small specialist tour operators with limited capacity cannot expect racking. One suggestion has been that agents should develop something similar to a 'delicatessen' counter in supermarkets which offer 'tasters'. In the case of the travel agents this would be a variety of specialist holidays such as painting, cycling, climbing or 'gourmet' holidays.

(f) Customer Incentives

In Chapter 2 we noted that the Monopolies and Mergers Commission (MMC) decided in 1986 that travel agencies could offer whatever 'pecuniary inducements' they wished. All multiples and many independents now take advantage of this ruling and make incentive offers which range from money off to low deposits or 'value added' inducements such as the offer of free insurance, transport to airports or discounts on ancillary travel products. There is now a yearly battle, often led by Lunn Poly, to offer the most attractive discounts. All would probably prefer not to do it and most have tried to attract customers instead through value added offers, but none of the multiples is prepared to lose market share by abandoning a practice which the customer has now grown to expect. Such discounting applies primarily to inclusive tour holidays and it is worth repeating again that it still remains the right of operators to fix the price of their packages and leave it to the agents to decide if they wish to 'give' something back to the customer. Examples of customer incentives include:

- low deposits

- cash discounts

- free insurance

Low Deposits

If agents choose to offer low or no deposit deals to customers they still have to pay the full amount of the deposit to the operator. As the difference must come from the agents this can seriously affect their cash flow. The agents will collect the full deposit as part of the final balance or, as with Lunn Poly's £5 low deposit offer of February 1992, the full deposit became due by 2nd March. When the multiples first introduced such incentives there were problems as some customers subsequently decided to cancel. Having paid only £5 or perhaps nothing at all the customer simply cancelled and refused to pay any more, leaving the agent to make up the difference to the operator. Now multiples such as Lunn Poly ask the customer to sign a deposit indemnity agreement under which the full deposit must be paid upon cancellation. If the customer then refuses, the agent will take legal action to recover the money. Low deposits may look attractive in adverts but in effect the agents is giving nothing away except a period of extended credit.

Cash Discounts

After the customer has booked, the operator raises the invoice showing the full cost of the holiday. When the balance is due, the agent deducts any cash discount offer it has made to the customer and receives that amount from the customer. The agent must then pay the full amount, less commission, to the operator. This incentive, like others, is financed by the agent's commissions and overrides (see Chapter 1) from the suppliers. These average between 1% and 3% over the base rate of 10%. The agent will also gain a commission from the sale of insurance, which can be anywhere between 30% and 45%. Such higher commissions, and perhaps a contribution from the agent's marketing budget, will go to finance the cash offer.

For many agents the knock-on effect has, of course, been to reduce their profits and to undermine their financial stability. Without the benefits they gain from incentive commissions and compulsory insurance it would be a completely pointless and ruinous exercise. If, for example, you take the average selling price of £300 per head for a European beach holiday, taking two adults on a base commission level of 10% that would mean an income generation of £60. With a £20 discount per person this would leave a net margin that would be so slim that it would probably not cover the cost of the sales consultant's time and the office overheads. However, if the agent was enjoying substantial incentives from the operator and a high commission level from insurance sales then the figures would look much more healthy as shown below:

Financing a Cash Discount

Income to agent

Holiday costs received from customer	£600.00	
less discount @ £20 per person	£40.00	£560.00
plus insurance premium from customer, 2 @ £23	£46.00	
Total income	£606.00	£606.00

Agent's outgoings

Holiday costs invoiced by operator	£600.00	
less incentive commission at 13%	£78.00	£522.00
Insurance costs 2 @ £23	£46.00	£568.00
less commission at 45%	£20.70	
Total outgoings	£547.30	£547.30
Difference – net margin		£58.70

With the benefit of extra commission offered by the operator as an incentive and the commission from the sale of the insurance the agent's margin has now increased by some £38. However, this example is based upon the top end of the commission scale, some holidays will not carry such a high rate. When the discount offer is not available the margin increases to £98.70 so it is understandable that most multiples and especially independent agents would like to see an end to discounting. There is, however, no sign that in today's competitive environment any individual agents could break ranks and stop discounting altogether.

The majority of the major tour operators agree that the MMC's decision did not really uphold their right to maintain price control because it allowed agents the right to discount the price of their product. There is, however, an agency agreement in force which states that agents will sell holidays at the price specified by the operator. Therefore, as we noted earlier, the operator will invoice the agent for the deposits and balances specified in the brochure and, as far as some of operators are concerned, if the agents then wish to discount their products out of their own pockets it is the agents' own choice, although clearly the operators are delighted because the customer can buy their holidays more cheaply. What they do not want to do is to contribute to this reduction in price.

The operators' major concern, however, is that discounting leads to a fall in the profits of the agency sector and a subsequent de-stabilisation leading to the collapse of a major agency chain. Many believe it is dangerous practice and that if agents trade without a sufficient return there will be an eventual decline in the standard, training and salary levels of agency staff. For some operators discounting is seen as a downward spiral which conditions the public to pay less for their holidays and to leave their bookings to the last minute. Holiday makers may now feel that they are entitled to the same cheap holiday that they had last year, and discounting may simply drive down quality. This situation gives the public a false impression of the true cost of going on holiday and as such is artificially changing the market.

Most suppliers are resigned to the fact that discounting is here to stay and that in retrospect it would have been better if the MMC's decision had been against discounting, as this would have preserved a fragmented agency sector. As it is the decision has helped to accelerate the process of concentration within the agency sector, so shifting the balance of power away from the operators.

Free Insurance

Free insurance is another customer incentive offered by both multiple and independent agents. While the customer is issued with a free insurance policy the agent still has to pay the premium to the insurance company. Thanks to the very high rates of commission on insurance, however, only between 50% and 60% of the premium is actually paid by the agent to the insurance company. Again such offers are usually linked to a minimum spend by the customer and to holidays offered by those operators who are giving an extra override. This type of offer is often compulsory to enable the agent to offset the discount through the extra commission earned. However this practice was being investigated by the Office of Fair Trading in 1997 which, if the compulsion is stopped, may have serious financial consequences for travel agents.

(g) Own-label Products

During the 1980s, as the 'March of the Multiples' gathered momentum, one interesting marketing development was that the multiple chains persuaded the operators to have their product overprinted with the agent's name. This became known as 'own-labelling'. Sometimes it was simply a sticker on the cover of a package holiday brochure, while in other cases a complete new cover was printed and 'wrapped around' an existing brochure. The practice was yet another reflection of travel agents adopting policies developed by their high street retailing neighbours. There are two main types:

- own-branding
- own-labelling

Own-branding

Perhaps the best examples of own branding are to be found within the supermarket and large retailing chains such as Sainsburys and Marks and Spencer. Because their names are so well known the chains can buy huge amounts of a product, say for example hair shampoo and chocolate buttons, with their name already on the packaging, rather than that of the manufacturer. Although customers do not know who produced the product they will still buy it because of the reputation of the chain. The concept of true own-branding is therefore to have products on the shelves in the retailers name but not having produced them. How does this then relate to the travel agency business?

This concept has been applied to travel in two main ways:

(i)   Some holidays are produced, managed and sold entirely by the travel agent. In effect the travel agent is a tour operator in its own right. Of the multiples only Thomas Cook actually has its own brand in this sense. Since its inception, the company has been involved with the production and operation of inclusive tours. Since the company ended its Mediterranean short-haul holidays in the late 1980s, because of the excessive competition in the market, its main products were long-haul packages such as the Thomas Cook Faraway programme. However in 1996 the company bought Sunworld and Time Off thereby adding to its own branded portfolio.

(ii)   An alternative form of own branding occurs when holidays are produced by a tour operator exclusively for a specific travel agent and are branded throughout with the agent's name. This means that not only must the brochure be branded with the travel agent's name, but the invoice, tickets and resort representatives must also bear the agent's brand. In theory the customer should not know that it is not the agent's own holiday package. There are very few examples of this in the travel business because operators are generally unhappy to lose their identity and agents have limited resources to ensure branding throughout. So what most do is to "own-label"

Own-labelling

Own-label operations involve the supplier in agreeing to either print the name of the agent on the cover of an existing brochure or replace the outside cover with an agent's own 'wrap-around' cover. The product is not exclusively sold through a single agent and can be purchased at other travel shops. The invoice and tickets are provided by the tour operator and, of course, at the resort all representation will be under the operator's name and not that of the agent. Once the customer has purchased the product the agent's name ceases to have the same significance as it did under 'own-branding'. Most of the major multiples are engaged in some sort of own-labelling, especially in the specialist product areas such as short breaks, long haul, villas and apartments and cruises. The benefits to the agent of own-labelling include:

- a higher profile for the agent as a specialist in a specific segment of the market;

- the usual benefits of override commissions and incentive deals;

- a potential customer picking up an 'own-labelled' brochure is less likely to take the booking elsewhere;

- counter staff are generally more motivated when it comes to selling the product if it is labelled as their own and will make more effort to be familiar with it.

The major reasons why operators join such schemes are that:

- they hope that it will lead to an increase in sales;

- by having their product endorsed by a major travel agent the operators trust that customers will hold it in higher esteem;

- it will ensure greater product visibility and staff attention.

There are, however, distinct disadvantages for operators in own-labelling, the most important of which is the potential loss of identity. Additionally it is the operators who must carry the costs involved in overprinting and in giving the agents extra commissions and incentives. Many suppliers have found themselves in a 'catch 22' situation, in that if they do not co-operate with a multiple in an own-labelling programme, their competitors will and yet if they do, their costs increase. Most therefore are against own-labelling in principle but are forced to do it in order to compete. Some will not do it as they are not prepared to 'devalue their brand' and will cite as examples companies such as 'Heinz' who do not allow retailers, of whatever size, to sell their products in containers without the Heinz name on them. Other operators prefer to maintain the distinction between operators and agents arguing that it is the operator who puts together the product, takes the risk, sells the product and controls the price, and that own-labelling is merely an extension of giving the customer travel agency ticket wallets.

In the future, however, computer technology will allow a further expansion of own-branding. The agents, and especially the multiples and the consortia, will be able to place a product on their internal viewdata screens without the operator's name on it. The potential customer will merely see a list of available holidays on the counter screen under the agent's name. The customer need never see a brochure and the agent will receive a special discount rate on the sale of such holidays.

(h) Holiday Clubs

Because of changes in the rules relating to discounting and incentives some multiple agents and independents have linked up with credit card organisations to develop alternative direct booking systems. It was, however, an independent agency, Page & Moy of Leicester, who first pioneered this concept and this resulted in the company becoming the country's largest single-unit travel agency in terms of business turnover. The company came to the conclusion that many of their customers used their high street travel agency merely as a conventional booking point for a pre-determined holiday chosen from tour operators' brochures, and consequently did not require any further advice or information. The company decided therefore to try and reduce costs substantially by cutting out the high street expenses and to transact the order by telephone. To do this customers merely used their credit cards, in this case Barclaycard. Page & Moy's concept was relatively simple:

- All Barclaycard customers would receive a publicity leaflet with their monthly statement giving details of the scheme and listing participating operators.

- Customers would then request a holiday brochure either from Page & Moy, directly from a tour operator or by obtaining one from a travel agent.

- Customers would choose their holiday from the brochure and telephone in their booking directly to Page & Moy quoting their credit card number in order to pay for the deposit or balance.

- Page & Moy would then book the holiday and give the customer a cash discount because of the saving on overheads.

This method of booking is said to be ideal for the sector of the consumer market which is composed of experienced travellers who know what they want and do not require the services of the high street travel agent. As the clients are credit card holders, there is likely to be a higher proportion of high earners who are consequently more likely to purchase higher value products. Such clients are often more aware of price and may be less loyal to a particular brand. They have confidence in their own ability, need little advice and the transaction is carried out in a very business-like manner. Although the concept may not initially have been about building a sales consultant-customer relationship it has now developed into a high quality service geared specifically to the special needs of the target market. Page & Moy for example train their telephone sales staff to a very high standard using a qualified Training Manager. The agents involved in such schemes benefit from the extra business they generate from credit card holders and, by using low cost, off-the-street office accommodation and by only accepting telephone bookings, their overhead costs are considerably reduced. The credit card companies and their respective banks benefit by providing an additional service which raises their profile in a competitive market and of course they earn interest on any outstanding balances customers may have on their credit card accounts.

As you might expect, such developments were, at the time, greeted with considerable criticism from those travel agents not in any such scheme. They felt that the schemes are to some extent a betrayal of travel agents by their own colleagues. As customers still need to obtain brochures they will naturally go into a convenient local agency, pick up a brochure, maybe even spend time getting advice, then return home to telephone someone else to do the booking. However the holiday club agents argue that they may be actually doing the reverse by driving potential customers into High Street agencies who then have the first opportunity of capturing the business. If they fail at that point then they have few grounds for complaint. Some suppliers feel this practice is unfair not because of the innovative way the agents are giving their deals, but because they are being supported by the people who they may be putting out of business. Brochure distribution is at the heart of the problem, for although the holiday clubs offer a full brochure distribution service, a proportion of the public will use local agents as an unpaid distribution and advice point. Many operators, however, seem to agree that if the market demands this form of trading then the opportunity should be provided for people to buy in this way. They do not concern themselves with where the business actually comes from but merely reward any agent which produces business. If they can get exposure through such deals they are likely to take it.

It is important to remember that any cash discount enjoyed by the customer is paid for by the agent and not the credit card company. The savings needed to provide the discount are generated in exactly the same way as in the agency shops, that is by special deals made with suppliers for enhanced commission, incentive deals and by the sale of insurance which is often compulsory. In Table 25 we show a comparison of discounts between retail travel agents and holiday clubs. This analysis shows that discounts on lower value holidays are greater in travel agents than they are with the holiday clubs, whereas higher value products attract a higher discount from the holiday clubs. This reflects the overall higher value business that is generated from direct customers using credit cards, who will usually be from higher socio-economic groups.

Table 25. Scale of discounts given by travel agents/holiday clubs

Holiday Spend Club	Travel Agent	Holiday
£	£	£
200-399	30	20
400-599	45	30
600-899	60	40
900-1199	75	60
1200-1649	95	80
1650-1999	110	100
2000-2499	150	150
2500-3499	180	200
3500-4499	200	250

Source: Industry, average discounts on selected offers

Thomas Cook, previously owned by the by Midland Bank, soon followed Page & Moy into this lucrative market, establishing a link with the Midland and Lloyds Mastercard/Access Group. A. T. Mays joined forces with TSB Trustcard and Pickfords with Girobank/Visa. As each scheme was announced there were howls of protest from other agents. They even persuaded ABTA to close its account with Barclays because of its links with Page & Moy and many chose to move their travellers cheques business from Thomas Cook as a protest. Such actions have not deterred the continued development of such schemes, with others being extended to trade union members and large commercial companies. Lloyds Bank, however, withdrew from the Thomas Cook/Access scheme in May 1989, describing the scheme as a "marketing flop", with their research showing that it had a very low level of customer awareness. At the time, the trade's most outspoken critic of the scheme, Harry Chandler, was quoted as saying:

> "Lloyds have discovered that people do not want to pay soaring interest rates on holiday purchases. It has realised tour operating is quite different from banking and decided it does not want the hassle."

> *(TTG, 1989)*

It is interesting to note however that Lloyds Bank have since re-entered to Holiday Club market by linking with an Independent travel agent, Apollo Travel based in Rotherham, South Yorkshire.

Table 26. Holiday club/credit card schemes 1997

Agents	Bank/Financial Institutions
Page & Moy	Barclaycard
Retail Travel	Midland/Royal Bank of Scotland
(Thomas Cook)	
Apollo Travel	Lloyds/TSB

Source: Industry

You must remember, however, that despite the outcry bookings through holiday clubs still remain relatively small when compared to the overall market. Estimates for 1989 were that holiday clubs accounted for 1% of the market with only some 10,000 holidays attributed to the Barclaycard and Access schemes. By 1997 this sector was estimated to be generating around 60,000 holidays.

(i) Direct Telesales

Originally called phonecentres this was a further innovation launched by a number of multiples. The scheme was aimed at attracting holiday bookings direct from the customer's home. A direct freephone number was available and in some cases the service was open all day including weekends. Led by Thomas Cook, who established five centres across the U.K. in the mid 1980s, it was intended to relieve pressure on agency staff in the shops, serve holiday makers isolated from those shops and provide all the same booking and service facilities. According to Thomas Cook the need for phonecentres arose because of difficulty answering telephone calls promptly in branch offices caused by pressure of business on the counter. Too much revenue was being lost through engaged telephone lines. A pilot scheme was set up in the Birmingham area which had a 'cluster' of branches surrounding it. By using a technique called 'local holding' incoming calls to branches were diverted to a telephone centre. It was found to be a success – the centre generated sales of about 10% of the combined sales of all the branches from which calls were diverted. In other words the system effectively produced the equivalent of an extra branch.

The system has similarities with the holiday clubs, whereby the customer will probably use other agents as brochure collection points then phone in direct. As a consequence the scheme received similar protests from other agents, who stated that this was a most unethical thing to do. An essential difference, however, is that there is no discount available for using this service over and above those already on offer via the branches. Other multiples such as A.T. Mays with its 'Fastphone Holidays' and Pickfords with 'Holidayline' followed Cook's lead. It was reported that Thomas Cook spent at least £250,000 to set up each of its five centres.

There are, however, a number of drawbacks to phonecentres. For example, how is the service to be kept in front of the public's view without spending a massive amount on advertising each year? Productivity is a problem as phonecentres receive enquiries on all aspects of travel, including rail and accommodation. It is estimated that a conversion rate of only one booking for every forty calls can be expected at phonecentres. Finally, there is the obvious resistance from the companies' own high street shop managers who see it as another form of competition and a dilution of their business.

By the nineteen nineties Phonecentres were replaced by the Direct Telesales Units a much more sophisticated and focused operation. The major multiple to lead the way was Thomas Cook who started up a four man operation in 1988 in Peterborough. The objectives were changed from providing a travel agency service over the telephone to a direct sell operation. They mirrored the Holiday Club concept established by Page & Moy and linked up with the Midland Bank and other third parties such as Marks and Spencer. The system was exactly the same, mail-out to third party customers offering a direct booking service with the added attraction of discounts. From that four man operation Thomas Cook Direct now employs over 200 staff in high technology premises and accounts for some 10% of the retailers total sales.

Lunn Poly responded in 1994 by opening a direct sell centre in Coventry (closed in 1996), this closely followed by A.T. Mays in Glasgow and Going Places in Stockport. However it must be remembered that some of the largest telesales centres in the UK were in fact started by small independent travel agents especially in the North East of England. Airtours, parent company of Going Places, bought out the largest, Late Escapes, in 1995 for £6m. It is now renamed Going Places Direct. The major sources of business for telesales units are:

Teletext

A high growth market because it is so easy for customers. View at anytime of the day or night then telephone the number shown on the television screen. Research shows of the 17m teletex viewers some 5.8m tune into the holiday section on ITV and Channel 4. 17% of users are in the AB social category while 27% are in DE.

Credit cards

Most of the major credit card companies offer their customers this service as explained previously under Holiday Clubs.

Advertising

This covers not only through the media, newspapers, magazines etc but also through own brand and own label brochures. This supports the retail high street network by providing an alternative booking service.

Third party promotions

The potential of those "closed user" groups is enormous. For example a link with Freemans mail order catalogue produced for Going Places telesales a potential customer base of 1.6m people. If only 1% responded that is 16,000 customers. Cooks have Sky

Televisions holiday channel, Nationwide Building Society and Orange Telecommunications.

Independent Agents

The effects of the 'March' on the smaller independent travel agent has been dramatic. From a fairly cosy position where they dominated the industry whilst being protected from the excesses of competition by their own regulator ABTA, they have faced an assault from multiples and from Government through the removal of restrictive practices. The major effects on and responses from independent management's include:

- excessive competition

- reduced market share

- pressure on profits

- formation of consortia

- franchise schemes

(a) Excessive Competition

Over a period of last fifteen years the number of travel agency branch offices in the UK has doubled as can be seen in Table 27. The multiples proportion of branch offices has risen from 20% in 1975 to around 30% in 1995. When these figures are related to the U.K. population it can be seen that each individual branch now has far fewer potential customers than in previous years. This is shown in Table 28. Whereas Independents previously had a virtual monopoly in smaller towns, suburbs and villages, they are now likely to have a multiple branch around the corner.

Table 27. ABTA Travel Agent Members 1979-1995

Year	Members	Branch Offices	Total	%Increase (Decrease)
1979	1896	2305	4210	
1982	2211	2884	5055	20%
1985	2647	3372	6019	19%
1988	2932	4477	7409	23%
1991	2750	4049	6799	(8%)
1994	2430	4547	6977	3%
1995	2219	4719	6938	(1%)

Source: ABTA

Table 28. Agencies related to population 1971-1995

Year		Potential Customers
1971	One agency for every	15,900
1979	One agency for every	13,302
1988	One agency for every	7,693
1995	One agency for every	8,359

Source: ABTA/CSO

(b) Reduced Market Share

Research carried out by ABTA in the mid 1980s showed that turnover from all travel agents rose to £4.5 billion. However, 3% of agents accounted for 51% of sales compared to 69% accounting for only 17% of sales. The majority of small independents were therefore receiving a smaller slice of the cake each year and it was estimated that on average this meant a 10% to 12% drop in Summer holiday numbers each year in the late 1980s because of the dilution of business. In 1994 it was reported that 57% of all inclusive tours sold were by the four major agency multiples who controlled 30% of the travel agency branch outlets. As the independents share declines, so does their ability to compete, their profit margins being squeezed to a position where for some, it is no longer economic to trade. However, it has to be said that there are some very successful independent agents who are coping well and thriving on the competition. It is the overall picture that places a question mark over the size of the independent travel agency sector.

(c) Pressure on Profits

A breakdown of the turnover figures for those agents receiving under £1 million in turnover revealed a disturbing situation for many small independents when related to average base commission earnings of 10% (see Table 29).

Table 29. Turnover/base commission breakdown, ABTA agents 1996

Proportion of agents		Turnover (£)	Commission (£)
2%	turnover less than	200,000	20,000
8%	turnover less than	400,000	40,000
24%	turnover less than	800,000	80,000
13%	turnover less than	1000,000	100,000
53%	turnover more than	1000,000	100,000 plus

Source: ABTA

It can be seen that 34% of agents were only taking in around £80,000 in commission, out of which they have to pay salaries, office space and other expenses. Little wonder then that these agencies are often only staffed by the owner and a few juniors on very low pay.

This overall lack of profit means that the small independents find it very difficult to participate in the price war by offering discounts, low deposits, free insurance, etc. An extremely limited advertising budget will be available and only small investment in new technology is possible. Salaries for staff have to be kept to a minimum and therefore a reliance on young inexperienced school leavers is necessary. Many take advantage of the Travel Training Companies "Travel Training Programme" formerly known as Youth Training (YT) which enables these youngsters to acquire all the basic qualifications. Unfortunately for the independents these people often then move on to multiples for better pay and conditions.

However, as stated before, it cannot be ignored that some individual branches of independent agents are often more productive than branches of multiples. British Airways Holidays confirmed in 1997 that their top ten performing agents were all independent branches.

(d) Formation of Consortia

Obviously having come under such pressure from the 'March of the Multiples' the independents have been seeking ways of fighting back. One alternative has been to link together and form an association or consortium. Taking the grocery trade in comparison, when faced with the growth of the supermarkets, many small shopkeepers joined together under such banners as Spar and VG Stores. The principles and objectives are therefore the same: forming a group of independent organisations to work together to achieve a common aim, i.e. to compete with the multiples through collective bargaining. However, the corner shop survived by working longer hours and attempting to give a better service but could not offer the same extensive choice as supermarkets. In the travel agency trade the question of choice is often the other way around as the independents' strength is the ability to offer all products. What differentiates the agency consortia from most of the multiples is that they are run by people who have a 'personal' financial stake in their businesses.

One of the largest groupings is NAITA, the National Association of Independent Travel Agents now trading under the name of Advantage Travel Centres. In 1989 this consortia had reached a total of 420 companies with 840 outlets, making it in fact, at that time, the largest U.K. multiple. By negotiating collectively Advantage Travel Centres have been able to obtain some of the benefits enjoyed by the multiples, for example, override commission, consolidated fares, a high earning insurance scheme, free advisory service on matters relating to licensing, bonding and disputes with principals, joint advertising, a closed-user computer system, and own label products marketed under the banner of "Advantage". Membership costs £730 a year, but only those agencies who are members of either ABTA with a minimum turnover of £750,000 or of IATA with a turnover of at least £500,000 are considered. These requirements will exclude quite a sizeable number of small independents but the consortia wish to retain an elite organisation. Advantage Travel Centres is controlled by an elected 'National Council' and administered by a Secretariat similar in many ways to ABTA. Although falling back in terms of members in 1997 Advantage announced a strategic alliance with a smaller consortium based in the South West of England bring its total branches to 720.

Another leading national consortium is ARTAC, the Alliance of Retail Travel Agents Consortia, now trading under the banner of ARTAC Worldchoice. It was originally formed by combining various existing travel agent consortia across the UK. Unlike Advantage membership it is open to any licensed business, no matter what its size. Again it looks for similar benefits from suppliers as those given to multiple chains. It has introduced a preferred suppliers scheme which covers not only tour operators but ferry, car hire and cruise companies, plus a closed user-group viewdata system. ARTAC has been very active during the nineties forging new alliances within the trade. For example they have joined forces with Association of Independent Tour Operators (AITO) to combat the threat of vertical integration. The deal gives ARTAC Worldchoice members:

- guaranteed minimum commission rates

- joint point-of-sale material

- training and educationals

- joint promotions and public relations support

By 1997 ARTAC Worldchoice membership has grown to 600 members controlling around 700 travel shops. In that year the Association staggered the trade by announcing a remarkable alliance with a top multiple agent A. T. Mays. Overnight this new alliance produced the largest grouping of travel agents ever known in the UK with around 1,000 shops and an estimated market share of 12%.

Consortia have also emerged on a regional basis where small independents, who are known to each other, have joined together to fight collectively for market share. An example in the South West of England is SWIFTA, the South West Independent Federation of Travel Agents with 73 shops Yet another is Fairway Travel Alliance in Scotland with only 18 members and 28 branches. Although these small consortia are likely to link up with the large national groupings such as Advantage and Worldchoice they will no doubt retain a measure of their independence which they hold so dear.

(e) Franchise Schemes

An alternative for the independent travel agent to the consortium is to become a franchisee. As Davidson (1988) explains, franchising is an ownership format that generally attempts to combine some advantages of independent business ownership with chain ownership whilst minimising the disadvantages. It involves a contractual relationship between an independent businessperson (franchisee) and a sponsoring or wholesaling organisation (the franchiser). For an initial fee and a percentage of gross revenue, the franchisee is granted both the right to operate a business under an established name and the use of established operational methods.

In travel this gives the independent travel agent (the franchisee) the opportunity of developing his own business whilst under the umbrella of a larger well-known organisation (the franchiser) that could be either regional or national. Once in the scheme the independent agent is expected to remove his own name from over the shop and replace it with that of the franchiser. Likewise the inside of the shop must reflect the corporate identity of the group, so that the customer assumes it is part of a chain. All the facilities of the group will then be available such as central marketing and accountancy, training and technology. However the scheme and its advantages are available at a price, for example a once and for all franchise entry fee, followed by a management charge or royalty. Using the now defunct Exchange Travel franchise scheme (1990) as an example the entry fee was around £10,000 and the royalty one and half percent of sales turnover, the charge being payable by monthly deduction from commission earnings.

There is again a comparison to be drawn with other high street shops where franchising is popular, especially in fast foods such as McDonalds and Pizza Hut. However, the difference is that in travel the franchiser is not in a position to control and purchase stock so it becomes difficult to set oneself apart in terms of identity to the customer. The participants in the franchise scheme have no product identity unless they enter into own-labelling; even then they are no more distinct than other multiples that do the same. Other forms of high street franchising are marketed on the basis of an exclusive product such as the 'Big Mac' and 'Kentucky Fried Chicken'.

The largest travel agency franchise scheme was operated by Exchange Travel, which unfortunately went into liquidation in 1990 leaving many of its seventy five franchise offices facing ruin. Some were taken over by Co-op Travelcare, but there is no doubt that the crash did much damage to whole concept of franchising in retail travel. However, by 1994 new schemes were emerging with the A.T. Mays "Associate Programme" offering independents the backing of a major multiple but in contrast a business travel franchising company, Uniglobe collapsed in November of that year with debts of nearly £2m!

Supplier Concerns About the Independent

The general view of the state and future prospects of the small independent travel agent is that they can compete and survive by concentrating on service and quality rather than price. This is the supermarket/small grocer analogy, where the latter survive by offering the customer a local, convenient and very specialised service including extended hours and home calls if necessary. Independents should thus include all ancillary products and not just inclusive tours. They should take the view of the enterprising retailer, such as the small grocer run by an ethnic family, who has identified its market and provided quality products and local customer service of the highest order. Whereas the multiples are designed to appeal to a national audience, the independent should target the local community. It is essential therefore to research local needs and link them to innovation. Some of the market is cut off because of discounting, but some customers do not always go to the cheapest retailer, for example for Hi-Fi equipment. In this case the discount retailer will probably not provide the service choice or back-up, because of narrow margins, whereas the specialist will.

However, not all suppliers agree with these sentiments, believing that "service is just an inadequate swap for the sacrifice of the discount". In other words people in general would prefer 15% off the holiday by booking at a multiple than the personal service at the corner travel agent, especially when nine times out of ten the so-called personal service is no better than that offered at multiples. These suppliers also think it a fallacy to say that personal service is the sole preserve of the corner shop – it can be very good in multiples, especially when used in conjunction with an advanced database providing additional information over and above that given by the small independent.

Suppliers are generally in agreement that a strategy of concentrating on niche marketing – segmenting the market and selecting those products upon which a reputation for service and quality can be built, is a useful way forward. For example, cruising, long-haul holidays, villas and apartments, U.K. holidays and skiing. The problem is the size of the segment and which other products are sacrificed to give that specialisation. The question is how effective the niche agent can be about offering something different compared to other agents without having to go down the discount route.

Although most suppliers are of the opinion that independents should try to steer clear of discounting, it should be remembered that they are just as eligible to go and ask for a special deal on commission and overrides in exchange for productivity. Overall, on a shop for shop basis, it appears that the independent is not being discriminated against. It is not a question therefore of multiples versus independents, but between those who have been lying on a feather bed and expecting to get money easily and those who are going out and working for it.

Supplier opinion on the consortium concept is varied. It is viewed with some scepticism. A definition is important before discussing the issue: to work properly a consortium should be "a group of like minded people trading under one brand name, with a proposition to the consumer which is unique and which is backed by very heavy advertising". Suppliers suggest that in the U.K. travel agency scene the independents are not very like minded, with no common brand name and no unique offer to the consumer because each one of the members of the consortium "wants to do his own thing". To be successful in any business, means starting by bearing the consumer in mind. If the consortia do not offer anything unique to the consumer then they are not offering anything at all. The grocery consortium, Mace, tried to create a virtuous circle where they could shift volume through discounting and then go and jointly buy substantial volumes of product. If businesses cannot shift extra volume, as in, say, a travel consortium, then there is little the suppliers can offer over and above existing commission rates. It was suggested that "a consortium is only as good as its weakest member, which is usually not very good", however, suppliers will deal and negotiate with them on the same basis as they would with a multiple and providing they got the support together, produced the volume and hit the targets, they would in return receive extra support.

In conclusion suppliers expect that the independents will survive, though in reduced numbers and possibly through banding together in consortia or by joining a franchise. For the leading tour operators, independents are among their top agents for productivity and remuneration proving they can match, and in some cases, beat the multiple.

Business Relationships

An important aspect of any distribution system is the business relationship that exists between the supplier and middleman. In the travel business this relationship follows the acceptance by the supplier of the agent as a sales outlet for its travel products. There will be a business agreement, sometimes written, sometimes verbal, which will include, amongst others, the form and level of remuneration and support services. This section highlights the major features of the business relationship and provides supplier evidence on the problems and effects.

Agency Appointment Policy

There are usually three types of appointment policies available to a supplier, these are exclusive, selective and intensive (see Chapter 4). If the supplier agrees to sell only through one agent this would be an exclusive arrangement. Alternatively the supplier may wish to appoint only those who meet certain criteria, or to limit the number of outlets available – this would be a selective policy. Finally by using all known agency outlets (usually ABTA appointed) the supplier would be employing an intensive policy.

To date no supplier has gone down the exclusivity route, preferring not to put all their eggs in one basket. All that is except Thomas Cook, a tour operator in its own right, who decided a few years ago to sell its own products 'in-house', i.e. holidays can only be bought through their own retail branches or direct by telephone. The rationale was that it saved commission being paid to other agents, saved agency distribution costs and support services, and gave the company total control over product production, distribution and sales. They were only in a position to do this because of their large network of branches, some 300 plus. If Thomson Holidays were ever to do the same using their 'in-house' agency, Lunn Poly, then that would bring ruin for many travel agents. The company has always denied that this was a possibility, stating that its network of 700 branches would still not be enough to provide adequate distribution. However, many agents are still very uneasy about the long-term intentions of the operator despite reassurances from the management.

In the airline business the agency must hold an IATA licence before it is allowed to sell tickets for international journeys. For domestic routes, however, the decision is left to each individual airline. There is therefore a selective policy in operation, as only those agents meeting specified criteria, including financial stability, security and staffing will be appointed. Although creating a closed shop, the majority of airlines would be reluctant to see this changed or removed as it gives security and confidence in distributing a potentially high value product around the world. If all agents were allowed to sell international airline tickets the chief concern would be security of ticket stock, because the fraud potential is enormous. Second the selling of airline tickets is still a skilled business, and beyond a one sector journey becomes complicated, therefore qualified staff are needed. Finally there is the basic right of the airlines to choose who they should distribute through.

The old British Rail's distribution policy was reflected in its agency appointment system, which was to provide outlets only where they did not impinge too much on existing rail station availability. It was a discretionary decision based upon location, target market, aptitude of staff and financial stability. Once appointed, agents were given a target of revenue in the first year and should they fail to meet this, their licence could be withdrawn.

A National Express licence is attractive to new agents as it helps to promote their services, and gets people into the office, enabling them to build up their first client base. The conditions of entry are, however, quite stringent with checks on credit status and the provision of a banker's guarantee. Generally though the policy is intensive: anyone who applies will be given serious consideration.

Ferry operators have intensive policies tempered by the requirement of ABTA membership. Some operators have no formal application or agreement system. Again this type of product is a useful source of revenue and publicity for newly formed agents. As with all transport operators ferry companies do not have to join ABTA to distribute through its members, so they are free to channel bookings through whichever outlets they see fit.

A similar situation exists with hotels, where no formal application or agreement system is in operation. It is left to the discretion of the individual hotel or hotel groups. They may check on ABTA or IATA membership but their major concern is the agent's method of payment, vouchers or cash and level of commission required. It is perhaps the most loose of all appointment systems. Holiday centre organisations act more like traditional tour operators, wanting ABTA membership before accepting bookings.

Finally in this section, tour operators who are ABTA members will generally employ an intensive method of distribution using the offices of ABTA travel agency members. However some operators have adopted selective policies in response to the agents' preferred schemes and to control the high cost and wastage of expensive brochures. The control mechanism is the unique ABTA number given to agents upon appointment. The principle is: no number, no booking. It is impossible, for example, to enter most tour operator's computerised reservations systems without an ABTA number and password. The problem for new agents is that they cannot apply for ABTA membership until they have actually opened for business. This means that there is a time lag during which no ABTA tour operators' products can be sold whilst the application is being vetted.

Commission/Overrides/Incentives

Historically the basic financial arrangement between suppliers and agents has been one of payment on results by way of a commission. Since their inception agents have struggled to negotiate increases in these commission rates yet the basic levels have remained relatively static (see Table 18, Chapter 2). This situation has presented a serious problem for agents as return on sales has not kept pace with the general rise in inflation and overheads. Running costs such as salaries, rent, rates, communication costs, etc. have risen much more rapidly than the relative rise in the cost of an inclusive package holiday. The only way of squeezing out more commission from suppliers has been through special deals negotiated between individual companies. These special deals take the form of an override or incentive.

Override

An override can be defined as moving up the standard percentage of commission from, say, the base at 10% to 11% and declaring this on invoices. It would not be conditional upon performance as in an incentive deal, but in return the supplier, such as a tour operator, would expect some guarantee of product visibility, i.e. guaranteed racking. It has the advantage of being credited directly to individual agency branches whereas an incentive payment usually goes straight to the head office of the agent.

Incentive

An incentive deal is more complex as it is based upon performance and that is linked to a growth factor on previous years' business. It is company wide and is paid retrospectively upon achievement therefore invoices show the standard base rate and individual branches may not see it as being as beneficial as an override. However, the operator knows that his product will be visible and that the incentive to perform will be strong. In addition the operator sets aside the money, which earns interest, and if the agent fails to meet the target, keeps it.

Most suppliers refer to both deals as overrides and are naturally very reluctant to reveal details as they are such a commercially sensitive issue. They came about mainly as a result of the March of the Multiples – the larger the company the more pressure on suppliers to pay more for the use of the agency's expanding distribution network. The multiples are in a stronger position than the smaller independents to negotiate a deal. These negotiations have now become an annual event leading to some very hard bargaining between supplier and agent. Sometimes the supplier will not give in to the agent's demands and this can lead to a complete breakdown in the relationship, resulting in the product being removed from the agent's racks. Multiples have appointed professional buyers to do the job for them and suppliers have key people to respond to them known as account executives. The deals are closely linked to the agents' preferred operators and racking policies which were discussed earlier in this chapter.

Airline overrides

The level of override varies considerably, with the airlines giving the highest, up to 20% and even higher in some cases, especially the third world airlines requiring hard currency for their respective countries. Deals are available to all but are targeted, some agents getting more than others. There are many small independent agents receiving very high overrides with particular airlines on specific routes because they specialise in supporting them. These agents include consolidators as described in Chapter 3. The situation has parallels with the corner grocery shops and supermarkets in that the latter, who buy in bulk, will always receive the bigger discount. Likewise the more airline seats bought the larger the override. Sometimes they are referred to as revenue growth programmes, based upon an individual target performance and revised each year. Most airlines agree that because of the high level of competition they are all locked into the incentive business for the foreseeable future.

Transport overrides

National Express bases its override on achievement of a judgement target, offering an additional 10%, whilst car hire, with a high basic commission rate of 20%, offers overrides of between 5% and 10%. British Rail's policy caused a problem when in the mid eighties they introduced a sliding scale of commission payment based upon results, ranging from 7% to 9%. The top level of 11.5% was scrapped causing a deterioration in relationships between themselves and their agents, some agents sending back their licences. However, a major review took place in 1989 to rectify the problem and return commission levels to a more realistic figure. Their override level is up to a maximum of 1% only. Ferry operators pay up to 2.5% provided the agent achieves a pre-determined and realistic target. It is common, however, for the vast majority of agents not to make the target and therefore to receive no extra payment.

Inclusive tour overrides

Inclusive tour operators pioneered the bonus commission deal on the basis of a growth reward. The policy is to support agents in return for increased sales whether they be multiple or independent. Surprisingly the largest operator, Thomson, does not pay override commission but instead makes what is termed as a marketing contribution which its competition believes is just the same thing. Operators accept that overrides, on average between 1% to 2.5%, are an important part of the agent's financial base. However, they are concerned that they are used for other purposes, such as discounting, which reduces agents' margins and consequently their stability. The last thing operators want is to be linked to agents who go bust, leaving their customers exposed to financial loss. The majority of operators use the incentive method of extra payment, setting targets to be achieved and paying out retrospectively. However, a number actually agree on a higher fixed rate of commission irrespective of the amount of business produced just to guarantee racking of their brochures. In conclusion then suppliers are generally concerned and somewhat unhappy about the override/incentive situation as can be seen from the following selection of quotes:

> *"At the end of the day we are paying to get our brochures on the rack. Override policies are funding agents' suicidal discounting offers."*

> *"Override commissions are the weakest form of incentive known to man. The more I give the more I am going to encourage the agents' discount war."*

> *"I don't believe that giving incentives stimulates extra sales, I cannot find any mathematical correlation between the two. We have a 'jaundiced' view on the whole topic."*

> *"Tour operators' overrides have precipitated the ability for retailers to discount, that in itself is a retrograde step."*

Agency Support Services

Distribution is also about the back up services provided by the supplier to its distributor. For example, it is important that the manufacturer of soap powders ensures that the supermarket always has a sufficient supply of the product to meet demand. There should be an easy re-ordering process, point of sale materials provided should match the stores' marketing and special promotions campaigns. The manufacturer's representatives should be able to up-date the store on new lines and deal with complaints and finally there should be an efficient payment system. This example compares well with the relationship between suppliers of travel and their agents, the major difference being the intangible nature of the product and its replacement with pieces of paper called the brochure and the ticket.

Brochures on the rack are as vital to the supplier as soap powder on the shelves. An empty rack or shelf means little or no chance of a sale, since brochures are the only way the tour operator has of showing his product. These are expensive to produce considering the research, planning and printing that goes into them. Approximately £5 goes into the cost of a holiday with a large tour operator to cover production and publication. It is therefore essential that there is careful control on the number of brochures produced and the way they are distributed amongst all the agents. Obviously it would be quite uneconomic to supply every agent with the same number of brochures so in most cases this is closely linked to productivity.

Before its demise in 1991 the International Leisure Group (ILG), whose products included Intasun, Club 18-30 and NAT Holidays, stated that every ABTA agent, that was 7,000 plus, received a file copy of every brochure they produced, but beyond that they were very carefully graded, those producing the business receiving more brochures. It is quite clear why such a policy was necessary when you consider that 80% of ILG's business came from only 20% of its agents. Another leading operator stated that brochure distribution was not a question of whether or not an agent was part of a multiple or a small independent, rather it was their commitment to the product.

Even smaller short break operators use a very sophisticated brochure distribution system based upon performance. For example one operator has four different grades but within each grade they have different brochure pack sizes. An A grade independent may receive a fifty pack size whereas an A multiple would receive a 200 pack size as both are top producers relative to their size of operation. One short break operator has no less than twenty two grades!

The operators use specialist brochure distributors who can interpret the grades by ABTA membership number and ensure correct deliveries are made. The top end of the grades will receive regular top up whereas those who do not produce much, and new agents, get a launch pack. An example of a grading system is shown in Table 30.

Table 30. A brochure distribution grading system

No of customers booked	Grade
Over 250	A
200	B
150	C
100	D
50	E
25	F
10	G
1-9	H

Source: Industry

Although in recent years many travel suppliers have cut back another major support service is that provided by the sales representatives. Representatives are often the only physical link between supplier and agent so they have a very important job to do in image building for the company. They have to establish a rapport with travel agency managers and staff, offer help and advice on products, arrange displays and promotions and entertain staff as a reward for doing good business through educational visits and leisure activities. One of their most important jobs is to ensure product visibility, i.e. racking, which may mean trying to override racking policies. Finally they will be expected to investigate and feed back details of performance and agency staff opinion of their competition. Representatives are expensive (salary, car, entertaining) therefore once again suppliers will link the number of visits made to travel agents to productivity. A car hire firm, for example, had agents divided into three grades linked to bookings as shown in Table 31.

Table 31. A sales visit grading system

Category	No of bookings per month	No of visits
A	10 plus	every 6 weeks
B	5 to 10	every 12 weeks
C	4 and below	every 18 weeks

Chapter 6

Technology and Change

New Technology and its Impact on Retail Travel

In this chapter we will consider the importance of new technology for travel retailing and the changes which it has brought and will bring to the sector. We begin with an interesting quote from the 'Travel and Tourism Analyst' of 1987.

> *"During the eighties the distribution and selling of travel products were subject to rapid change due to the development of new electronic databases and their exploitation in private computer and telecommunication systems. These are now essential ingredients both in the search for competitive advantage and in the satisfaction of consumer demand. After a century of relatively peaceful existence, travel selling and distribution now finds itself under challenge."*

> *(Welburn, Travel and Tourism Analyst, July, 1987)*

Welburn went on to identify the following reasons for this:

- state of the art advances in electronics, delivering higher processing speeds, greater capacity and lower cost;

- the exploitation of such technological advances in private computer and telecommunications systems, especially computer reservations systems;

- the improvement of public telecommunication systems;

- increased computer literacy among both travel staff and the general public;

- liberalisation and competitive pressures among airlines;

- counter-competition pressures, seeking to preserve dominant market positions.

Such technological changes have, up to now, been generally restricted to the means of communication between suppliers and agents. The major threat, however, is seen as the use of this technology by an increasingly sophisticated leisure and business traveller turning to home-buying and self-ticketing machines. Suppliers are constantly searching for more efficient and cost effective methods of distribution and in the context of this book one major question we must ask is whether new technology will lead to an increase in the sale of travel and tourism products through direct sell methods or whether it will further cement the supplier-agent relationship. This section attempts to address some of these issues whilst reviewing travel technology developments.

The Use of Technology by Suppliers and Agents

Travel agents are constantly being offered an ever increasing range of newer and more sophisticated systems. Some have responded positively by embracing the technology for both sales and administration purposes whilst others still rely on out-dated terminals or manual systems. Giant multi-national computer reservations systems (CRS) have been developed by the international airlines to provide global networks for the sale of both air travel and other leisure products. These CRS companies have for a number of years now been locked into a fierce battle to secure the distribution networks provided by the travel agents. The original Viewdata system is under threat from the more 'intelligent' CRS but some agents, especially the smaller independents are resisting the change because of the higher costs involved and many are yet to be convinced of its benefits.

In the late seventies microfiche systems proved to be a great aid to travel agency sales providing flight and holiday availability from a limited number of suppliers. A microfiche is a thin sheet of film which has tiny pages of information spread across it. A special viewer enlarges the film for reading. The system used by travel agents was similar to those used in libraries and press archives.

At that time airlines were already advanced in their use of computers for reservation and administration. In the U.K. British Airways and British Caledonian decided to link agents directly to their systems through leased telephone lines. They established 'Travicom', the predecessor of today's **Global** CRS known as 'Galileo'. At the same time the Post Office (later British Telecom) developed the Viewdata system which it marketed as 'Prestel', where agents could be linked through the normal telephone system to thousands of pages of travel information held on central computers.

It is important to understand therefore that there are two basic forms of technology available to the agent:

    (i)   airline backed CRS linked direct to agents who use the so-called 'intelligent' personal computer terminals;

    (ii)   Viewdata linking suppliers through telephone lines to agents who use 'dumb' terminals. These links mostly through specialist network providers such as Istel and Fastrak.

Each has gone its own separate way in development leaving agents to make difficult choices based on their business type, their level of demand for such a system and each system's respective costs.

The Development of Computer Reservations Systems (CRS)

Computer reservations systems were originally developed in the l960s by airlines as an 'in-house' facility aimed at increasing internal organisational productivity. In the U.S.A., American Airlines and TWA hooked their offices up to their systems which were to become known as 'Sabre' and 'Pars'. Many European airlines also began to develop their own systems. Sabre was introduced to travel agents in 1976 and was quickly followed by the U.K.'s Travicom in 1977. The first agents to introduce these systems were IATA appointed business agents who, because of their high volume of business and their need to service their customers quickly and efficiently, could afford to invest in the expensive equipment required.

Basically the system operated by linking the agents to a central computer, or controller, which then linked them onward to a whole host of independent airline computers. We show a diagrammatic representation of the system in Figure 18. The controller, or central computer, was used to interpret information from the airlines' computers into a common language which could be received by the agents.

Figure 18. An early Computer Reservations System (CRS)

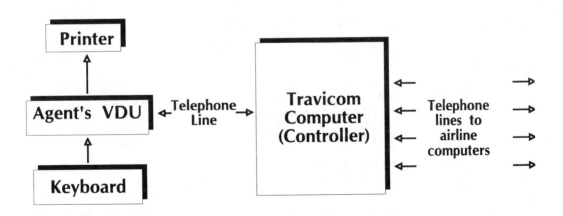

As the industry moved into the 1980s more sophisticated versions of CRS were developed and the most important of these were those which incorporated the capacity to print tickets, issue invoices and deal with payments to suppliers. A further enhancement offered by major suppliers, such as British Airways through its Travicom system, was to introduce other leisure products, such as package holidays, accommodation and car hire into the system. As Viewdata had already established a hold on this market, however, there was generally a low take up of the systems from leisure travel agents. Sales of CRS were therefore targeted at business travel agents who essentially only needed an airline reservation system. As you will see from Table 32, by 1986 just over 1,000 agency locations had been connected to the Travicom Executive System with around 2,000 terminals processing an estimated 70% of all IATA business. Entry into the Travicom system was also available through viewdata using a new adaptation called 'Skytrack' and we shall discuss this later in the chapter. Travicom's name disappeared soon after the Galileo CRS company was formed in 1987 but this multi-access system did not finally end until February 1994. By this time over 2,400 agencies were using some 12,000 terminals.

Table 32. Travicom/Galileo usage, 1986-1995

	1986	1990	**1995**
Number of agencies connected	1030	2000	2,400
Number of terminals in use	2400	9000	12,000
Number of airline users	42	380	

Source: Travicom/*Galileo*

Also in the mid-eighties a number of US airlines began to make in-roads into the U.K. market with systems which were labelled 'mega-CRS'. These included American Airlines' Sabre system, United Airlines with its Apollo system and TWA with its Pars system. As a result of this increased competition from across the Atlantic, the major European airlines divided into two camps to launch a new generation of CRS in 1987 to compete with the Americans. These were:

(i)   'Galileo', the new name for Travicom which was now backed by British Airways, Alitalia, Swissair and KLM;

(ii)   'Amadeus' supported by Lufthansa, Air France, Iberia and SAS.

The formation of these new companies heralded the start of a substantial marketing campaign to win the business of the travel agents. All the players in this market are now seeking to offer the most sophisticated and comprehensive systems to meet agents' needs fully in the 1990s. All systems of this sort are now referred to as global distribution systems or GDS for short and this name change reflects their world-wide and multi-product application. A customer can now make a booking in a UK travel agency including flight and hotel with instant ticketing and then change it at another agency say in Australia and add a car hire. Agents in different Continents can call up an individual customer record, called a PNR (Personal Number Record) which has been created by another agent in another country. In effect CRSs can 'talk' to each other. Through a single keyboard and a single language these systems provide the agent with access to the world's most comprehensive range of travel services including:

- schedules and seat availability for hundreds of airlines world-wide;

- international fare quotes;

- world-wide hotel and car hire facilities;

- tours, ferry and rail bookings;

- travel related services including currency conversions and theatre and sporting event tickets.

The standard terminal in the agent's office is now referred to as an 'intelligent workstation', and is a personal computer (PC) using specially developed software. As they are developed such systems will be fully integrated with the agency's management system. The aim is to free the agents to concentrate on their primary role of selling and servicing customers.

Figure 19 shows how today's systems are now much more sophisticated than that shown in the previous figure.

Figure 19. A Global Distribution System (GDS)

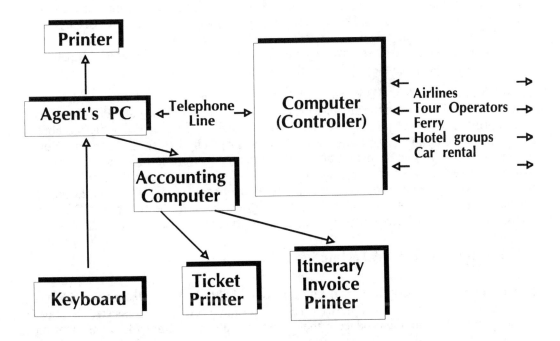

The problem facing agents is not only the choice between the various systems but their respective cost. Such considerations are particularly important in difficult economic times like the early 1990s. A quote from the 'Travel Trade Gazette' sums up the agent's dilemma:

> "High powered selling by CRS vendors does no good if agents cannot afford to invest. This especially applies to the smaller agent who would need an annual air product turnover of £250,000 just to pay for the Travicom system."

> (Nichol, TTG, 1989)

In this article the author went on to note that the majority of ABTA agency members have turnovers of less than £1,000,000 and would need to concentrate on a technology system which was more appropriate to their business mix and income.

The question of investment cost was further highlighted in an article in 'Travelnews' which said:

> "The majority of agents have invested in Viewdata of which there are around 27,000 terminals, to replace them would cost the trade close to £30 million."

> (Purdom, Travelnews, 1989)

The compatibility of systems is another issue facing the agents. They want a so-called 'one-stop' terminal enabling them to access all possible systems through either their existing Viewdata sets or through PCs. The CRS companies moved in this direction by linking up their systems to one of the Viewdata network providers and we discuss this development later in the chapter. As airline backed CRS continue to compete for the attention primarily of business travel agents, so Viewdata systems are set to compete for the business of the remainder of the retail travel market.

By 1997 the emphasis for GDSs was consolidation and concentration on the development of new products. For example all were bringing out Automatic Ticket and Boarding Pass (ATB) printers that issue joint tickets and boarding passes. However, even this was about to be challenged by the new Electronic Ticketing launched by British Airways on Galileo which does away with a paper ticket altogether. All were promoting the use of Windows-based technology where agents can quickly change between different applications on screen. Non-air products are also now being provided by GDSs such as hotels, car hire, ferries and even special events. The biggest threat to the future of GDSs may be from the Internet with suppliers offering a cheap and easier form of electronic booking.

CRS Laser-disc/CD ROM Technology

Initially new developments such as the introduction of CRS laser-disc technology allowed television-quality pictures to be shown on a CRS terminal screen. This assisted the travel agent by both showing the product to the customer and overlaying booking information. Cruises and hotel accommodation are two products which are particularly well suited to this type of technology. For example, using CRS Utell, the world-wide hotel reservation service, an agent could show customers pictures of hotels, bedrooms and facilities with local maps and sightseeing attractions. Cruise operators could take their potential customers on a 'tour' of one of their ships, showing types of cabins and other facilities in the comfort of the travel agency. As the system can be adapted to show holiday destinations and hotels it could supplement or even replace the traditional holiday brochure.

The USA lead the field in this technology and were the first to have integrated full-screen colour moving images and pre-recorded narration at the touch of a button. The most notable was Worldspan's Pars 'Integrated Reservation Imaging System' (IRIS). It worked on laser discs, each containing 54,000 images. They installed the system in 300 US locations but in the U.K. and Europe there was generally a lack of interest from travel agents. Again we quote 'Travelnews':

> *"The problem seems to be that agents do not want to spend time showing videos to potential customers when, at the end of the day, the customer will take brochures home and choose."*

> *(Burnham, Travelnews, 1992)*

This technology has today being superseded by the now familiar CD ROM, an acronym for Compact Disc Read-only Memory but the amount of discs tailor-made for the travel agent is negligible. Reed Travel Group have produced a CD covering all scheduled airline timetables, together with information on destinations. Aimed at the business travel agent it only provides data not graphics. For the leisure agent CD ROMs are seen as slowing down the reservation process and costly for example "a 300-branch chain would need an average 1,500 computers at £1,000 a unit and though CD ROMs cost only £60 this cost increases significantly with a decent monitor, graphics card and memory" (Cogan, Equinus, Travel Weekly Supplement 1996/7)

Top four CRS Suppliers 1997

In this section we will give a brief description of the top four CRS suppliers in 1997:

- Amadeus
- Galileo
- Sabre
- Worldspan

(i) Amadeus

Founded in 1987 by Air France, Lufthansa, Iberia and SAS, Amadeus has developed substantially in some European markets but its commercial launch in the U.K. was not until January 1991. In November 1990 the system provider signed an agreement with Sabre for joint products and marketing which was expected to give Amadeus a stronger position in the U.K. However, this joint agreement was abandoned in the following year. Rivals say it will now be very difficult for Amadeus to catch up but the company at that time was aiming for a 15% share of the market. As Table 33 shows by 1997 Amadeus had secured a 10% share of the UK market with 135 locations, however its World-wide share is estimated at around 26%. Founding member airline SAS has been replaced by Continental Airlines of America. In 1997 Amadeus was promoting a new Windows-based system giving access to as wide range of global schedules and fares.

Table 33. Major global computer distribution companies 1997

Company	UK Locations (%)	World Share (%)	UK Agents (%)
Galileo	40	32	Carlson Wagonlit
Worldspan	38	12	Dawson/Sanderson Going places A.T. Mays Thomas Cook
Sabre	12	30	American Express
Amaedeus	10	26	Lunn Poly

Source: Industry

(ii) Galileo

Formerly called Travicom, which originally acted as the U.K. distributor for the system, Galileo was formed in 1987 by a consortium of British Airways, KLM, Swissair, United Airlines now joined by USAir and Alitalia. Its first test bookings were made in January 1991. Its major global links were with the Apollo system of United Airlines until they combined in 1992 to create a full global distribution system (GDS). More than 60 airlines can be accessed through the system. In the U.K. there are about 2,400 Galileo users, although many of these are primarily business house travel agents. It is far and away the most successful CRS provider in the U.K., with an estimated 75% of booked business travel segments. Galileo launched its new CRS leisure product system in June 1990 offering travel agents an innovative way to make bookings. Today Galileo's users are now be able to book many leisure products such as package holidays, ferries, European rail journeys, car hire and accommodation through its links with Viewdata based systems.

(iii) Sabre

Unlike all other GDS's Sabre has only one owner, the AMR Corporation based in the USA who also own and operate American Airlines one of the Worlds leading carriers.

Sabre has been marketed in the U.K. since 1985 and was the first competitor to the old British Airways system, Travicom. It only has an estimated 10% share of UK locations but 30% World-wide. In 1996/7 Sabre is offering business agents a new easy-to-use booking system called "Turbo Sabre". The product is aimed at reducing keystroke usage by up to 25% and eliminating the need for agents to remember complicated commands. In addition to airlines reservation access Sabre offers car hire, hotels, rail companies and ferries. Other software packages include managing travel expenditure and customer profiles all needed as part of the move towards a paperless environment.

(iv) Worldspan

The Worldspan system was introduced in February 1990, bringing together the Pars system, jointly owned by TWA and Northwest Airlines, and the DATAS II system of Delta Airlines. Abacus, a far Eastern CRS consortium of eleven airlines, later joined and took a financial stake. Pars was fully operational in the U.K. for about five years, but DATAS II was never sold here. Pars was transformed in 1993 into the new Worldspan system. At present there are around 2,700 locations in the U.K which include the leisure agents Going Places, A.T.Mays and Travelcare and Thomas Cook. This breakthrough into the leisure agents market has virtually closed off the competition achieved by offering low cost access from existing viewdata equipment into a major CRS. In addition to its central booking system for airlines, hotels, car hire, ferries and rail. Worldspan's product range includes:

- Worldspan FareDeal PC-based automated negotiated fares database.

- Worldspan Power Pricing finds the three lower-priced alternatives to itineraries within a few seconds.

- World Dial Link - a dial-up system for agents who do not wish to invest in their own line. This is a disc than can be inserted in an existing personal computer.

- Worldspan View was the first product to allow access to a CRS from Viewdata equipment.

- World Gateway - this allows agencies which already have a personal computer for accounts and administration to access the CRS through a gateway board.

- Commercial World - an easy to use dial-up system for business houses to use jointly with their agent.

- World STP - a satellite ticket printing facility which can be located on the premises of business houses.

- Worldspan Compass – gives branch agency executives access to productivity and revenue statistics on an immediate daily basis.

- Worldspan Gateway Plus – full access to the Internet, E-Mail and file transfer.

Development of Viewdata

Viewdata is the generic term used to describe an 'information service transmitted by telecommunication lines', such as New Prestel Viewdata. The information in the system is stored as pages in a database. A television set or visual display unit (VDU) is used to recall pages through an instructions input from a keyboard. Viewdata should not be confused with Teletext, e.g. the BBC Ceefax and ITV Oracle services, which is an information service transmitted through the television network. The major difference between the two systems is that Viewdata allows a two-way communication using a telephone line, with a microprocessor converting the signal into a picture and text on the screen.

The first Viewdata system in the U.K. for the travel business was introduced by the Post Office in the late 1970s. 'Prestel' provided thousands of pages of travel related information stored on a number of central computers. By purchasing a VDU and joining Prestel (originally owned British Telecom) the agent, using a secret numeric password, could access this information. Travel suppliers such as airlines and tour operators were able constantly to update their product information and communicate with travel agents. This early system is illustrated in a diagram in Figure 20.

Figure 20. An early example of the viewdata system

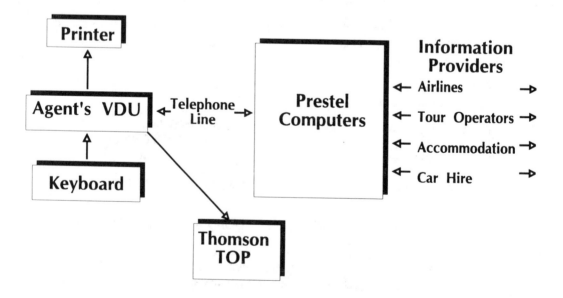

The message to agents was clear

> *"tune into Prestel or fall behind in the travel industry age"*

> *(Booth, TTG, 1981)*

By 1981 over 2,000 terminals had been installed in agencies.

The big breakthrough for Viewdata came when Thomson launched its 'Open-Line' programme, known as 'TOP' in October 1982. Agents were supplied with a telephone number which, when programmed into their Viewdata sets, linked them directly to the Thomson computer, bypassing Prestel. This is shown in Figure 20. The agent could now make instant reservations and very shortly after its introduction 45% of Thomson business came through the new system. By the end of 1982, 3,500 of its 4,000 appointed agents were connected to the system and this led Thomson to prohibit telephone reservations from its agents in 1986. In every way 'TOP' changed the face of holiday sales distribution.

In fact Thomson was not the first tour operator to introduce direct Viewdata reservations, as Olympic Holidays' 'Sparta' system went on trial towards the end of 1980. Sealink was another organisation who offered these facilities, using its 'STARS' reservation system, and it can claim to have been the prime mover in introducing Viewdata through its policy of subsidising many agents in purchasing their first Viewdata set. Airline reservations were also available using a direct dial system, called 'Skytrack' which was offered by British Airways Travicom, a cheaper alternative to leisure agents than its sister 'Travicom Executive' and 'President' systems.

Pan Am introduced its 'Panther' system, while Thomas Cook and Horizon Holidays joined the growing number of suppliers anxious to use the new sales and marketing technology. In the early 1980s a problem which emerged was the inability of these relatively unsophisticated VDUs to be programmed with more than about four direct dial-up telephone numbers. New models had to be developed and a way found to give multi-access on one telephone call. This became possible with the introduction of the Prestel 'Gateway' service, "a facility enabling the Prestel user to communicate directly with the computer of an Information Provider as well as the Prestel general database". Until this innovation was introduced it must be remembered that agents and suppliers only communicated directly with the Prestel computer, which then sent messages on their behalf to the suppliers' systems. Once Prestel Gateway was launched it was possible to dial-up the 'Gateway' service, be presented with a variety of computerised reservations systems and link up directly to all of them on one local telephone call.

Although Prestel's Gateway was the first available 'network' it was soon joined by a number of competing systems. These included 'Istel', then a British Leyland subsidiary and 'Travinet' owned by the Thomas Cook/Midland Bank group. These organisations worked very hard to build up their list of suppliers, which encouraged agents to dial-up their network. Soon the original innovator, Prestel, began to lag behind its rivals.

By 1987 there was so much business coming through to the networks that the systems began to fail under the strain. Agents often found the dial-up phone number engaged or, when they did connect, could not link with the supplier, then after a few minutes of waiting time the line was automatically disconnected. To overcome this problem the concept of 'hard wiring' was introduced by Istel, quickly followed by Travinet, now called 'Fastrak', and Prestel. Hard-wiring is: "a permanent Viewdata connection between the agency, who pay a fee for this service, and the network provider, without incurring the cost and trouble of dialling up through a telephone line". The advantages are a guaranteed instant connection, a better quality picture with no line interference and an increased speed of communication. The Viewdata system took a mighty leap forward with hard-wiring and we illustrate this in Figure 21.

Figure 21. The viewdata hard-wiring system

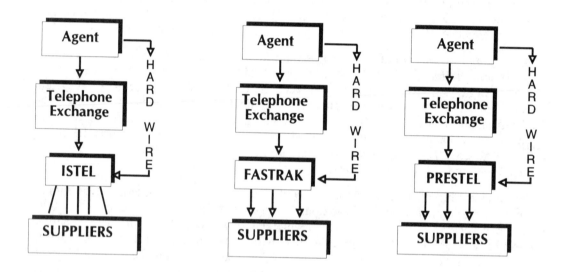

Hard-wiring was aimed at major users of Viewdata who, according to the network suppliers, would soon recoup their outlay and begin to make savings. You should recognise, however, that although hard-wiring can secure an instant connection to a supplier's reservations system, this does not mean that the booking process will be any quicker once the agent has been connected.

One of the problems still facing agents is which of the networks to hard-wire. The choice is about the respective cost and the number of suppliers available on each system. To complicate matters certain large tour operators chose to line up with one specific network. The networks also started to develop automatic in-agency invoice and ticket printing, data transfer, electronic mail and funds transfer. By 1997 AT&T Istel and Imminus Fastrak were the leading viewdata networks:

(i) ATT&T Istel

Istel emerged into the 1990s as the UKs leading system. By the end of 1990 1,900 agents had hard-wired to Istel. Its unique selling point is that it offers connection to Thomson from their top selling agents. Leading multiples already signed up included Lunn Poly and A.T. Mays. Istel is now owned by the American telecommunications giant, AT&T, and this has given the system a degree of international credibility.

Cross-connections are now possible with CRS providers such as Galileo and Worldspan. Istel is also available to business agent users of all four UK CRSs through a software connection. Useage of Istel was said to have grown by 400% over the five years up to 1995.

(ii) Imminus Fastrak

Fastrak's direct connect hard-wire service is called 'Fastlink' and in 1992 had about 1,000 users in the U.K., including the Thomas Cook branches. It claimed at that time to have the largest and fastest growing number of suppliers on its system which included, until its collapse in 1991, the International Leisure Group (ILG). A company was been formed called the Travel Technology Initiative to develop a standardised system for ticket printing and documentation in agencies which it hoped would give Fastrak an edge over its rival, Istel. This system, called 'Fasticket', was launched in November 1991 with Sealink-Stena Line as the first principal involved and Owners Abroad. Travel agents would be able to 'customise' tickets with their own name to offer a more personal service. The main benefit to agents of printing tickets themselves is that customers could make late bookings and could walk out with tickets in their hand, rather than face the uncertainty of collecting them at the port or airport. Imminus, formerly Midland Network Services) introduced its Chameleon Linkmaster in 1993 which allows agents to handle various functions including front and back office administration, branch to branch communication and access to CRS databases. By 1995 it had more than 500 users and is now diversifying into home shopping by providing technology for booking services through cable and satellite television. In 1997 Imminus was bought by communications and television group General Cable for £33m.

(iii) Prestel

Although first on the scene, British Telecom's Prestel service failed to become the dominant force in travel industry technology. It allowed its rivals, Istel and Fastrak, to overtake it especially in respect of hard-wiring. It did launch a hard-wiring service in 1988 but withdrew it within a year despite incurring major expenditure. In 1994 BT sold off Prestel and its buyers renamed it New Prestel. Looking to win business from independent agents its new products include a revamped flight-only directory and a comprehensive destination database owned by Thomas Cook. New Prestel still offers however, the largest information database available in the U.K., with over 300,000 pages, and still has over 7,000 travel subscribers and a 'Gateway' facility through to a number of suppliers.

Co-operation

From an agent's point of view the rivalry between viewdata suppliers is as frustrating as the battle going on between the CRS suppliers. Ideally agents would prefer one network and one hard-wire, which would link all travel suppliers. At the moment they have to choose and in so doing they must consider the links currently available, the respective costs and the future prospects.

Viewdata network suppliers were beginning to acknowledge the dilemma faced by agents in 1990 when Prestel and Fastrak reached a commercial understanding for closer co-operation. This **included** a joint distribution of services through each other's networks and the promise of co-operation in the future in such areas as the level of service, product development and a common standard for secure printing. The main beneficiaries of this co-operation **were to** be the agents, for those who use Fastrak **would** be able to obtain information from, and make bookings with, suppliers using Prestel and vice versa.

Istel on the other hand decided to join the Travel Technology Initiative, which it saw as a significant first step towards co-operation with its rival, Fastrak. Istel's decision was expected to give a massive boost to TTI's development of secure ticket printing and a travel agency booking system using electronic data interchange (EDI).

Competition Between CRS and Viewdata - Future Developments

Many in the industry see Viewdata as an outdated system which is slow, inefficient and uses the so-called 'dumb' terminal. One commentator described viewdata as "Stonehenge technology". By the year 2,000 it is said that personal computers (PCs) linked to sophisticated CRS systems will have taken over. There must be a radical change of approach, however, if CRS is going to replace Viewdata. Among agents specialising in the leisure market for example, in 1992 only one in three U.K. agents, about 2,300 out of 6,900 ABTA agency outlets, had CRS. As a spokesperson for Galileo said:

> "Agency terminals must become more affordable with a wider range of non-air services such as car hire, hotels and tour operators. They must be 'user friendly' designed for sales consultants who normally use a telephone. Pop-up menus, fast responding overlays of on-screen held, larger screens and full language prompts are all essential features if CRS is to gain wider

acceptance. There is no doubt that the considerable power of a PC linked to CRS poses a real threat to Viewdata in the near future".

(Webster, Galileo, Travelnews, 1989)

Viewdata network suppliers still believe their system is viable provided it has new enhancements which will speed up the response time and eliminate time wasting graphics. A spokesperson for Istel commented:

"Viewdata was initially designed to be used by agency staff who were anything but computer literate. Speed was sacrificed for a user friendly screen and laborious prompts. But computers hold no terrors for today's school leavers who don't require a screen designed to look like the booking form in a brochure. CRS demands investment which the trade cannot support given current economics. There are 25,000 Viewdata sets in use, to replace them all with PC's is a pipe-dream. It's not just the cost of the new equipment but also the responsibility of managing it. Agents would have to employ higher grade staff to cope with CRS complexities. Rather than replace Viewdata suppliers should be looking at ways to improve it".

(Tuach, Istel, Travelnews, 1990)

The ideal solution from the agent's point of view was to have the opportunity to access both CRS and Viewdata by cross-connection,. For the majority of leisure travel agents this would mean having the ability to access CRS from their Viewdata sets. For the minority, primarily business agents already using CRS, it was the ability to get into Viewdata through CRS. June 1991 saw the first steps in such a development with the link up between Galileo U.K. and the AT & T Istel. One leased line or hard-wire connected agents to both the scheduled airline, hotel and car hire system of Galileo and the predominant tour operator system of Istel. This cross-connection was only available, however, when an agent used a personal computer, not a Viewdata terminal. Low cost personal computers, in 1992 costed at £44 per month, and were offered to agents who signed up for the GalileoLink service. This cross-connection is now common place mainly thanks to the efforts of Worldspan who offer the link into their CRS free of charge.

Payment Systems

Another important aspect of the distribution relationship between suppliers and agents is the ability to have an easy and efficient payment system for the settlement of debts and payment of commissions. Once again new technology has allowed this to happen without the adverse effect on cash flow which many agents feared. Agents rely for additional income on the time lag between the collection of moneys from customers and the time of payment to suppliers.

Thomson Holidays led the field with its automatic banking system in the mid 1980s. Instead of writing cheques and posting them to Thomson, agents agreed to a weekly debit of their account through an electronic transaction linked into the Viewdata reservation network. There was no additional cost to the agent for this facility and Thomson believed at that time that it would reduce the cost of processing a cheque by between a third and a half, thereby enabling agents to reduce their bank charges.

Additionally the system helped agents to tighten up on administration. As agents have a confidential 'diary' on the electronic system telling them of the state of confirmed bookings, when balances are due and their payment date to Thomson. Other major operators were also moving towards this system of payment using new technology.

Competition Policy

Computer reservations systems have now become the primary means of disseminating air travel information to the agents. These systems have also had a major impact on competition within the airline industry. Those airlines who operate CRS, either alone or as part of a group, have a distinct commercial advantage over their rivals who do not. For example, smaller airlines have to pay for the privilege of being 'screened' in the same way as travel agents must pay to access CRS. This differs from other products, e.g. inclusive tours, selling through Viewdata where each tour operator maintains its own individual system and does not charge the agents to access its systems. There are two competitive aspects to this:

- the issue of bias within a CRS;

- the commercial relationship between CRS suppliers and travel agents.

Both problems can affect the interests of the consumer.

(i) Airline CRS Bias

Whilst CRS has no doubt benefited the customer, CRS providers can also use their systems to influence and perhaps distort the way in which information is presented to the agent and the customer through the Visual Display Unit (VDU). This has become known as 'screen bias', which can affect the customer's choice and make it more difficult for agents to match the available travel services to their customer's requirements.

Bias can occur in a number of ways. It has been defined as:

> *"the inclusion of parameters in software packages to favour the services of the CRS owner and certain carriers over other services".*

> *(CAB Report to Congress, 1983)*

Examples of bias include:

- employing display criteria designed to give greater prominence to selected services;

- declining to display the services and fares of another carrier;

- displaying false and misleading information;
- limiting or completely excluding the display of information such as alternative connections;
- refusing to permit reservations or ticketing on behalf of certain carriers to be made through the system;
- employing contract terms which prevent travel agents supplementing information by using another CRS on the same premises at the same time;
- 'screen-padding', that is presenting information regarding selective services in a highly detailed fashion with the objective of filling most of the space available on the 'first' and 'second' screens.

(Airline Competition, HMSO, 1988)

The issue of 'screen bias' has been highlighted by reports which suggest that 90% of CRS bookings in the U.S.A. are made from the first screen of information called up by the travel agent and 70% from the first three lines of the display. It is only natural that a busy agent will not want to go through screen after screen of information to satisfy a customer's enquiry. What the agent and the customer want, however, are the best alternatives, at the time requested, to be shown first, irrespective of carrier. Another common method used by carriers to encourage incremental bookings through their CRS is to use the so-called 'halo-effect'. This term refers to the tendency of travel agents to book flights on the carrier providing the system.

In 1988, the U.K. Government's Transport Committee decided to conduct an enquiry into airline competition and began with an examination of the impact of CRS. It took the view that:

> *"the anti-competitive use of CRS was not in the interests of either the consumer nor the long-term health of a competitive airline industry".*

(Airline Competition, HMSO, 1988)

The committee's recommendations included the possible separation or 'arms-length' relationship between airlines and their CRS companies, an open market for agents to use alternative CRS and, where information about a route is not comprehensive, that this should be clearly stated on the display.

The publication of the Government's report was soon followed by new regulations from the European Commission under European Competition rules. EC transport Ministers produced a CRS code of conduct, designed to eliminate on-screen bias. These provided that:

- all carriers should be given equal rights to have flights displayed on a non-discriminatory basis;
- CRS should be made available to travel agents on equal terms;

- data displayed on CRS must be accurate;

- flights displayed should not be biased towards services by any operator;

- information generated by CRS must not be used to gain an unfair commercial advantage by any airline.

By 1992 the EC were becoming increasingly concerned that anti-competitive practices were still being carried out by the major CRS organisations, especially in that they were not allowing those airlines which were not part of the CRS agreement to have their full schedules or flight opportunities displayed.

A system representative replied, however, that:

> "an individual CRS could not force an airline to distribute through a particular system, it would be their right to choose"

The Impact of New Technology on the Relationship Between the Travel Agent and Customer

The Government's 1988 Committee of Enquiry were also concerned about the three way relationship between the agent, airline and the customer. It found that:

> "despite the impression generally given to the public it was clear that the travel agent has two sets of principals: the traveller who buys the ticket and the airlines whose ticket he sells"

> (Airline Competition, HMSO, 1988)

Unfortunately the agency/supplier commission system gives agents an incentive to breach their responsibility to the customer in favour of the airline with whom they have a close working relationship and a possible incentive commission agreement. (Such agreements were discussed in Chapter 5.) Agents are not necessarily rewarded directly for the time and effort involved in finding the best buy for the customer, instead there is clearly an incentive to sell those airline seats which are the easiest to find and process.

We have already noted that there is a temptation for travel agents to direct their customers to the supplier which gives them the greatest commission. The new CRS systems increase this temptation and compound the dilemma of the principal-agent relationship. It is easier for a travel agent, acting purely as the agent of the customer, to find the cheapest flight than it is for a travel agent which regards itself as the airline's agent. The Committee recommended that the most effective policy to overcome the problem of the three way relationship would be to clarify the role of the agent. As the CAA noted:

> "the consumer is interested in knowing that the agent is his agent and not the agent of a particular airline. Disclosure of a relationship with a particular airline might be useful"

Such a situation would be known as a process of 'polarisation of interest', whereby those agents electing to be 'agents of an airline' would be restricted to selling seats of that airline. Those agents electing to be 'agents of the passenger' could sell seats for scheduled flights of any airline. All agents would be under a legal obligation to 'know their customer' (that is whether the customer wanted the cheapest or the quickest flight) and to offer the 'best advice' and all agents would continue to provide general travel advice and to sell non-scheduled seats/package holidays, as they currently do. The Government's Committee recognised that even under the 'best advice' rules this would not necessarily prevent an agency favouring one airline or being paid an over-riding commission by an airline or operator which may influence the agent's decision on which supplier to recommend. Currently there has been no implementation of such a policy.

The Transport Committee were concerned that all alternatives should be made known to the customer even if those were not shown within the CRS. They suggested that the agent has a 'duty to perform' and recommended that agents should make more effort to provide such information, for example by giving the customer access to the ABC World Airways Guide or OAG timetable.

The Travel Customer's Use of Technology

Electronic Point of Sale and Self Ticketing

During the 1980s cash dispensers transformed the face of high street banking. Now similar sophisticated stand alone units are at the forefront of a possible new revolution in retail merchandising. Known as 'Interactive Transaction Processing Systems' (ITPS) they provide the customer with user friendly, touch sensitive, screens and keyboards. For the leisure traveller the computer offers the customer graphics with text, video and other digital images and provides the supplier with new and interesting business opportunities. Such systems help customers to enter their own specific requirements and then perform calculations and search through vast amounts of information before selecting options that match the customer's requirements. Such systems also accept credit card payment and issue a confirmation and tickets.

Just as the public benefit from having the choice to shop in a number of non-traditional ways, so retailers will gain by not having to pay for unnecessary floor space or the training of staff. ITPS addresses these problems through advanced technology. It puts computerised selling precisely where retailers need it – at the point of sale.

The dilemma for the travel agent is whether ITPS will be a boon or a disaster. This may well depend on who chooses to use the system. If suppliers decide to place terminals at non-agent locations such as other stores, in shopping precincts or transportation terminals then they will deprive the agents of business. If, however, the agents themselves use them in the same way that counter top reservation systems are used they will become an additional selling tool. For example, the agency's ITPS unit could connect through networks such as Istel and Fastrak, and complete a booking with the agent's commission being credited in the usual way. They can make the booking process at least 50% faster and release staff to handle more complex enquiries.

Ideal targets for such systems are low margin products such as flight only deals, ferry and theatre seat bookings. Following a market research exercise in the late eighties Thomas Cook found that the most popular usage was 'through the whole in the wall' after the shops had closed, in a similar way to which cash points are used in banks. The system was set into the agent's shop front for out-of-hours business.

Of course, this kind of innovation can also be provided by CRS organisations. For example early in the 1990s Sabre announced its 'Sabrevision' system which comprised a video screen set into a small booth. Linked to Sabre's main database, a browsing client could access a whole range of products shown through a full colour, narrated video. The system could accept credit cards and issue tickets. As one supporter put it:

"It takes the place of the brochure and is the way of the future."

(Shankman, Travelnews, 1990)

Airline Electronic Ticketing

Perhaps the biggest threat to agents came from the airlines introducing ITPS self ticketing at airports. Widely used in the US they were introduced by British Airways on domestic routes and called "Timesaver" Air customers could use a self-service machine located in the departure area of key airports. Primarily such machines are aimed at frequent travellers who use high frequency domestic shuttle services. The airline was at pains to point out that they had no wish to undermine their agents, fearing a possible backlash on sales to prime overseas destinations if they extended the facility. To avoid this the machines were designed to take only B.A. branded cards which were issued by travel agents themselves (although they could accept standard credit cards such as Visa and Mastercard) thus protecting the travel agent's commission. Two comments from B.A executives at that time emphasised their concern:

"We do not see ourselves taking over from travel agents."

(Strong, BA Marketing Director, TTG, 1989)

"There are no plans at the time being to use other credit cards."

(Marshall, BA Chief Executive, TTG, 1989)

But behind these assurances there was of course the possibility of companies such as B.A developing direct sell strategies. The future depended on the level of competition between carriers and the demands of the suppliers' management to save distribution costs primarily the agent's commission. In 1995 a significant event took place in the US when American Airlines became the first major carrier to make a ticketless option available on all its domestic flights. Called the "Electronic ticket or E-ticket" the process begins when a reservation is made. The travel agent or airline creates an electronic ticket in its internal database and gives the passenger a confirmation number. The passenger checks in with the confirmation number and personal identification. The airline verifies the electronic ticket record and updates the database to show that the coupon is used. The passenger then obtains a boarding card from the carrier through a self-service machine or check-in desk. We have illustrated this process in Appendix L.

On the 12th of March 1997 British Airways introduced E-ticket on all its domestic services as an alternative to the normal booking and ticketing methods. The entire network became fully bookable as it once was before the introduction of turn-up and go Shuttle services. Around 40,000 Executive Club cards were distributed to travel agents who will issue them to passengers at the time of booking for identification purposes in self-service machines and check-in desks at airports. Although primarily for the business agent the airline will be making the facility available for leisure agents via their Viewdata networks. The benefits and in some cases dangers for the travel agent include:

- Easier distribution of tickets to travellers based in non-traditional locations and flexibility to make changes.

- Increased productivity for the traveller who may be able to make travel arrangements from the road with a laptop computer or mobile phone.

- Less stress involved, electronic itinerary delivered, no need to have tickets collected and/or delivered.

- Lower agency costs for labour and postal charges, which can be passed onto the traveller.

- Lost ticket problems avoided.

- Lower airline distribution costs e.g. it costs on average £5 to process a conventional paper ticket by less than £2 for an E-document.

(Adapted from Ogden, N., Business Travel World, October 1995)

For the agent then the threat is clear, travellers especially for business purposes, dealing direct with airlines through Electronic Data Interchange (EDI), having no need of a paper ticket and using their own PCs for information and reservations. The airlines however have been quick to reassure their agency partners, speaking at the Business Travel 1977 exhibition, BAs Distribution Manager for the UK, Gavin Halliday said "E-ticket will revolutionise ticketing procedures for all agents. We are working with our GDS and agency partners to bring everyone on-line as soon as possible" However David Radcliffe, Managing Director of Hogg Robinson Business Travel was more cautious, stating that "clients still want the security of a piece of paper, all E-ticketing does for the travel agent is to swap one piece of paper for another. Electronic ticketing is probably suitable for BA Super Shuttle routes but, if the passenger is connecting to another flight, it is not used for the rest of the journey. It will be the customer who decides whether to use it or not"

Touch-Screen Kiosk

For leisure product suppliers such as tour operators the opportunity for increasing direct sales is being developed through technology based "Home-shopping" which we discuss in the next section. However there have been attempts at offering the customer a stand-alone booking machines in the late eighties and early nineties all of which came to nothing. One company however, Thomas Cook in collaboration with Olivetti, has pioneered the "self-service booking kiosk". Launched in July 1994 a prototype multimedia kiosk was placed inside their retail travel agency branch at Marble Arch, London. This integrated holiday booking system contained an Olivetti computer with a large memory for storing the many still images seen on the screen. A laser player contains the video images and a touch-sensitive screen is used to narrow down holiday selection. The unique feature of this system is an integrated video link with Thomas Cook Direct consultants at their headquarters in Peterborough. The process is therefore two-way with both customer and consultant being able to see each other. Payment is made be inserting a credit card into the system and finally a printed confirmation is issued from the machine. In the first four months of operation it was said to have produced over £20,000 of business.

The prototype was followed a year later with a more advanced kiosk placed in three branches of NatWest Bank and a Department Store whilst self-service banking tills were placed in three Thomas Cook branches. In 1996 Thomas Cook were planning to introduce hundreds of interactive travel booking kiosks worldwide. Again this new technology now posses a real threat to travel agencies with an announcement that British Airways and Thomson were to sell direct to the public through 200 BT kiosks installed around London. Although "experimental" it will be extended to the rest of the UK if successful. One of the main differences with the BT kiosk is that users will pick up a handset and dial a freephone number as opposed to a video face to face link. Supporters say that "time would tell how confident users would be about spending large sums of money at a kiosk. To go into a travel agency is not always the most wonderful experience. You might have to wait a long time" (Anne Machin, BT Manager for kiosks TTG, 1996)

Critics say "that the problem with technology, despite all the grand promises, when the kiosk is not working it is about as useful as an empty cardboard box. The kiosk did not fill me with much enthusiasm as a vehicle for booking a holiday. It was a bit like looking at a giant video game and as inspiring. Somehow a bustling hotel foyer is not the place for leafing through details of a get-away-from-it-all break. Its function is more suited to checking out where the nearest McDonalds restaurant or foreign exchange bureau is. But for those more indulgent moments in life, kiosks hardly seem to fit the bill" (Rachael Jolly, TTG, 1996)

Travel Shopping at Home

In the 1980s one of the travel agents greatest fears was that the emerging new technology would allow people to shop from the comfort of their own home. By linking their television set to the telephone through special adapters, potential travellers could link up to a variety of databases, view the products and buy directly simply by quoting their credit card numbers. The need to go out to a travel agent would therefore be eliminated.

British Telecom's Prestel service was a first attempt to access this potentially vast market. Perhaps to the surprise, and no doubt to the relief of many in the agency sector, it proved a very slow process and ground to a halt by the end of the 1980s. The problem seems to have been one of cost. In addition to line charges and usage fees, adapters for domestic TV sets cost around £300 at 1987 prices, much more than a set with teletext facility. While the teletext system is relatively low-cost it has one way communication only, with the customer viewing the products on the screen then telephoning in the orders. Prestel, on the other hand, while of relatively low cost for the intensive business user such as a travel agent, was comparatively much more expensive for the home user, and had limited impact despite its possibilities for home shopping, banking and other transactions. The banks pulled out of the Prestel system and instead concentrated their efforts on sophisticated 'hole in the wall' machines and telephone banking. Most travel suppliers recognise, however, that unlike banks, which are in the main used for cash transactions, customers want the personal advice and service delivered by the travel agent.

If, however, the U.K. had followed the lead taken by the French, home buying of travel products might have been entirely different. France Telecom, the country's Government owned phone company, started offering a service called 'Minitel' in 1984. This system involved a telephone linked monitor and keyboard which were supplied free of charge. The Government's plan was literally to bring the entire nation on line, with no more outdated phone books and the opportunity to develop home shopping, banking, news updates and access to professional databases. Yet even here the optimistic predictions did not materialised and although four million terminals were in circulation in 1989, this still represented only 15% of the country's telephone subscribers. There were over 9,000 service providers on the system, but most of the business and news services flopped. While Minitel was simple to use, involving a four-digit number and a code for the desired service, surveys found that most owners rarely use the system. More than half of the calls on the system were to services offering simplistic games, horoscopes and messages, many of them 'pornographic'. The system had some successes, however, with the electronic phone directory, which was free to use and consequently unprofitable for the Government, receiving thirty five million calls every month. Catalogue sales via Minitel were booming, and La Redoute, one of France's biggest catalogue stores, reported at that time that 10% of its 100,000 daily orders coming in this way.

It is unlikely that we shall see a similar development in the U.K. in the foreseeable future because of the very high cost of development and installation. Stark predictions for the retail trade made some ten years ago now have simply not materialised. An example appeared in 'Counter Travel Weekly' in December 1987.

> *"A retailing revolution, booking travel and holidays via computer from home looks set to become a reality for around five million U.K. households. The trade ought not to regard it as a nightmare, ABTA should enter into urgent talks with British Telecom."*

In 1990, after 18 months of trials, yet another attempt was made to enter the home shopping market by an organisation called Keyline. With a give-away home computer the company signed up banks, bookmakers, building societies, retail chains, mail-order houses and insurance companies with the promise that they would have recruited some 500,000 home customers by the end of 1991 for round-the-clock transactions. A special computer was central to this system. It was smaller than an A4 sheet of paper, lighter than a novel and was been designed to look like a toy. It avoided time wasting menu structures and bewildering search codes. The main barrier to such new developments was the U.K.'s antiquated local telecommunication system. Until the standard copper wire was replaced by the limitless capacity of optical fibre cables, the full potential of such systems could not be realised.

In 1995 the kiosk pioneer Thomas Cook launch a home shopping trial with British Telecom. Using interactive videotext and the telephone to make bookings the product allowed customers to research destinations and make reservations. Placed into 2,500 households in East Anglia it had a 25% response rate within the first few days, however little has been reported of its progress since.

In 1997 the old Teletex system was about to be revolutionised by "digital television" bringing in new channels and Internet services. Instead of the dark screens and Lego-look teletex there will be colourful screens full of photographs and easy to use instructions. It will be modelled on the Internet style and Windows-based computer screens. However, as with so many previously tried home shopping schemes only time will tell if the public can trust a non-human method of booking. As Thomas Cook reported in 1997 after years of trying out new distribution ideas only 15% of sales were coming through the phone compared to 85% from their shops.

Payment System between Customers and Agents

A separate and unrelated development to supplier/agent systems is EFTPOS (Electronic Fund Transfer at Point of Sale). This is the process whereby payment by the customer's plastic card initiates the automatic transfer of funds from the customer's account to the agent's, without the need for paperwork. The problem for the travel agent and for other high street retailers is the initial cost of installing the equipment needed and the processing charge levied for each transaction.

All the major banks now offer their customers this payment card facility. Barclays issues its 'Connect card' while Lloyds and the Midland offer 'Switch' cards. A point to remember about these cards is that they do not offer credit; the money is deducted from the customer's bank account within a couple of days. To date travel agents seem to have avoided this system, although it has been taken up by supermarkets, petrol stations and some leading high street stores. The banks are in a strong negotiating position, however, knowing full well that as they gain widespread acceptance of their plastic by customers and other retailers, the travel agents will be forced follow suit.

Payment Systems between Customers and Suppliers

There can be little doubt that new technology has revolutionised travel documentation. For example, the conventional airline ticket may eventually be replaced by the so-called 'smart card'. Such cards, already in use with some major airlines, are be programmed to carry financial credit. They allow the passenger to reduce the time spent at the check-in, generally recognised to be one of the most unpopular stages of air journeys and hotel visits. Instead of queuing the holder simply walks through a card identification control which validates the holder's card and debits the customer's account. It is expected that desk top controls will be made available for travel agents to join such a system.

Appendix A   *Travel Agents' Code of Conduct*

Reproduced by kind permission of the Association of British Travel Agents

All members of the Travel Agents' Class (hereinafter referred to as travel agents) shall comply with this Code of Conduct.

AIMS

To ensure that the public receive the best possible service from travel agents in the belief that properly regulated competitive trading by and between travel agents will best serve the public interest and the well being of the travel industry.

To maintain and enhance the reputation, standing and good name of the Association and its membership.

To encourage initiative and enterprise.

To ensure that travel agents and their staff are familiar with this Code and the Articles of Association.

CONDUCT BETWEEN TRAVEL AGENTS AND MEMBERS OF THE PUBLIC AND OTHER MEMBERS OF ABTA

1.1   Standard of Service

(i)   Travel agents shall maintain a high standard in serving the public and shall comply with all relevant statutory requirements.

(ii)   Travel agents shall make every effort to ensure that accurate and impartial information is provided to enable their clients to exercise an informed judgment in making their choice of facilities. In addition every travel agent is required to display in a prominent position a notice to read "we act as agent only for selected operators" in the form set out in the Appendix to this Code.

(iii) Travel agents shall make every effort to ensure that their clients are sold tours, holidays and travel arrangements compatible with their individual requirements.

1.2   Advertising

(i)   All advertising by travel agents shall comply with the Codes or regulations of recognised organisations or associations such as the Advertising Standards Authority, the Code of Advertising Practice Committee, the Independent Broadcasting Authority, the Independent Television Companies Authority, and the Association of Independent Radio Companies which regulate the standards and practices of travel agents in relation to advertising.

(ii)   No advertisement, document or other publication, whether in writing or otherwise, shall contain anything which is likely to mislead the public.

(iii)   A travel agent shall not advertise in such a manner as to suggest that other travel agent or tour operator members of the Association may become insolvent.

(iv)   A travel agent shall show his ABTA number in all his press advertisements for travel business but shall not be obliged to do so where these advertisements are in classified run-on form unless such advertisements contain any reference to ABTA.

1.3   Alterations to Travel Arrangements and Emergency Contact

(i)   When alterations are made to travel arrangements for which bookings have already been accepted, travel agents shall inform their clients immediately they are advised of the situation and act as intermediaries between their principals and clients in any subsequent negotiations.

(ii)   To facilitate emergency contact by principals, travel agents shall on request supply a telephone number where they may be contacted outside office hours.

1.4   Booking Conditions

(i)   Travel agents shall draw the attention of their clients to booking and other published conditions applicable to their travel arrangements before any contract is made. Where a package travel booking is made by telephone, the travel agent shall ensure that at least the details given in the ABTA guidelines to the Package Travel Regulations 1992 (issued February 1993) shall be communicated to the client before the contract is made. Further with regard to package travel arrangements, travel agents shall ensure that all clients receive a written set of booking conditions on or before confirmation of the booking.

(ii)   Travel agents shall ensure that their conditions of booking are not in conflict with this Code of Conduct. When acting as a tour organiser, travel agents shall ensure that their conditions comply with the Tour Operators' Code of Conduct of the Association.

1.5   Counter Staff

Travel agents shall ensure that their counter staff carefully study travel brochures and other literature concerning the services provided in their agency, so that they are able to impart accurate information to their clients.

1.6   Booking Procedure

(i)   Travel agents shall ensure that booking procedures are complied with in every detail and in accordance with any relevant agency agreement. In particular agents must ensure that any special requests related to disabilities or medical conditions are noted and passed on effectively to tour operators and in accordance with any agency agreement.

(ii)   All booking references shall be shown.

(iii)   Travel agents shall ensure that with regard to package travel arrangements, details of the relevant arrangements that are in place for the security of the consumer (e.g. ABTA/ATOL bonding) are communicated to the consumer before any contract is made.

(iv)   When dealing with unfamiliar principals travel agents shall ensure that there is in fact financial protection in place where a company is not a member of ABTA, an ATOL holder, a member of Association of Independent Tour Operators (AITO), the Confederation of Passenger Transport (CPT) Bonded Coach Holiday Scheme or the Passenger Shipping Association (PSA) and shall not book travel arrangements on behalf of the consumer where a principal cannot provide evidence of specific financial protection.

1.7   Insurance Facilities

(i)   Travel agents shall draw the attention of their client's to insurance facilities and cover to suit their client's requirements.

(ii)   (a)   Travel agents when providing insurance which is not arranged through the principal (e.g. tour operator) concerned, shall ensure that within 48 hours of the booking being made, clients are given an insurance document showing the effective start date of cover, the premium paid whether by client or agent on his behalf and the insurance company's name, address and reference number. Written details of cover and claims procedures including emergency contact number shall normally be given to clients prior to departure.

(b)   Travel agents shall comply strictly with the terms of their agreements with insurance companies and make prompt sales and other financial returns as required under these agreements.

(c)   In respect of package holidays, travel agents shall use their best endeavours to ensure that in cases where the principal requires insurance and where neither the principal's nor their insurance is taken by the client, an indemnity against liability for the benefit of both the principal and agent shall be signed by the client in the form set out in the Appendix to this Code.

1.8 Travel Documents

(i) Travel agents shall ensure that all documentation received from principals is checked before delivering them to their clients and that any points requiring clarification are explained to their clients.

(ii) Travel agents shall as required by their principals pass on to clients within four working days of receipt, documents intended for them and in particular shall assist their principals in complying with their requirements under Air Travel Organisers' Licences applicable in this regard. Travel agents shall not materially alter, amend or delete, any part of any principal's documentation or fail to pass on any documentation from a principal intended for the client.

1.9 Passports, Visa and Health Requirements

(i) Before a contract is made, travel agents shall inform their clients of health requirements which are necessary for the journey to be undertaken and shall draw to the attention of clients travelling abroad the availability of the D.o.H. leaflet Advice on Health for Travellers.

(ii) Before a contract is made, travel agents shall as far as practicable advise their clients of passport and visa requirements (or advise where such information is available) for the journey to be undertaken.

1.10 Transaction and Correspondence

Transactions with clients shall be treated as confidential and in the event of a dispute between a travel agent and a customer, all correspondence shall be handled within the following time limits:

(a) No later than 14 days from the date of receipt for an acknowledgement to be sent; and

(b) not later than 28 days from receipt for a detailed reply to be sent.

1.11 Correspondence from the Association

All correspondence from the Association about complaints and companies with the Articles of Association and this Code shall be handled within the same time limits shown in 1.10 unless indicated otherwise by the Association.

1.12 Disputes

(i) In the event of a dispute with a client, travel agents shall make every effort to reach an amicable and speedy solution.

(ii) Travel agents shall make every reasonable effort to deal with complaints of a minor and general character with a view to avoiding recourse to principals. When complaints are of such a nature that reference to the principal is necessary a travel agent shall use his best endeavours acting as an intermediary too bring about a satisfactory conclusion.

(iii) Any dispute arising out of an alleged breach of contract or negligence by a travel agent may be referred to arbitration arranged with the Chartered Institute of arbitrators. It shall be subject to such time, financial and other restrictions as from time time shall apply to the scheme arranged for Tour Operators.

(iv) Where a client indicates in writing that he wishes to refer an unresolved dispute to arbitration, the travel agent shall reply to the Association within 21 days enclosing a cheque and documents and shall comply with the terms of the Arbitration Scheme referred to in sub-paragraph (iii) above and in particular with all the relevant rules and regulations of the Chartered Institute of Arbitrators for the time being in force.

1.13 Misleading Use of the ABTA Symbol etc

A travel agent shall not, directly or indirectly, cause, permit, assist or encourage any person, company or firm not in membership of the Association to represent itself as a member by the use of the ABTA symbol or any ABTA number or by any other means. Where a travel agent is alleged to be in breach of this provision the travel agent shall comply with any requirement placed upon it by the Association with any time limit that may be specified.

1.14 Trading Names

Before employing a trading name (which for these purposes means a name which is not either the correct corporate name or in the case of an unincorporated business, the name under which ABTA membership is enjoyed) a travel agent shall ensure that he has notified ABTA of such trading name in compliance with ABTA's regulations for such notification.

1.15 Notice to Customers - Financial Protection

Travel agents shall display in a prominent position at each of their offices which is open to the public, a notice in the form set out in the Appendix to this Code or in such other form as the Travel Agent's Council may from time to time approve.

1.16 Payment of Accounts

Travel agents shall settle all accounts without delay or within an agreed period, if any. A continued failure to settle accounts as they arise shall constitute prima facie evidence of an inability to meet liabilities under Article 16(1) of the Articles of Association.

1.17 Refunds

Where travel agents receive refunds, they shall normally remit such refunds within six working days of their receipt from the tour operator.

1.18 Vouchers

Where a voucher is published by or on behalf of a member and it contains any reference to ABTA, it must include the appropriate statement as listed below. This statement must feature in capital letters and bold print in a size no smaller than 10 point.

(i)   Where the voucher is given away for free or offers a discount, the following phrase must be used:

"THIS VOUCHER IS NOT COVERED BY THE ABTA FINANCIAL PROTECTION SCHEME"

(ii)   Where the member is paid the face value of the voucher, it must carry the following phrase:

"THIS VOUCHER IS ONLY COVERED BY THE ABTA FINANCIAL PROTECTION SCHEME ONCE IT HAS BEEN REDEEMED AGAINST A SPECIFIC HOLIDAY BOOKING"

TRAVEL AGENTS ACTING AS PRINCIPAL/TOUR ORGANISING

2.   Travel agents acting as a principal to a contract with a client or organising their own package travel arrangements shall in addition conform to the Tour Operators' Code of Conduct in respect of such travel arrangements, including the provisions of that Code relating to arbitration and surcharges.

INFRINGEMENT AND ENFORCEMENT

3.1   If any infringement of this Code of Conduct is alleged against a travel agent, the facts shall be reported to the Secretariat for preliminary investigation.

3.2   The travel agent against whom the allegation has been made shall provide, at the request of the Secretariat, such further information or documents as may be required within such a period as may be specified.

3.3   If, after the preliminary investigation, the facts alleged against the travel agent appear to the Secretariat to constitute a prima facie infringement of this Code, the facts shall be dealt with in accordance with paragraph 3.4. below or submitted to the the Code of Conduct of the Travel Agents' Council (hereinafter called the Committee) in accordance with paragraph 3.5 below.

3.4   (i)   Where the Secretariat after due investigation have reason to believe that a travel agent has committed a fixed penalty offence as set out herein below, the Secretariat may issue the travel agent with a fixed penalty notice in respect of the offence.

    (ii)   The following breaches of this Code by a travel agent constitute a fixed penalty offence and attract a fine of £300 which may increased by the Travel Agents' Council from time to time.

       1.2(iv)   requirement to display ABTA number in advertisements.

       1.8   failure to pass and check on documentation from principals.

       1.10(a)(b)   dealing with complaints and correspondence from clients.

       1.11   complaints and correspondence from the Association.

       1.14   failure to advise of trading name.

       1.15   requirement to display financial protection notice.

       1.17   requirement to remit refunds within six working days of receipt.

Breaches of the remaining paragraphs of this Code are not fixed penalty offences and therefore shall be referred to the Committee in accordance with paragraph 3.5 below.

    (iii)   The secretariat has at all times the discretion to refer directly to the Committee in accordance with the procedures laid down at 3.6 below all alleged breaches of this Code including repeated breaches of this Code which would normally constitute a fixed penalty offence.

    (iv)   Where the Secretariat issues a fixed penalty notice in the standard form as set out in Appendix 2 hereto indicating what clause has been breached, the fine that is to be levied in the time period in which the fine must be paid, the travel agent may:

       (a)   pay the fine within 28 days as set out in the fixed penalty notice, or

        (b)   request in writing to the Secretariat that the matter be referred to the Code of Conduct Committee.

    (v)   Where the travel agent fails to pay the fine within the specified fixed period notice, or requests the matter be referred to the Committee, or fails to respond to the fixed penalty notice, the Secretariat shall refer the matter to the Committee in accordance with the procedures laid down in paragraph 3.6 of this Code. The Secretariat shall not refer the matter to the Committee until the period specified in the fixed period notice has expired.

3.5   Where the Secretariat after due investigation has reason to believe that the fats alleged against the travel agent constitute a prima facie infringement of this Code, the facts shall be submitted to the Committee who shall give the travel agent at least 14 days notice in writing of the time and place of hearing of the complaint. The travel agent shall be entitled to make representations at the hearing either personally (with or without legal representation) or in writing. The Committee shall have the power to impose a reprimand or fine.

3.6   If the Committee shall decide upon a reprimand or fine they shall notify their decision to the travel agent, who shall have the right, exercisable within 14 days after the service of the notice upon him, to appeal against such decision to the Appeal Board who shall make such arrangements as it thinks fit for the conduct of the appeal. The decision of the Committee to fine or reprimand a travel agent shall take effect on the expiration of the period of appeal. If the travel agent has not then appealed, he shall thereupon be liable to pay the fine or sustain the reprimand.

3.7   In cases where the Committee decide that the appropriate penalty for the alleged breach of the Code could be termination or suspension of membership, the ddecision shall beb submitted to the Travel Agents' Council which may ratify the decision or impose an alternative penalty.

3.8   The Travel Agents' Council shall notify their decision to the travel agent, who shall have the right, exercisable within 14 days after the service of the notice upon him, to appeal against a termination or suspension of his membership, a fine or a reprimand, to the Appeal Board who shall make such arrangements as it thinks fit for the conduct of the appeal. The decision of the Travel Agents' Council to terminate or suspend the membership of a travel agent or to impose a fine or reprimand shall take effect on the expiration of the period allowed for appeal. If the travel agent has not then appealed, he shall thereupon cease to be a member, be suspended as a member, be liable to pay the fine or sustain the reprimand.

3.9   If the travel agent shall appeal against a fine, reprimand, termination or suspension of membership, the decision shall not take effect unless and to the extent that it is confirmed or varied by the Appeal Board, which shall determine the appeal by exercising the powers of the Travel Agents' Council in such manner as in its discretion it thinks fit.

3.10 The Appeal Board shall be constituted inaccordance with Article 17 of the Articles of Association.

3.11 After the decision of the Appeal Board has been made known to the appellant, that decision shall be communicated to the Travel Agents' Council.

3.12 The Council shall arrange for decisions to penalise a travel agent and the reasons therefore to be published.

GENERAL

4.   Service

Travel agents shall ensure that the public receive the best possible service and shall take no action which does not maintain or enhance the reputation, standing and good name of the Association and its membership.

5.   Compliance

Travel agents shall not engage in any activity that is expressly or potentially in conflict with this Code of Conduct or any other Rule, Article, Code or Regulation of the Association for the time being in force.

Appendix B   *Job description for a travel sales consultant*

Reproduced by kind permission of the Thomas Cook Group Ltd.

PERSON AND ROLE PROFILE		
ROLE TITLE: SALES CONSULTANT - TRAVEL **DEPARTMENT: RETAIL** **MANAGER: MANAGER** **SECTOR: UK RETAIL** **DATE: MARCH 1996**		
FACTOR	**PROFILE OF THE IDEAL PERSON**	**FACTOR LEVEL**
KNOWLEDGE & EXPERIENCE	Sound knowledge of relevant products sold. Good working knowledge of travel geography with experience of overseas travel. COTAC I and II and/or BA fares and ticketing 1, 2 or 3 or equivalent experience. Experience of cash handling and acceptable payment methods. Capable of arranging complex itineraries. Multi-skilled. Audit, security, legal and company regulations fully understood - good awareness of current affairs. Sound knowledge of in-branch accountancy documentation, sources of reference and security procedures.	C
HUMAN RELATIONS SKILLS	Able to communicate face to face, by phone and in writing mainly with customers, with speed, accuracy and tact. Able to achieve rapport quickly and provide high level of customer service whilst closing the sale. Selling skills vital, including tenacity when dealing with all customers. Able to work as a member of a team, including training of peers.	D
THINKING & REASONING	Selection of preferred products after assessing customers needs with consideration for company profit and cost incurred whilst maintining quality service. Able to identify additional opportunities for sales and revenue generation e.g. Foreign Exchange. Decide application of company marketing policies whilst having recourse to guidance via Manager/Customer Service Manager.	B

NUMERICAL LOGIC & I.T. SKILLS	Ability to use defined systems e.g. TIB, TOPS, PAL, PLATFORM and/or CRS. Knowledge of manual and automated ticketing. Good numerical ability for simple arithmetic calculations (including percentages) requiring accuracy and calculate complex booking quotes. Able to use a calculator.	A
PERSONAL QUALITIES	Able to operate in a pressurised environment with unpredictable customer flow patterns. Must be able to remain calm when dealing with customers. Capable of taking decisions within defined limits with little supervision. Pride in appearance and presentation with enthusiastic, outgoing and friendly personality which will maintain and enhance the company's reputation in the eyes of the general public.	B
PHYSICAL SKILLS	Dexterity in use of keyboard, paperwork and cash. Use of VDU for prolonged periods. Mainly sedentary work requiring limited walking and lifting. Quick reaction to frame requests.	C
	OVERALL ROLE LEVEL	3

ROLE-87

Appendix C   *U.K. Residents currency allowances, 1945-79*

Year	Expenditure (£ million)	Annual Currency Allowance		
		Date	Amount	Notes
1945	-	Oct 1945	Fixed at £100	To include dollar area
1946	42	Mar 1946	Changed to £75	
1947	76	Aug 1947	Changed to £35	
		Sept 1947	Withdrawn	
1948	66	Apr 1948	Fixed at £35	To exclude dollar area
1949	75	Apr 1949	Changed to £50	
1950	85	Dec 1950	Changed to £100	
1951	104	Nov 1951	Changed to £50	
1952	83	Jan 1952	Changed to £25	
1953	89	Mar 1953	Changed to £40	
		Nov 1953	Changed to £50	
1954	101	Nov 1954	Changed to £100	
1955	125			
1956	129			
1957	146	July 1957		To include dollar area
1958	152			
1959	164	Nov 1959	Changed to £250	Further amounts granted
1960	186			
1961	200			
1962	210			
1963	241			
1964	261			
1965	290			
1966	297	Nov 1966	Changed to £50	Plus certain additions; no limit for sterling area
1967	274			
1968	271			
1969	324			
1970	382	Jan 1970	Changed to £300	Per journey
1971	442			
1972	535			
1973	695			
1974	703			
1975	917			
1976	1,068			
1977	1,186	Nov 1977	Changed to £500	Per Journey
1978	1,549			
1979P	2,091	June 1979	Changed to £1,000	Per journey £5,000 per journey for business
		Oct 1979	No limit	All exchange controls removed

Source: Board of Trade for estimates of expenditure 1946-63; Department of (Trade and) Industry, *International Passenger Survey,* from 1964.

Appendix D   *U.K. Residents population figures 1985-95*

Age	1985	1987	1988	1989	1990	1995
0-7	3,610	3,671	3,725	3,800	3,862	4,118
5-9	3,398	3,536	3,601	3,608	3,615	3,858
10-14	3,888	2,508	3,386	3,371	3,408	3,617
15-19	4,540	4,372	4,241	4,066	3,898	3,413
20-24	4,747	4,791	4,738	4,657	4,548	3,898
25-29	4,103	4,373	4,501	4,626	4,724	4,510
30-34	3,770	3,831	3,885	3,959	4,069	4,673
35-39	4,144	3,958	3,845	3,790	3,752	4,039
40-44	3,424	3,854	4,007	4,074	4,119	3,722
45-49	3,171	3,151	3,208	3,296	3,382	4,066
50-54	3,041	3,024	3,053	3,089	3,104	3,312
55-59	3,079	3,031	2,998	2,959	2,929	2,995
60-64	3,146	2,986	2,942	2,908	2,889	2,758
65-69	2,540	2,748	2,862	2,952	2,841	2,628
70-74	2,400	2,,297	2,177	2,076	2,174	2,454
75-79	1,826	1,854	1,865	1,876	1,881	1,737
80+	1,791	1,908	1,972	2,036	2,096	2,347

Source: CSO

Appendix E   *Socio-economic groups*

A Upper Middle Class

Forming 3% of the population, social class A covers higher managerial, administrative and professional occupations. The head of the household will be a successful business or professional person or may have considerable inherited wealth. They would normally live in expensive detached houses in provincial areas or if in London, in expensive flats or town houses in the better parts of town. Social class A occupations include barristers, bishops, brain surgeons and top businessmen and women.

B Middle Class

Defined as intermediate managerial administrative or professional occupations. social class B covers people who are quite senior but not at the top of their profession and could include younger people, destined for social class A who have not yet climbed so far up their career ladder. They are well off but their life-style is respectable rather than rich and luxurious.
Ten percent of Britons are in this class including most people in management and 'teachers over 28 years of age'!

C1 Lower Middle Class

Covering supervisory, clerical and junior managerial positions, often called white collar jobs, the lower middle class will often be significantly less affluent than classes A and B and includes 24% of the population. Teachers under 28 years of age, most nurses and many civil servants would be in social class C1.

C2 Skilled Working Class

The largest class with 30% of the population, it consists mainly of skilled workers. Tending to be of lower educational attainment and status than social class C1, they can nevertheless often be higher earners. Print workers, fitters, electricians and plumbers would be classified as skilled working class.

D Working Class

Consisting entirely of manual workers, semi-skilled or unskilled, this class includes assembly line workers and farm workers and unskilled workers in service industries.

E Those at the Lowest Levels of Subsistence

Social class E is made up largely of the unemployed and the poorest pensioners. Together, social classes D and E comprise one third of the population.

Appendix F   *ABTA Membership growth*

	Members
1950	97
1955	200
1960	432
1965	614 (Stabilizer introduced)
1966	815
1967	1,334
1968	1,522
1969	1,591
1970	1,652
1971	1,736
1972	1,851
1973	1,963
1974	1,979
1975	1,915
1976	1,881

ABTA Membership - Travel Agents Class Only

	Members	Branch Offices	Total Offices (Head & Branch)
1977	1,771	2,143	3,914
1978	1,807	2,182	3,989
1979	1,896	2,305	4,201
1980	1,950	2,448	4,398
1981	2,094	2,687	4,781
1982	2,211	2,844	4,055
1983	2,396	2,903	5,299
1984	2,537	3,196	5,733
1985	2,647	3,372	6,019
1986	2,086	3,657	6,463
1987	2,889	4,107	6,996
1988	2,932	4,477	7,409
1989	2,965	4,548	7,513
1990	2,914	4,302	7,216
1991	2,750	4,049	6,799
1992	2,712	4,178	6,890
1993	2,572	4,405	6,977
1994	2,430	4,547	6,977
1995	2,219	4,719	6,938

Source: ABTA

Note: Breakdown of figures into separate travel agents class not available until 1977.

Appendix G   *ABTA council structure*

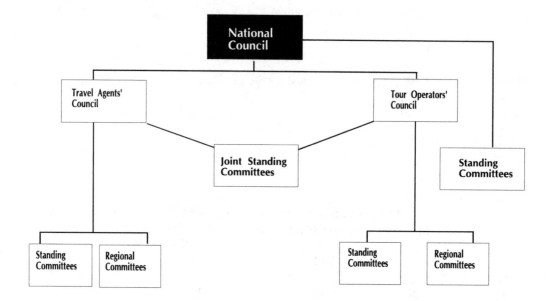

Appendix H   *Middleton's 'Tourism Channel' chart*

Zero level channel	Principal ——————————	Customer (on producer's premises). Typical of attractions, cafes, museums, guest houses, taxis.	Principal is retailer at own location.
Zero level channel	Principal ——————————	Customer (at home) All forms of direct response marketing practised by hotels, some tour operators.	Principal is retailer via reservation system.
Zero level channel	Principal ——————————	Owned retail————Customer (on producer's outlets/premises) multiple units. Typical of car rental companies, railways, airlines (in part) and hotels with multiple units acting as referral system.	Principal owns the distribution system.
One level channel	Principal ——————————	Independent————Customer (on retailer's retail premises) outlets Typical of many tour operators, holiday centres, airlines (in part) hotels.	Principal pays commission to retailers.
Two level channel	Principal Tour —————————— Operator/ Wholesaler	Independent————Customer (on retailer's retail premises) outlets. Typical of resort hotels, some camping and caravan sites, charter airlines.	Principal negotiates bulk sales or allocation of production to another principal.

Appendix I   *Examples of agency discount offers*

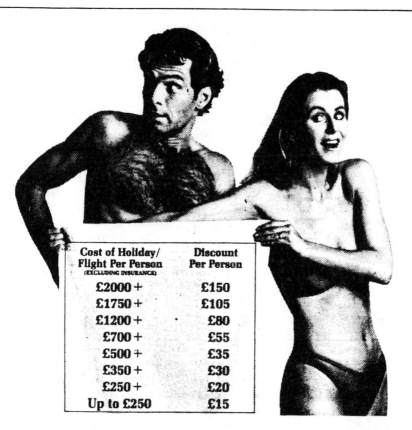

Cost of Holiday/ Flight Per Person (EXCLUDING INSURANCE)	Discount Per Person
£2000 +	£150
£1750 +	£105
£1200 +	£80
£700 +	£55
£500 +	£35
£350 +	£30
£250 +	£20
Up to £250	£15

From Dec. 27th to Jan. 12th, no one takes off more.

As Britain's largest travel agency, Lunn Poly offer bigger discounts to more people than anyone else. Now for a limited period, we are offering our biggest discounts ever. And unlike many travel agents, we'll give everyone in your party a discount.

The offers are for all overseas Summer holidays and flights. All we ask is that you book between December 27th and January 12th, and take out our holiday insurance.

So if you want to see more taken off, take off to Lunn Poly now.

ABTA 18057 ATOL 0010.

Getaway for less at *Lunn Poly*

Appendix J   *Example of a Third Party promotion leaflet*

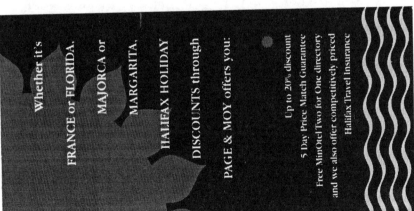

Reproduced by kind permission of Page & Moy Ltd

Halifax Holiday Discounts for holidays to remember at prices you won't forget

Book your 1997 holiday simply by calling 0116 250 7700.

As a Halifax customer, Page & Moy (ABTA No. 99529) can offer you a range of valuable discounts, a 5 Day Price Match Guarantee and convenient operating hours so - you'll be walking on sunshine right through to your holidays!

You can also take advantage of our competitively priced Halifax Travel Insurance and Travel Money Service

Save up to 20%

As a Halifax Visa cardholder you could save up to 20% if you book certain holidays through Page & Moy from selected brochures of the holiday companies listed below before 31st March 1997.

Inspirations - First Choice - French Life - Sunworld

Alternatively, you can save up to 15% off selected brochures from a wide range of holiday companies also when you book before 31st March 1997. Here are just a few of the holiday companies you could choose from:

Airtours - Celebrity Cruises - Crystal - Cosmos - Magic of Italy - Meon Villas - Sunworld - Unimed Vacations - Virgin Holidays and many more.

Please note: These discounts are limited to selected holidays and departure dates. Please call for details of holidays to which this offer applies.

Take a look at the table opposite to see how much you can save.

Break away for less

Book your holiday with Page & Moy before 31st March 1997 and you'll receive a free MinOtel Two for One UK Hotel directory.

This will entitle you to two nights bed and breakfast for the price of one in a wide selection of hotels across the UK. Many hotels even allow longer two for one stays.

You'll always save with Halifax Holiday Discounts

If you choose a holiday which isn't included in the above offers, you can still save up to 10% off the total basic holiday cost with most other major ABTA tour operators.

And the great news is that the up to 10% discount doesn't just apply to holidays booked before 31st March 1997 - it applies right through the year. So, even if you book at the last minute, you'll still save money.

Call 0116 250 7700 for details of the discount applicable to your holiday.

Save and be safe with Halifax Travel Insurance

Comprehensive insurance is vital when you go abroad. Book your holiday and travel insurance before 31st March 1997 and avoid paying the increased rate of Insurance Premium Tax. Even if you cannot book your holiday before this date ask about our Travel Insurance at your local Halifax branch

Halifax Travel Insurance offers some of the most competitive premiums around.

Just phone and go!

There are just three easy steps to booking your holiday.

Choose your holiday, remembering to make a note of any flight or hotel codes.

Telephone 0116 250 7700 with your holiday details and quote Ref: HAL/VIS 75D. Page & Moy will check availability and confirm details. You will be required to pay at least the deposit and travel insurance premium, why not pay the easy way with Halifax Visa.

Complete the booking form in the brochure and send it to: Page & Moy (Halifax Holiday Discounts), PO Box 155, Leicester LE1 9GZ

You will normally receive your tickets and travel documents 7-10 days prior to departure.

You can call Halifax Holiday Discounts seven days a week, all year round (except Christmas day) anytime between 8am-9pm Monday to Friday, 8am-5pm on Saturdays and 10am-4pm on Sundays and Bank Holidays.

5 Day Price Match Guarantee

Page & Moy offer Halifax customers a simple low price promise.

"We guarantee that if, within 5 days of booking your holiday with us, you show the identical holiday or cruise was available at a lower price elsewhere (after deducting all discounts) we will refund the difference".

No more travel money worries

Wherever you're going, the Halifax will take care of your travel money requirements too, we can offer:

Competitive buy back service.

American Express Travellers Cheques and foreign currency.

Next day delivery service (subject to certain conditions).

American Express 24-hour Worldwide Refund Delivery Service for lost or stolen travellers cheques.

Say good-bye to your travel money worries by calling in to your local Halifax branch who will be able to give you full details.

Remember book your holiday the easy way call 0116 250 7700.

Total basic holiday cost*	Up to 20% Discount**	Up to 15% Discount**
£250-£349	£70	£55
£350-£399	£150	£90
£400-£449	£175	£110
£450-£499	£230	£135
£500-£599	£300	£160
£600-£699	£350	£180
£700-£799	£420	£225
£800-£899	£450	£250
£900-£999	£460	£275
£1000-£1099	£1000	£475
£1100-£1199	£1150	£650
£1200-£1299	£1350	£578
£1300-£1399	£1550	£840
£1400-£1499	£1730	£1185
£1500+	£200	£1285

* see points 5 in Points to Note section

** offer applies to holidays booked before 31st March 1997 & departing between 1st May and 31st October 1997 only unless Page & Moy specifies otherwise at the time of booking.

Appendix K   *Capabilities of a modern CRS*

Travel agents, consumers and businesses can use SABRE to access information, make bookings and issue tickets or vouchers for a side range of travel suppliers. The following pages describe the travel services offered through SABRE.

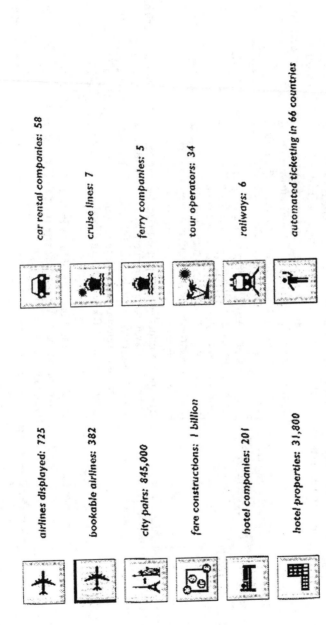

airlines displayed: 725

bookable airlines: 382

city pairs: 845,000

fare constructions: 1 billion

hotel companies: 201

hotel properties: 31,800

car rental companies: 58

cruise lines: 7

ferry companies: 5

tour operators: 34

railways: 6

automated ticketing in 66 countries

SABRE's core products meet the needs of the different groups that want access to a reservation system, from consumers to business travellers to travel agents. All SABRE's products involve the travel agent as an integral part of the booking chain.

Product	Market	Characteristics	Available
Dial SABRE[SM]	Smaller or leisure-based travel agencies	Low-cost, easy-to-use version of SABRE. Agents buy a software package, which runs on a standard PC and modem, and then pay only for the time they are connected to the system. The Windows[TM] based software means only minimal training is required to master the system.	Europe, Australia, New Zealand
Professional SABRE[SM]	Travel agencies	Full access to SABRE system through personal computer, using either DOS or Windows[TM] platform. SABRE provides all computer equipment and connection to system for monthly lease cost. Agents can earn 'credit' against these costs through the productivity-based agreement.	Worldwide
Turbo SABRE[SM]	Larger,more productive travel agencies	The most productive CRS platform on the market, improving travel agency productivity by more than 25 per cent. Subscribers use a dedicated 'keypad' on the PC keyboard to select options, removing the need to remember any CRS booking commands.	North America, Europe (UK) (*October 1995*)
Business Travel Solutions	Corporate travel	A fully integrated package of three PC-based modules for travel planning, travel expense reporting and pre-travel decision making.	USA

Product	Market	Characteristics	Available
Commercial SABRE®	Travel agents' corporate custtomers	User-friendly version of SABRE for corporate travel departments. The traveller inputs booking details on his/her PC, which are then transmitted to the SABRE travel agent, who reviews the travel plans and issues the travel documents.	North America, Europe
SABRExpress by mail SM, SABRExpress by faxsm	Travel agents' corporate custtomers	Business travellers can use e-mail, or specially designed fax forms, to make travel requests. Booking details are transferred automatically to SABRE, where the booking is made, with the Passenger Name record returned to the travel agent for quality control and ticket issue.	Europe, North America
easy-SABRE®	Consumers	The world's first home booking system (introduced 1985) for travel available through a number of on-line information systems, including America On-Line and CompuServe. Consumers can view travel information and can make bookings directly in SABRE. Travel agent or airline then provides ticket issue.	North America
SABRE Electronic Ticketing	Consumers	Provides passengers and their travel agents with the means to make a reservation, pay for airline tickets, obtain a passenger receipt and an invoice/itinerary, go directly to the airport and board an airplane according to each participating carrier's boarding procedures, without the required paper flight coupon of an airline ticket document.	USA (United Airlines, Shuttle by United)

Appendix L   *How does electronic ticketing work?*

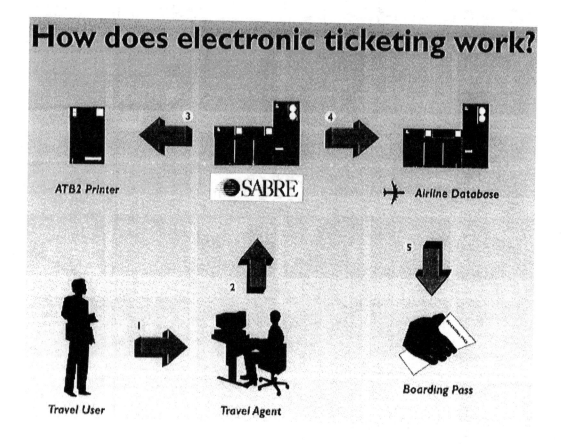

Reproduced by kind permission of "Business Travel World"

Bibliography

Books

Alderson, W.,   *Co-operation and conflict in Marketing Channels,* Dynamic
                         Marketing Behaviour, New York, Irwin, 1965.

Baker, M. J.,   *Marketing: An Introductory Text,* 4th Ed. London, Macmillan,
                         1985.

Bishop, J.,   *Travel Marketing,* Folkestone, Bailey & Swinfen, 1981.

Boone, L. E., and   *Marketing Channels,* New Jersey, General Learning Press, 1973.
Johnson, J. C.,

Burkart, A. J., and   *Tourism, Past, Present and Future,* 2nd Ed, London, Heinemann,
Medlik, S.,   1984.

Callaghan, P.,   *Travel and Tourism 3rd Edition,* Sunderland, Business Education
and others,   Publishers Ltd., 1997.

Corke, J.,   *Tourism Law,* Huntingdon, Elm Publications, 1987.

Carter, J.,   *Chandlers Travels,* London, Quiller Press, 1985.

Cowell, D.,   *The Marketing of Services,* London, Heinemann, 1984.

Cundiff, E. W.,   *Fundamentals of Modern Marketing,* 4th Ed, New Jersey,
and others,   Prentice-Hall, 1985.

Davidson, J. H.,   *Offensive Marketing,* London, Penguin, 1987.

Davidson, W. R.,   *Retailing Management,* 6th Ed, New York, Wiley, 1988.
and others,

Elvy, H.,   *Marketing,* London, Heinemann, 1984.

Evans, J. R., and   *Marketing,* 3rd Ed, New York, Prentice-Hall, 1987.
Berman, B.,

Foster, D.,   *Travel and Tourism Management,* London, Macmillan, 1985.

Giles, G. B.,   *Marketing,* 3rd Ed, Plymouth, Macdonald and Evans, 1978.

Golzen, G., and   *Taking up a Franchise,* 3rd Ed, London, Kogan Page, 1986.
Barrow, C.,

Guirdham, M.,   *The Management of Distribution Channels,* Oxford, Pergamon, 1972.

Christopher, M.,   *The Strategy of Distribution Management,* Aldershot, Gower, 1985.

Holloway, J. C.,   *The Business of Tourism,* London, Pitman, 1994.

Holloway, J. C.,   *Marketing for Tourism,* London, Pitman, 1988.
and Plant, R. V.,

Hodgson, A.,and   *The Travel and Tourism Industry, Strategies for the Future,*
others,   Oxford, Pergamon, 1987.

James, D. L., and   *Retailing Today,* 2nd Ed, New York, Harcourt Brace Jovanovich,
others,   1981.

Keegan, W. J.,   *Global Marketing Management,* 4th Ed, London, Prentice-Hall, 1989.

Knee, D., and   *Strategy in Retailing, Theory & Application,* Oxford, Phillip
Walters, D.,   Allen, 1985.

Kotler, P.,   *Marketing Management,* 3rd Ed, London, Prentice-Hall, 1976.

Kotler, P.,   *Principles of Marketing,* 2nd Ed, London, Prentice-Hall, 1984.

Lavery, P.,   *Travel and Tourism,* Huntingdon, Elm Publications, 1987.

McIntosh, R. W.,   *Tourism; Principles, Practices, Philosophies,* (4th Ed, with
                       Goeldener, C R., Wiley, New York, 1984), Grid, Ohio, 1972.

Middleton, V. T.   *Marketing in Travel and Tourism,* Oxford, Heinemann, 1988.
C.,

Morrison, A. M.,   *The Tourism System,* New Jersey, Prentice Hall, 1985.
and Mill, R. C.,

Myers, J. H., and   *Consumer behaviour and marketing management,* Houghton
Reynolds, W. H.,   Mifftin Co, 1967.

Ornstein, E., and   *The Marketing of Leisure,* London, Associated Business Press,
Nunn, C. A.,   1980.

Stapleton, J.,   *Teach Yourself Marketing,* Sevenoaks, Hodder & Stoughton, 1984.

Swinglehurst, E.,   *Cooks Tours: The Study of Popular Travel,* Poole, Blandford
                       Press, 1982.

Wahab, S.,   *Tourism Management,* London, Tourism International Press, 1975.

Walters, D. W.,   *Strategic Retailing Management,* New York, Prentice-Hall, 1989.

Yale, P.,   *The Business of Tour Operators,* Harlow, Longman, 1995.

Special Reports

ABTA:	*Report of the commission of enquiry into ABTA*, June, 1969.
	Travel Agents Remuneration Survey, 1980-83, Thornton Baker Associates, Nov 1984.
	Resale Price Maintenance & Stabilizer. A discussion paper. Robertson, Parker & Associates Ltd, June 1976.
	The 1988 Holiday survey, An independent survey into customer satisfaction with package holidays, 1988.
BR:	*Passenger Marketing Fact Books*, Vols 1-3, 1988/9.
Euromonitor:	*The Travel and Tourism Industry*, 1983.
	The U.K. Package Holiday Market, 1986.
HMSO:	*Department of Transport, Review of arrangements for protecting the clients of Air Travel Organisers*. Report and recommendations to the Secretary of State for Transport. Sir Peter Lane, June 1984.
	Transport Committee, *Airline competition: Computer Reservation Systems*, Vol 1, 1988.
	M.M.C., *Foreign Package Holidays*, Cmnd 9879, Sept 1986.
	M.M.C., *Thomson Travel Group and Horizon Holidays*, Cmnd 554, Jan 1989.
Inland Revenue:	*Travel Agents*, Business Economic Notes, BEN 1, 1988.
Istel:	*Technology & the Travel Agent*. 1987.
Jordans:	*British Travel Agents & Tour Operators*, 1977.
Keynote:	*Travel Agents and Tour Operators*, 1987, 1994, 1995.
	Airlines, 1993.
	Market Review, U.K. Tourism and Holiday Travel, 1987.
Mintel:	*Tour Operating*, Leisure Intelligence, Vol 3, 1987, Vol 3 1989.
	Inclusive Tours, Leisure Intelligence, April 1996.
	The Holidaymaker, Special Report, 1987.
	Travel Agents, Retail Intelligence, Vol 5, 1988.
	Travel Shopping, Leisure Intelligence, Vol 1, 1989.

Travel Agents, Retail Intelligence, Vol 3, 1990, Vol 2 1992, Vol 1 1994.

TOSG: *Tour operators study group, an introduction,* November, 1988.

Touche Ross: *Tour Wholesaler Industry Study*, 1976.

Statistical Sources

BTA: *Digest of Tourist Statistics,* Nos 1-20.

CAA: *Airlines Annual Statistics,* 1973-94.

Air Holidays and Expenditure, News Releases, 1981-1990.

ATOL Busclass 1992-1996.

HMSO: *Overseas Travel and Tourism,* Business Monitor, MQ6, CSO, 1979-1996.

CSO, *Annual Abstract of Statistics*, 1970-96.

Plus special reports as above.

Annual Reports

ABTA: Annual Reports, 1969-1996.

Members Handbook, 1985-97.

Thomson Travel: Annual Reports, 1985-96.

Thomas Cook: Annual Reports, 1987-96.

Journal Articles

Barrett, F.,   Bucket Shops, Kicking the Bucket, *Executive Travel*, 18-19, Nov 1984.

Baxter, J.,   Travel retailing is put on the line, *Travel Agency,* 6-7. Feb 1987.

Bitner, M. J., and Booms, B. H.,   Trends in Travel & Tourism Marketing, The Changing Structure of Distribution Channels. *Journal of Travel Research,* Spring 1982.

Boberg, K. B., and Collison, F. M.,   Computer reservation systems and airline competition, *Tourism Management.* 174-183, Sept 1985.

Bruce, M.,   New Technology and the Future of Tourism, *Tourism Management,* 115-120, June 1987.

Buttle, F. A.,   Travel Agency Merchandising, *International Journal of Hospitality Management*, Vol 5, 171-175, 1986.

Buttle, F. A.,   How Merchandising Works, *International Journal of Advertising*, No 3, 139-148, 1984.

Elton, M. A.,   U.K. Tour Operators & Retail Travel Agents - ABTA and the public interest, *Tourism Management*. 223-228, Sept 1984.

Evans, J. L.,   Teleshopping: Implications and applications for the retail travel agency, *Journal of Institute of Certified Travel Agents* U.S.A., Vol 5, Part 2, 15-24. 1984.

Feldman, J.,   Transport. CRS & Fair Airline Competition, *Travel & Tourism Analyst*, EIU, No 2, 5-22, 1988.

Fitch, A.,   Tour Operators in the U.K. Survey of the industry, its markets and product diversification, *Travel & Tourism Analyst*, EIU, 29-43, March, 1987.

Gauldie, R.,   1992 & The European Travel Industry, *Travel & Tourism Analyst*, EIU, No 3, 66-78, 1988.

Graham, M.,   Technology, why the trade is spoilt for choice, *Travel Agency*, 15-16, Dec 1988.

Hammond, B.,   Bucket Shops, will they stop you buying from this man, *Executive Travel*, 21-23, Sept 1982.

Harding, M.,   Independents, time to stop feeling small, *Travel Agency*, 8-9, June 1987.

Heap, R.,   Marketing Tourism in the Nineties. Inclusive Tours - An Untapped Market, *Tourism Management*, 169-170, June 1987.

Lockwood, C.,   Automated air ticketing, *Travel Agency*, 9-10, Feb 1989.

McEwan, J.,   U.K. Travel Agencies - future marketing strategies, *Tourism Management*, 171-173, June 1987.

Middleton, V. T. C.,   Product Marketing: Goods and Services Compared, *Quarterly Review of Marketing*, Vol 8, No 4, July 1983.

Middleton, V. T. C.The Marketing Implications of Direct Selling, *International Tourism Quarterly*, No 2, 1980.

Moutinho, L.,   Consumer Behaviour in Tourism, European *Journal of Marketing*, December, 1987.

Nicholls, J. A. F.,   Airline deregulation, Computerised Reservation Systems and Travel Agents, F.I.U., *Hospitality Review*, Vol 3, Part 2, 61-65, 1985.

Peisley, T.,   Have shopping trolley will travel, *Travel Agency,* 8-9, May 1987.

Ray, P.,   Paying by plastic-an explosive issue? *Travel Agency,* 8-9, Jul/Aug 1987.

Ray, P.,   A plan for cornering the top of the market, Four Corners concept, *Travel Agency,* 6-7, Dec 1988.

Richardson, D.,   Technology, Waging the War against Paper, *Travel Agency,* 42, Oct 1987.

Richardson, D.,   Technology, Screen Test. Market Report, *Travel Agency,* 11-12, June 1986.

Saltmarsh, G.,   Travel Retailing in the U.K. Survey of the agents, their costs, markets and mergers, *Travel and Tourism Analyst,* EIU, 49-62, Sept 1986

Saltmarsh, G.,   Smallmen rule OK?, *Travel Agency,* 6-9, Sept 1984.
and Ray, P.,

Shafer, E. L.,   Technology, Tourism & the 21st Century, *Tourism Management,* 179-182, June 1987.

Stafford, J.,   Technology, High-tech for Higher Profits, *Travel Agency,* 11-12, May 1987.

Index

A

A. T. Mays, 19, 62, 63, 138, 142, 158
ABTA, 12, 25, 26, 29, 30, 43, 47, 53,
   54, 59, 61, 63, 67, 68, 69, 71, 72, 78,
   83, 97, 98, 156
   codes of conduct, 13
   members, 61
   youth training scheme, 12
ABTA Codes of Conduct, 8, 69
ABTA National Council, 71
ABTA Retail Code, 71
ABTA tour operator, 70
ABTA Tour Operators' Code, 71
ABTA's Articles of Association, 70
ABTA's bonding system, 72
Accommodation, 2, 92
Accuracy and Expertise, 16
Advance Booking Charters, 27
Advanced Booking Charter (ABC), 45
Advantage Travel Centres, 63, 120, 158
Advertising, 8
Advertising Standards Office, 59
Affinity charters, 44
Age groups, 40
Agency
   types, 18
Agency agreement, 7, 26
Agency income, 29
Agency remuneration survey, 29
Air 2000, 57
Air charter tour firms, 70
Air Europe, 45, 50
Air transport, 43
Air transportation, 27
Air travel, 31, 34, 76
Air Travel Reserve Fund, 71
Air Travel Reserve Fund Act 1975, 55

Air Travel Scheduled Services, 76
Airlines, 3
Airtours, 47, 120, 123, 124, 137
Airtours International, 6
All-travel service, 21
Amadeus, 175
Amenities, 2
American Civil Aeronautics Board
   (CAB), 45
American Express, 16, 19
Ancillary services, 11,13,15
By Appointment, 26, 27
Appointments, 20,161
Arbitration scheme, 69
ARTAC, 63, 120, 138, 158
Association of British Travel Agents
   (ABTA), 6, 68, 69, 71, 73
ATOL, 26
Australasia, 41
Automatic ticketing, 174
Automobile Association, 63
Aviation business, 51
Aviation fuel, 38

B

Bank of England, 36
Banker's bond, 69
BEA, 43
Benefits, 24
Blue Cars, 52
Blue Star Travel, 65
BOAC, 43
Boat trains, 46
Boeing 707, 43
Boeing 747, 44
Boeing 747 Jumbo Jet, 62
Bonding, 61, 70

Bonding scheme, 70
Brand Image, 137
Brand loyalty, 9
Break bulk, 5
Brian Perry, 64
Britannia, 6, 43
Britannia Airways, 46
Britannic travel, 24
British Airways, 4, 30, 31, 43, 45, 60,
    78, 79, 174
British Airways Holidays, 4
British European Airways, 43, 52, 54
British Hotels and Restaurants Associa-
tion, 39
British Overseas Airways Corporation,
    43
British Rail, 51, 68, 87, 162
British Railways, 50
British seaside resorts, 39
British Shipping Passenger Agency Con-
ference, 68
British Tourist Authority, 27, 28
Brochure conversion ratio, 83
Brochure distribution, 151
Brochures, 90
Brokers, 6
BTA, 42
Bucket shops, 77, 79, 80
Bus and Coach Council, 83
Bus ticket outlets, 63
Bus travel, 84
Buying process, 129
Type of business conduct, 20, 21, 23, 25
Business agent, 23, 24, 25
Business community, 10, 16, 17, 25
Business income mix, 28
Business relationships, 161
Business travel, 21, 25, 27, 32, 76, 78,
86, 87, 89
Business traveller, 16, 19, 50, 88

C

Canada, 41
Captain Ted Langton, 52
Car distributors, 9

Car ferry services, 47
Car hire, 32, 33, 49, 85, 86, 87
Car manufacturer, 9
Car ownership, 33
Car-carrying rail, 48
Caribbean, 41
Carlson Travel Network, 19
Carlson Wagonlit Travel, 16, 23, 78
Cartel, 68
Cash and carry wholesalers, 5
Cash discount, 7, 30, 60, 67
Catalogue firms, 59
CD ROM, 175
Chain of distribution, 2, 4, 6
Channel of distribution, 1, 14, 59, 60,
    77, 109
Channel Tunnel, 33, 48, 49, 51, 88
Channels of distribution, 76, 77, 79,
    81, 83, 85, 87, 89, 91, 93, 95, 97, 99,
    101, 103, 115
Charter, 78
Charter flights, 81
Charter airline, 4
Charter operators, 45
Choice of products, 11, 14
Civil Air Transport, 54
Civil aviation, 43
Civil Aviation Authority (CAA), 45
Clarksons, 54, 63, 71
Clipper flying boat, 43
Clothes shop, 6
Co-operative Travel, 61
Coach business, 49
Coach companies, 3
Coach Europe, 50
Coach industry, 49, 50
Coach operators, 34, 83, 140
Coach services, 49
Coach Tour Operators, 82, 84
Code of Conduct, 26
Code of Ethics, 69
The Comet, 43
Commercial accounts, 32
Commercial clients, 23
Commission, 3, 5, 6, 12, 21, 22, 25,
    30, 32, 62, 140, 143, 146, 147, 163

Committee of Tour Operators, 69
Common fund, 69, 70
Competition, 55
Computer reservation systems, 24, 25,
 62, 88, 91, 170, 171
Computerised
 booking machines, 10
Computerised booking system, 22
Concorde, 44
Conglomerates, 56
Consolidation, 81
Consolidators, 26, 76, 77, 78, 79
Consumer, 5
Consumer behaviour, 129
Consumer credit boom, 36
Consumer demand, 36
Consumer protection, 26, 68
Consumer protection schemes, 61
Contract of sale, 7
Consortia, 157
Convenience, 11, 13
Cooks, 63
Core product, 2
Corporate image, 141
Councils of ABTA, 68
Court Line, 71
Creative Travel Agents Conference, 50
(CTAC), 61
Cruise, 34, 41, 46, 47, 48, 89
Cruise and ferry operators, 4
Cruise holiday market, 53, 55
Cruising, 32
Cunard, 46
Currency exchange, 38
Customer needs, 21
Customer incentives

D

Dean and Dawson, 61
Definition, 4
Demographic trends, 41
Deposits, 67, 140, 145
Devaluation, 36
Devalued, 36
Developments in transport, 34

Direct and Indirect Selling, 8
Direct channels, 1
Direct Holidays, 81
Direct mail, 10
Direct response, 14
Direct response marketing, 8, 84
Direct sales, 78, 91
Direct sell, 3, 5, 11, 14, 59, 60, 79,
 81, 86, 90, 99
Direct sell operators, 11, 13, 59, 62
Direct sell tour operators, 12, 60, 102
Direct telesales, 140, 153
Direct selling, 8, 83
Direct television, 8
Disadvantages, 25
Discount travel tickets, 25
Discounting, 55, 67, 147
Discounts, 59, 69, 140, 146
Discretionary incomes, 33
Discretionary spending, 36
Disposable incomes, 40, 42
Distribution channel, 9, 48, 75, 110
Distribution system, 9, 77
Distributors, 36
Domestic holidays, 30
Domestic market, 30, 49
Domestic products, 26
Domestic resorts, 40
Dr Richard Beeching, 50

E

E.C. Package Tour Directive, 26, 70,
 73
Eclipse, 5, 9, 81, 97, 102
Economic, 35
Economic benefits, 17
Economic prosperity, 33
Economic trends, 35
Economies of scale, 53
Eddie Milne, 69
Electronic Ticketing, 174, 188
Ellerman, 65
Entry requirements, 39
Eurolines, 49
Eurostar, 33, 51

Exchange controls, 35
Exchange rates, 37
Exchange Travel, 66
Exclusive distribution, 115
Expert advice, 11
Express Coach Operators, 32, 84
Extended Credit, 17, 25

F

Factory shops, 8
Far East, 41
Fares, 79
Fastrak, 180, 181
Ferries, 32, 34, 47, 91
Ferry, 46, 47, 48
Ferry operators, 48, 152
Fiesta Tours, 70
Financial protection, 73
First Choice Holidays, 5, 97, 117
Florida, 40
Food manufacturers, 9
Foreign currency, 28, 35
Frames, 61, 64
Franchise, 76, 159
Franchiser, 117, 159
Freddie Laker, 44
Free insurance, 69, 67, 140
Free transfers, 67
Freemans Mail Order, 59

G

Galileo, 88, 172, 174, 176
General agents, 20, 21, 22, 23
General public, 10
General/leisure agent, 20
Global, 52
Going Places, 5, 19, 65, 137
Greece, 37
Group 20, 63
Group charters, 44
Growth of tourism, 33
Gulf war, 36

H

Happy Traveller's Club, 59
Harry Chandler, 59
Harry Goodman, 45
Historical development, 59
Hogg Robinson, 19, 23, 25, 64, 65, 78
Holiday agents, 22
Holiday centres, 95
Holiday clubs, 150, 152, 154
Holiday entitlement, 42
Holiday Programme, 41
Holiday Shop, 21
Holiday Shop concept, 65
Holiday travel, 76
Home agency system, 59
Home shopping, 190
Hong Kong, 41
Horizon, 52
Hotels, 3, 4
Hovercraft, 34, 47
Hughie Green, 59

I

IATA, 20, 22, 26, 27, 44, 78, 79, 172
    agency investigation panel, 27
    Licence, 27
IATA Agents, 27
IGL, 55
Ilkeston Co-op Travel Agency, 67
Implant, 16, 24
Import and export of currencies, 39
incentive commissions, 79, 163
Incentive payment, 25
Incentives, 12, 30, 67
Inclusive coach tour, 50
Inclusive package holidays, 23, 30
Inclusive protection, 68
Inclusive tour, 27, 30, 36, 44, 51
Inclusive tour charters, 46, 54
Inclusive tour market, 22, 40, 56, 61, 66
Inclusive tour operators, 34
Inclusive tours, 29, 30, 36, 40, 60, 96
Incoming tourism, 28
Independent airlines, 43, 53

Independent charter flights, 43
Independent operators, 52, 100
Independents, 18, 20, 22, 23, 27, 50,
    61, 67, 155
Indirect Channels, 1
Indirect sell, 9
Indirect selling through an agent, 3
Inducements, 67, 69, 72
Inflation, 36
Institute of Travel Agents (ITA), 68
Insurance, 30, 147
Intasun, 36, 45
Intensive distribution, 114
Inter-City, 50
Interest rates, 36
Intermediaries, 1, 8, 9
International Air Transport Association,
    68
International airline tickets, 27
International Leisure Group (IGL), 50,
    53, 56
International tourism, 39
Istel, 180, 181
IT sales, 66
ITX fares, 78

J

James Maxwell, 68
Jetsave, 45
Jumbo Jet, 44

L

Laker, 45
Leisure division, 22
Leisure market, 76
Leisure multiples, 19, 23
Leisure shops, 22
Leisure travel, 25
Liberalisation, 81
Licences, 20, 53, 61, 68, 76
Licensing, 23
Line services, 32
Liner services, 46
Location, 11, 13, 126

Long haul destination, 41
Long-haul, 78
Low cost, 21
Low deposit, 7, 67, 140, 145
Low revenue products, 21
Lunn Poly, 1, 6, 19, 21, 65, 66, 124,
    141

M

Mace, 63
Mail order, 8
Mail-shots, 9
Manufacturers, 2, 3, 4
March of the Multiples, 19, 63, 64, 65,
    67, 135, 138, 140
Market concentration, 67
Market segmentation, 142
Market share, 28, 60, 136
Marketing incentive, 60
Marketing point, 15
Martin Rooks, 59, 60
Mass tour operators, 60, 99
Max Wilson, 47, 53
The media, 34, 41
Merchandising, 127
Merger, 20
Mergers, 56, 64
Miami, 40
Middlemen, 9
Midland Bank, 63
Miniples, 19
Monetary inducement, 67
Money back guarantee scheme, 63
Money discounts, 69
Money-off deals, 67
Monopolies and Mergers Commission,
    56, 67, 72
Motoring holidays, 47, 48
Motorways, 34
Multinational, 19
Multiple travel agents, 18, 20, 21, 22,
    23, 25, 27, 50, 53, 61, 64, 66, 67, 135
    141

N

NAITA, 63, 158
NAT Holidays, 50
National Bus Company, 49, 63
National Express, 49, 84, 152
National Express Service, 50
National flag carriers, 44
National multiples, 19
National Travelworld, 85
Natural disasters, 23
New technology, 10, 142, 169
Non-scheduled, 46, 81
North Sea Ferries, 31

O

Ocean liner services, 46
Office of Fair Trading, 25, 26, 67, 148
Office of National Statistics, 27
Operation Stabiliser, 70
Opening hours, 126
Organisation
   by size of, 18
Organisation and servicing of travel, 34
Organisation of Petroleum Exporting
Countries, 36
Outbound and domestic tourism, 28
Outbound international market, 30
Over capacity, 57
Overheads, 22, 25
Override comission, 61, 163
Overseas Aviation, 52
Overseas hotel developments, 34
Own-branding, 148
Own label, 148, 149
Owners Abroad, 57

P

P & O, 32, 46, 47
P & O North Sea Ferries, 31, 91
Package holiday, 9, 26, 27, 54, 61
Package tour, 46
Package tour industry, 51
Page & Moy, 67, 151, 154

Pan American, 43
Passenger road transport, 48
Passenger Shipping Association, 32
Pecuniary inducements, 67
Pegasus, 52
Personal service, 11, 16, 21
Personnel, 128
Phonecentres, 153, 154
Pickfords Travel, 21, 61, 65, 124
Point of sale material, 15
Political upheavals, 23
Poly Travel, 62
The Polytechnic Touring Association, 61
Portland Holidays, 5, 9, 59, 60, 97, 102
Portrian Travel, 23
Poundstretcher, 45
Power and influence, 21
Preferred deals, 15
Preferred group rates, 79
Prestel, 181
Pricing policy, 128
Primary channels, 77, 97
Principals, 2, 3, 8
Principals as Manufacturers, 2
Principals in the Travel and Tourism
   Industry, 2
Principals/suppliers, 10, 14, 15, 139
Product, 4
Product discrimination, 143
Product visibility, 14, 140
Profits, 55
Provision One, 44, 54
The 'Pull' strategy, 10
The 'Push' strategy, 10

R

Rail inclusive offers, 50
Rail travel, 22, 32, 34, 50, 87, 88
Railway tickets, 50
Railway Train Operating Companies, 15
Rainbow Holidays, 29
The Readers Digest, 59
Reasons for development, 33
Recession, 24, 33
Redeemable couchers, 67

Regional multiples, 19
Registration bill, 69
Regulation, 49
Regulatory rules, 68
Renwicks, 65, 138
Reservation centres, 78
Restrictive practices, 67, 69, 71
Restrictive Practices Act (Services)
    Order, 71
Restrictive Practices Act, 1956, 67
Retail Price Maintenance, 67
Retail travel market, 28, 29, 31
Retailers, 2, 3, 5, 8
Retailing defined , 6
Road, 48

S

Sabre, 25, 176
Safety net, 55
Saga Holidays, 9
Salaries, 25, 142
Sale to tour operators, 3
Sales consultants, 12, 16
Sales promotions, 15
Sales representatives, 15, 25
Savings
    time and money, 15, 17
Scheduled air tickets, 27
Scheduled airline, 39, 52
Scheduled carriers, 44
Scheduled market, 76, 81
Scheduled routes, 44, 45
Scheduled service, 46, 52
Sea transport, 89
Seat only deals, 27
Seat only operators, 81, 102
Seat-only sales, 79
Secondary channels, 77, 79, 97
Self-ticketing, 80, 85, 88, 89
Selective distribution, 115
Shaw Saville, 46
Shearings, 50
Shipping, 46
Shop design, 126
Short break operators, 101

Short break inclusive tour market, 30
Short break package tour, 47
Short breaks holidays, 4
Short duration breaks, 40
Short-haul, 78
Siesta Travel, 50
Sir Henry Lunn, 52, 61, 62
Skytours, 59
Small independents, 22
Smart cards, 50
Socio-economic groupings, 42
Socio-economic trends, 38
Sole proprietor, 22
South Africa, 46
Spain, 37
Spar, 63
Specialised tour operators, 30, 41
Stabiliser, 70, 72
Stabilizer Resolution, 54, 70
Staff development, 141
Staff training sessions, 15
Standard of living, 40
Start-up and marketing costs, 60
Sub-agents, 77, 79
Sunshine currencies, 37
Suppliers, 4, 9
Suppliers of a service, 3
Surface Transportation, 31
Surface traveller, 34
Survival of, 22

T

Takeover, 20, 56, 65
Technology, 25
Telephone sales, 80
Telesales Units, 122, 123, 153
Teletext, 123, 154
Thailand, 41
The Travel Distribution Framework, 1
Thomas Cook, 1, 19, 38, 50, 52, 53,
    61, 63, 64, 68, 78, 117, 118, 139, **154**
Thomson, 46, 54, 55, 59, 60, 65, 79
Thomson Holidays, 6, 52, 97, 117
Thomson Travel Group, 5
Time-share villas, 41

Tjaereborg, 57, 59, 60
Tom Gullick, 55
Touch-screen kiosk, 189
Tour operating business, 56
Tour Operators, 2, 4, 6, 9, 12, 34, 36,
    39, 40, 51, 52, 53, 55, 57, 59, 61, 78
Tour Operators Study Group (TOSG),
    54, 70, 71
Tour Operators' Council, 69
Tourism and change, 35, 37, 39, 41
Tourism and motivation, 130
Train Operating Companies, 3, 86, 87
Transport, 2
Transport Act, 49
Transport Developments, 43, 45, 47, 49
Transportation suppliers, 13
Travel Agencies, 22, 30, 61, 63
Travel agency development, 35, 36, 38,
    40, 42, 44, 46, 48, 50, 52, 54, 56, 58,
    60, 62, 64, 66, 68, 70, 72, 74
Travel agent in law, 7, 8
Travel Agents, 2
    role and function, 6, 10
Travel Agents' Council, 69
Travel allowance, 35
Travel Club of Upminster, 59
Travel Company, 24
Travel geography, 22
Travel managers, 17
Travel market value of, 28
Travel sales consultant, 11
Travel Savings Association (TSA), 47
Travel savings club, 53
Travel technology, 17
Travel writers, 34
Travel year, 35
Travellers cheques, 28
Travicom, 172
Trust House Forte, 63
Turnover, 55
TWA, 43

U

U.K. Domestic Tourists, 28
U.K. Tourist Boards, 30

U.S.A., 43
Unbiased advice, 11, 12
Union Castle, 46
United States of America, 40
Universal Sky Tours, 52
Unlicensed agencies, 61

V

V form, 36
Value of tourism products, 29
Vertical Integration, 6, 12
Vertically integrated distribution, 117
Viewdata, 178
Vingressor, 59, 60
Virgin, 45
Visa restrictions, 39
Visits abroad, 38
Vladimir Raitz, 52

W

W. H. Smith, 63
Wakefield Fortune, 65
Wallace Arnold, 49
Walt Disney World, 40
Wayfarers, 61
Wealth of industrialised society, 33
Wheel of retailing, 123
Wholesalers, 2, 4
Wish you were here, 41
Workers Travel Association, 61
Worldchoice (ARTAC), 63, 158
Worldspan, 25, 176, 183

Travel and Tourism

3rd Edition

edited by Paul Callaghan, Phil Long and Mike Robinson

ISBN 0 901888 03 7 640 *pages*
published Autumn 1997 *Price £18.95*

The third edition of this important text book covers the main aspects of many courses in Travel and Tourism. The book looks at the nature of tourism, its history and development, its contemporary importance, the structure of the industry and the operation of its component parts, concentrating specifically on transport, accommodation, retail travel, tour operation, public sector tourism and the role of marketing in travel and tourism.

The third edition has been substantially expanded and updated to reflect the dynamic and changing nature of Travel and Tourism.

Travel Geography

Self Study Primer

Shelley C. Clough

ISBN 0 907679 53 6 640 *pages*
published August 1997 *Price £12.95*

This Self Study Primer on Travel Geography has been produced for those working in the retail leisure travel industry and particularly for candidates studying S/NVQ Travel Services.

It is divided into three sections:

- The United Kingdom

- Europe and Short Haul Destinations

- World-wide and Long Haul Destinations

It can be used independently, as part of a training programme or as part of a portfolio of evidence.